UNIONISM IN A DEVELOPING ECONOMY

Issued under the auspices of the
Shri Ram Centre for Industrial Relations

UNIONISM IN A
DEVELOPING ECONOMY

A STUDY OF THE INTERACTION BETWEEN
TRADE UNIONISM AND GOVERNMENT
POLICY IN INDIA, 1950-1965

C. K. JOHRI

ASIA PUBLISHING HOUSE

BOMBAY—CALCUTTA—NEW DELHI—MADRAS
LUCKNOW—BANGALORE—LONDON—NEW YORK

PRINTED IN INDIA
BY MEGH RAJ AT THE NEW INDIA PRESS, CONNAUGHT CIRCUS, NEW DELHI,
AND PUBLISHED BY P. S. JAYASINGHE, ASIA PUBLISHING HOUSE,
BOMBAY-1

To the Memory of
MY MOTHER

FOREWORD

TRADE UNIONS ARE AN IMPORTANT CONSTITUENT OF THE IN-
dustrial relations system in any society that permits decentralised decision-making and group interests to shape work
rules. Unions and their leaders are just one among several
sets of actors that together determine the nature of industrial relations and its output, *viz*. the work rules.

In industrialised Western countries, particularly in the
U.K. and the U.S.A., the evolution of unions has occurred
mainly in the context of the bilateral relationship between
workers and employers, which in turn has generally been
aided by government policy. In the U.S.A., in particular, the
statute has required the two parties to negotiate in good faith
and thereby promoted collective bargaining. In the U.K.,
this development has taken place spontaneously without
any significant assistance from the law.

In India, on the other hand, there has existed an extraordinary situation in which the maturing process of unions has
been simultaneously aided and obstructed by government
policy. There have, no doubt, been natural hurdles, such
as illiteracy among workers, their lack of commitment
to industrial life, poverty, unemployment, general apathy,
and victimisation by employers; and these have been discussed at length by the few scholars who have been interested
in the subject. However, the important role of the government in conditioning the behaviour of unions, and through
them of workers in general, and the response of the unions
to this policy have been neglected. The present book, it is
hoped, will fill the gap in this respect.

Readers may note that the relationship explored in this
book is an unusual one. It is customary to examine unions
in their dealings with employers. Indeed, the regulation of
employers is the very *raison d'etre* of unionism. However,
the framework within which this function can be carried
out is determined by the state either through the policy of
non-interference or, what is more common, through the
active direction in accordance with the statute. In India,
the government has taken the extraordinary course of using

statutory regulations in a manner that generally restricts the scope of collective bargaining. As a result, union and government interaction has become as important as the one between unions and managements. In fact, the latter is contingent upon the former.

This book explores some of the more important facets of the interaction process. Dr. Johri is, however, not content with just an analysis; he goes on to plead for a reorientation of government thinking in the direction of a new goal, *viz.* the promotion of professional trade unionism.

I am glad to note two important features of this book. First, its conclusions are based on a comprehensive review and a systematic analysis of the published data. It is well known that these are incomplete and inadequate in many respects, and yet with careful sifting and regrouping these can be made far more potent than is generally realised. This in itself is a painstaking, but essential, task in respect of significant researches. Second, the author takes an aggregative, all-India view of the problems of unionism. Global studies of this nature are necessary as aids in policy-making inasmuch as these give perspective and a sufficiently quantitative basis for assuming cause-and-effect relationships. Aggregative researches should be supplemented by case studies. The author has indicated the lines along which future investigations can be fruitfully directed.

The purpose of research in an applied field, such as industrial relations, is not merely to augment the stock of knowledge, but to lead, through better understanding, to more effective policies as well. It is our hope that this book will make a significant contribution in this respect and that its ideas will be eventually reflected in the making of new policies.

A. JOSHI
Director

Shri Ram Centre for Industrial Relations
New Delhi

PREFACE

THIS BOOK TREATS THE PROBLEM OF INTERACTION BETWEEN the government and the organised labour movement in the specific context of the developing economy of post-Independence India. As the title suggests, the book simultaneously deals with an important aspect of development in an underdeveloped economy, and one of its special manifestations, *viz.* trade unionism with its peculiar characteristics. The significance of research in unionism from such an unusual angle lies in the contradictory roles of labour in respect of democracy and development and the imperative necessity felt by the government in reconciling them. In the theoretical literature on the subject the conflict has been portrayed as between the consumptionist demands of unions and the productionist goal of the state. This is particularly acute in an underdeveloped democratic country, such as India, where the government operates under the constraint of preserving, even strengthening, people's institutions while seeking to develop the economy. A similar, though weaker, constraint operates on union leaders. They must cooperate with the government in order to further their collective interests but, in fact, cannot do so without clashing with it. The relationship between the parties is bound to be one of ambivalence.

This book is the result of an empirical exploration to give substance to the conflict in roles envisaged by theorists. As usually happens in such exercises, several interesting theoretical discoveries have been made. These relate to the effect of inflation on the degree of unionisation through conflicts operating as the intervening variable; and of the government labour policy on unionism by size and viability, on the one hand, and the postures of labour leaders on matters relating to planning and development, on the other.

An interaction process involves both conflict and cooperation. It is paradoxical that the two parties should generate conflict in the course of seeking cooperation. The paradox is the result of unresolved ambivalence in the relationship. As long as the interests of the government and unions clash as well as coalesce it is inevitable. The two can seek to reduce the quantum of the former and augment the latter but, in practice, such an outcome is largely contingent upon the growth of the economic pie which is hardly to be expected in the short run. And, yet, cooperation is meaningless if it is not on day-to-day matters which, however, more often than not, bears heavily on the distribution of the economic pie. Therefore, clash of interests is inevitable on the terms on which cooperation is sought by one and offered by the other. The problem is not how to overcome this tension on a permanent basis but rather to discover the art of living with it. In India, it will take a long time to learn and master this art.

It should be remembered that we are facing serious imbalances in the sphere of industrial relations. Undoubtedly these are, to some extent, manifestations of deeper crises in the economic system. The latter can probably be remedied by better planning, more careful ordering of priorities, and more effective implementation of policies. The initiative rests with the government, and one hopes that with a proper blend of policies the right results can be achieved. However, in respect of the former, the causes of imbalances are not self-evident, nor is the government policy potent in the short run. Trade unions and their leaders comprise an important element of the industrial relations system. The government policy must inevitably operate upon and seek the desired responses from them. But has it, or, can it work? In order to get the answer it is necessary to know the purpose of trade unions and the goals their leaders have set for themselves. There are union leaders who have narrowly viewed their purpose as the regulation of the factor market. But there are others who think that the purpose of unionism is conterminous with radical political movements aiming at the complete transformation of the social order, through either revolutionary or peaceful means, in order to achieve the emancipation of the working class. These are, however, polar positions that essentially demarcate the boundaries of unionism. Between these limits there are many strains of thought, different goals, and, accordingly, contending sets of labour leaders. What distinguishes one from the other is the time dimension the leaders attach to their goals and the seriousness with which they motivate the rank and file members to strive for their achievement. The more significant this characteristic of a union movement, the more complicated is the interaction process and the less certain will be the outcome of government policy, no matter how well it is conceived. This is because of three reasons. First, the impact of policy is not uniformly felt on different centres of the trade union movement. The heterogeneity of the latter in India has been sufficient to diffuse the impact. Second, it tends to evoke conflicting responses as different political centres seek to defend or advance their respective interests in the light of the policy. In fact, the competing union leaders are continually operating upon the government to bring about suitable modifications in policy to their advantage. Third, the response of leaders to policy is largely contingent upon their expectations of the probability of their continuing to enjoy (or increasing) workers' support. In this dynamic setting the outcome of any policy is bound to be uncertain.

It is evident that, as long as the total uncertainty about probable reactions to each other's behaviour remains undiminished, there is no hope of a constructive relationship developing on a durable basis between the government and union leaders. As a first step in this direction, it is necessary that the issues on which the two parties have interacted should be analysed and explained and the scope of mutually advantageous relationship clearly discerned. The present book is devoted to this purpose. We have endeavoured to explore the relationship of conflict as well as cooperation and finally proposed the modification of government policy to serve a new, socially accepted and widely upheld purpose, *viz.* to strengthen the professional core of trade unionism through an ideologically neutral policy on trade unions.

This book has a weakness. In India, the industrial relations system is a tripartite one. The government, the employers, and the unions simultaneously interact among themselves as well as bilaterally to achieve their respective goals. We have deliberately kept the focus of our research fixed on the bilateral interaction process between the government and the unions. This is an important and, as an area of research, a much neglected relationship. We believe that the more basic and traditionally studied area of labour-management relations derives its strength or weakness, as the case may be, from the nature of the former. Nevertheless, for completeness, the tripartite as well as other bilateral relationships should be fully researched upon and explained.

In the preparation of this book I have been helped by several colleagues. At the earlier stage, when I was meandering through various routes in chase of an elusive target, much help was rendered by Dr. C. P. Thakur, Abdul Aziz, Nand K. Tandan, and S. M. Pandey. At the later stage, when I finally came to grips with the problem, valuable support was given by Padma Venkataraman and Naresh C. Agarwal. To the former, in particular, this book owes much. A lot of initial work involving considerable amount of data collection and analysis was done by these friends. I am grateful to them. Among the critics who were deeply sceptical of the project and had profound misgivings about its destiny but, nevertheless, prodded me on, a grateful mention should be made of Prof. Fred C. Munson of the University of Michigan, formerly a Consultant at the Centre. Several friends have obliged me by finding time amidst their many obligations to read and make useful comments on the draft manuscript. In this connection, I would like to thank and express my deep appreciation to B. N. Datar, Vinay Bharat Ram, M. Atchutan, Fr. A. J. Fonseca, *S.J.*, Dr. V. B. Singh, and Santosh Nath. In our organisation, K. N. Vaid, Robert Gavin, and A. C. Nanda have given me encouragement, opportunities for clarification of ideas and specific comments. K. R. Seshagiri Rao has edited the final draft. The several drafts were typed by K. K. Gogia. I am happy to acknowledge their help. Finally, Arun Joshi, the Director of our Centre, has lent me a helping hand in satisfactorily completing the book. His comments on the study led to several important revisions in the text, a major change in the chapter scheme which led to further useful revisions, and many improvements in the presentation of the last chapter. Much that is useful in the book owes to the friends cited above. However, shortcomings have probably remained. For them, the responsibility is, of course, entirely mine.

July, 1967   C. K. JOHRI

CONTENTS

LIST OF TABLES

CHAPTER 1

INTRODUCTION

INDIAN ECONOMY IN A PERSPECTIVE

THE MAIN THEME OF THIS BOOK IS AN ANALYSIS OF INTERACTION of the labour policy of the government and trade unionism in the context of the stresses and strains of the developing economy of India. The analysis has been attempted at the national level and is based on the published data mostly by government sources. The period covered begins with 1950 which is the year preceding the First Five Year Plan, and ends with 1965 which is the fourth year of the Third Five Year Plan. This has been a period of a more or less stable growth of the economy accompanied by a steady increase in prices barring a short break between 1952 and 1955 and a quantitative expansion of trade unions. This has also been the most dynamic period of the Indian economy in the twentieth century if not over a much longer period.

In this century, for the first time, the national output, in real terms, began to grow at a rate faster than the increase in population. Over the last five decades the per capita income had, at best, remained constant. Considering that the population itself has been growing at a much slower rate, this is the barest minimum necessary for averting famines.[1] Due to the extreme weakness of the growth impelling factors and the indifference of the government, the society had settled down to a low level of economic equilibrium with its supporting values, social stratification, and customs.

---

1. In the Indian Union, as presently constituted, the population increased by a mere 5.75 per cent in the decade 1901-1911, declined by 0.31 per cent in the next decade, and rose by 11.0 per cent, 14.22 per cent, 13.31 per cent, and 21.51 per cent respectively in the subsequent decades. The latest census was that of 1961. See A. Mitra, *Census of India*, Vol. I, Part II-A(i), General Population Tables, 1964, p. 181.

By contrast, the period since Independence in 1947 has been marked by sustained governmental intervention in the economic affairs of the country. This intervention has been assisted by foreign capital in the form of grants, loans, and trade credits, usually accompanied by modern technology requiring new skills, changes in organisational structure, and leadership at all levels. As the successive five year plans have demonstrated, the government has entrusted to itself the most crucial tasks of economic development. The public sector has accepted the responsibility of expanding vastly the steel and machine tools, heavy electricals, chemical fertilizers, petroleum refineries, steam and diesel locomotives, aircraft, and electronic industries. In these and several other fields India has made major strides under the regime of planned economic development.[2] It is not necessary to catalogue the achievements of the Indian economy under government leadership, nor to ignore the fact that some other underdeveloped Asian countries have accomplished much more during the same period.[3] The Indian planners have often been rightly criticised for repeating mistakes, carelessness, faulty planning, resulting in misplaced priorities and avoidable waste.[4] The incontrovertible truth, neverthe-

2. Government of India, Planning Commission, *Third Five Year Plan*, pp. 452-509. Government of India, Planning Commission, *Third Plan Mid-Term Appraisal*, 1963, pp. 119-137.

3. U.N., *Economic Survey of Asia and the Far East*, Bangkok, 1965: See Chapter 1, Section 3, pp. 13-27. This survey shows that for 12 Asian countries India is second from the bottom, the country below being Indonesia. During the period 1952-1954 to 1961-1963 the GNP of Japan rose by 10.0 per cent per annum, China (Taiwan) by 7.1 per cent, Thailand by 6.0 per cent, and Burma by 5.0 per cent.

   For a comparison of India, Pakistan, and communist China, see K. N. Raj, *India, Pakistan and China : Economic Growth and Outlook* (Mimeographed), October 1966. Also see K. N. Raj, *Indian Economic Growth: Performance and Prospects*, New Delhi, Allied Publishers, 1965.

4. These are evident from the shortfalls in the fulfilment of the Third Plan. The criticisms have originated from a wide variety of sources and are often of a political nature. From among the academicians, too, there has flowed much criticism. Inevitably these are not free from ideological or doctrinaire underpinnings. For our purpose three outstanding inst-

less, remains that the country has been lifted from the mire of stagnation and pushed onto the growth path. The vicious circle of low income resulting in low savings and investments leading back to subsistence living has been broken. The economic structure is less imbalanced; the infra-structure has been strengthened; the opportunities of investment and gainful economic activity have multiplied; the educational achievements and the technical competence of large segments of Indian people have gone up significantly; and alongside has risen the level of aspiration and desire for better living.

The contrast between the economies of India prior to and after the ushering in of the planning era can be best brought out with the aid of a few relevant statistics.

The national income of the Indian Union at 1948-49 prices rose from 51.0 billion rupees in 1900-01 to 70.2 billion rupees in 1924-25. During this period the per capita income, in real terms, increased from 220 to 271 rupees yielding annual growth rates of 1.5 per cent and 0.9 per cent respectively.[5] Between 1924-25 and 1949-50 the national income went up by another 18.0 billion rupees while the per capita income registered a fall of 22.4 rupees. This was because while the growth rate of output fell by more than half, the increase in population was greatly accelerated by the declining mortality rate. On a note of caution it may be stated that the national income data over this period are not completely reliable. The data contain unknown margins of error due to paucity of source material. Nevertheless, the findings are supported by independent estimates of agricultural production and, therefore, they may be correct in

---

ances may be noteworthy. See B. R. Shenoy, "The Indian Economic Scene—Some Aspects" and D. R. Gadgil, "On Rephasing the Second Five Year Plan", *The Indian Economic Journal*, Vol. V, No. 4, April 1958, pp. 327-357 and pp. 358-368 respectively. Also see N. V. Sovani, "Planning and Planners in India", *The Indian Economic Journal*, Vol. XIII, No. 4, Jan.-March 1966, pp. 477-497.

5. See K. Mukerji, "A Note on the Long Term Growth of National Income in India, 1900-01 to 1952-53" in V. K. R. V. Rao, *et al* (ed.), *Papers on National Income and Allied Topics*, Vol. II, Bombay, Asia Publishing House, 1962, pp. 15-24. Also see H. C. Arora and K. R. R. Iyengar, *et al* (ed.), *Papers on National Income and Allied Topics*, Vol. I.

broad magnitudes and can be relied upon as indicators of long-term historical trends.[6]

It is, thus, clear that the economy, prior to Independence, had been stagnating for nearly half a century. This was reflected in the deteriorating occupational distribution of the working population. In 1931, 71.2 per cent of the working force were engaged in agriculture and mining whereas only 16.3 per cent were engaged in industry. By comparison, in 1951 the respective percentages were 73.0 and 13.0.[7] It may, however, be noted that the decrease in the share of industry in the working population was not reflective of the trend in industrial output, but rather of increasing pressure of population. This is shown by the fact that between 1900-01 and 1924-25 the index of industrial production rose by 133.6 per cent, and went up by 136.6 per cent between the latter year and 1949-50. For the whole period the industrial output increased at an average annual rate of 5.5 per cent.[8] Evidently, this was not adequate, particularly in the face of stagnating agriculture, to make a positive impact on the occupational distribution of working population.

Let us now take a broad view of the progress of the economy since 1950. According to the latest estimates the net national output at 1948-49 prices rose from 88.5 billion rupees in 1949-50 to 150.5 billion rupees in 1964-65 or at an average annual rate of 4.6 per cent.[9] To put the matters in perspective, the Indian economy had added a mere 37.2 billion rupees to the annual flow of goods and services over the entire half a century as compared to 62.0 billion rupees in a period

6. According to S. Sivasubramanian, the gross value of agricultural production in the undivided India rose from 7.5 billion rupees (in 1938-39 prices) in 1900-01 to 8.0 billion rupees in 1924-25. In 1946-47 it had risen slightly to 8.2 billion rupees. See his "Estimates of Gross Value of Output of Agriculture for Undivided India, 1900-01 to 1946-47", *Papers on National Income and Allied Topics*, Vol. I, (op. cit.), pp. 231-246.

7. See V. K. R. V. Rao, "Changes in India's National Income—A Stati Economy in Progress" reproduced in *Papers on National Income an Allied Topics*, Vol. II, (op. cit.), pp. 6-12.

8. See K. Mukerji, (op. cit.), pp. 18-19.

9. C.S.O., *Estimates of National Income* 1948-49 to 1962-63, February 196 p. 22, and *Estimates of National Income* 1963-64 (Provisional), April 196 p. 1, and K. N. Raj, *India, Pakistan and China*, (op. cit.), Table 1.

of just 15 years since 1950. Considering the Indian background, this is no doubt a remarkable performance. The fact that much of this gain has been wiped out by the spurt in population cannot hide the immense endeavour that has gone to make it possible.

THE INVOLVEMENT OF GOVERNMENT

In order to achieve this growth the government has tried to involve itself and the rest of the society in making three kinds of effort. First, the mobilisation of scarce real resources, such as skilled labour, machinery, raw materials, managers, and putting them into suitable organisational frameworks. Second, the mobilisation of financial resources, expressed through savings from current earnings, for the purpose of diverting real resources from idle or current uses to planned projects. Third, the creation of institutional complexes and the enactment of legislation for securing the transfer of real and monetary resources with either the maximum cooperation or the least resistance from the affected strata of population. Since the government clearly understood that the process of economic development could not but involve stresses and strains on the economy in general and on the sections of people in particular, that it must result in losses and gains accompanied by shifts of power, status, and influence among the more or less organised groups of economic interests, and the paramount necessity of maintaining political stability through the hegemony of state, it set upon fairly early in its career to formulate principles and policies in respect of the third kind of effort.[10] These have been developed for farmers, managements of companies, organised labour, and other interest groups to a greater or lesser degree depending upon not only their relative importance in the economic order but also their power to facilitate or retard the achievement of national objectives as perceived by the

10. See H. Venkatasubbiah, *Indian Economy since Independence*, Bombay, Asia Publishing House, second revised edition, 1961, Chapters I, III, V, and VI. Also see Government of India, Planning Commission, *First Five Year Plan*, pp. 7-27, pp. 420-443, and pp. 570-592.

authorities.[11]

In respect of regulating the interest groups the government did not, and in view of the constitutional transfer of power possibly could not, start from a clean slate. The British government of the undivided India had done much thinking during the Second World War on the problems of post-war economic reconstruction. The First Five Year Plan largely consisted of schemes that were already on the files of the war administration. Similarly, the government had experimented with controlling both organised industry and labour in the interest of war efforts. Moreover, the Indian National Congress had set up a National Planning Committee which in turn had constituted panels of experts for making recommendations to reconstruct the post-war social economy of the country. Most of these panels had submitted their reports by 1948.[12] Furthermore, the Congress governments under the provincial autonomy had acquired a brief but valuable experience in these spheres.

All of these together with the dream of a new India provided a basis for the enunciation of principles on regulating interest groups. By the year 1948, the government had laid down an Industrial Policy Resolution, an Industrial Truce Resolution, a five year plan of labour legislation, a policy on land reforms, and so on. All of these were bound together by the fundamental tenets of the Gandhian doctrine that had

11. The opening para on "Labour" in the *First Five Year Plan* (p. 50) reads as follows :

Our approach to labour problems rests on considerations which are related on the one hand to the requirements of the well-being of the working class and on the other to its vital contribution to the economic stability and progress of the country. The worker is the principal instrument in the fulfilment of the targets of the Plan and in the achievement of economic progress generally. His cooperation will be an essential factor in creating an economic organisation in the country, which will best subserve the needs of social justice. Certain rights and obligations are associated with this distinctive role.

12. The National Planning Committee had been set up by Jawaharlal Nehru in 1938 with himself as its Chairman. It produced 25 volumes on a variety of subjects including labour, several industries, land policy, and national planning. See K. T. Shah (ed.), *Report : National Planning Committee*, Bombay, Vora & Co., Publishers (P) Ltd., first edition, June 1949.

found general acceptance with the Indian National Congress, the liberal ideas of the national leaders which were mostly derived from the intellectual ferment in European countries, particularly in the thirties, the I.L.O. conventions, and faith in economic planning as the cure for India's manifold ills. One should not expect internal consistency in a set of beliefs originating from such diverse sources. But they moulded government policies. Inevitably, with the passage of time, these policies would be modified and tailored to meet the more clearly thought-out goals.

In this book we will be concerned only with those aspects of government policy that affect the organised labour. Since these form part of the overall government policy of achieving clearly stated social and economic goals, the national perspective will have to be kept in view. But the focus will be maintained on the interactions of government policies and the responses of organised labour. We will be concerned with three sets of questions: (*i*) What were the constituents of the government's trade union policy and the underlying desiderata? (*ii*) Given this policy, and its inherited strength and weakness, what were the responses of trade unions to (*a*) the problems generated by the developing economy, (*b*) the policy itself, and (*c*) the opportunities and challenges created by (*a*) and (*b*)? (*iii*) What has been the outcome of these interactions and what might be the lessons which the government could learn for devising a more purposive policy? These questions will be further broken down and analysed in smaller components in the following chapters. The remainder of this chapter will be devoted to stating the basic premises on which the entire edifice of the theme has been erected. The premises relating to the fundamental principles of government policy and the broad strategies of trade unions are stated in the following sections.

GOVERNMENT AND ORGANISED LABOUR

On the question of encouraging trade unions in a democratic society, the government had made up its mind as early as 1947. The Indian Trade Unions Act, 1926, had given workers the right to form and register trade unions, and to conduct trade disputes and promote the interests of their members through political, educational, and civic means without fear of involvement in either criminal or civil conspiracy.[13]   The desire to encourage trade unions was implicit in the Indian Trade Unions (Amendment) Act, 1947, which is on the statute book but has not yet been enforced.   This Act provides for compulsory recognition of representative trade unions and specifies unfair practices on the part of employers that are punishable with fine up to one thousand rupees.[14] Besides legal encouragement, the government also helped the trade unions through political patronage and moral support.   The latter has been based on moral considerations of assisting the weaker sections of the population to organise themselves against the strong, as well as on grounds of political expediency.

The second tenet of the government's labour policy has been to maintain industrial peace.   Rule 81-A of the Defence of India Rules achieved this aim during the Second World War.   It was later embodied in the Industrial Disputes Act, 1947.[15]   The government has not confined its interest in maintaining industrial peace merely to passing legislation. It has also tried to enlist the political support of central trade union federations and the parties that are behind them.   An early instance of this action is the tripartite Industrial Truce Resolution in December 1947.   Thus, even while encouraging the formation of trade unions, the government has been keen not just in balancing one party against the other but on preventing collusions.   This is clearly the continuation of the war-time policy to the era of planned economic development.[16]

13. Indian Trade Unions Act, 1926, Chapter III, sections 15, 16, 17, and 18.
14. Indian Trade Unions (Amendment) Act, 1947. See the "Statement of Objects and Reasons" and Chapters III-A and III-B including section 32-A.
15. See the "Statement of Objects and Reasons".   An essential feature of rule 81-A, now incorporated in the Industrial Disputes Act, 1947, was the power of the appropriate government to refer an industrial dispute for compulsory adjudication and to enforce the award thereof.
16. *First Five Year Plan*, (op. cit.), pp. 581-582, and Myron Weiner, *The Politics of Scarcity : Public Pressure and Political Response in India*, pp. 82-84.

The third tenet has been to involve trade unions in the formulation and implementation of five year plans. In order to make the labour leaders' participation more effective at all levels—national, industry, and plant—the government set up a Central Industries Advisory Council, the tripartite industrial committees, and works committees. It should also be noted that the labour portfolio in the Union Cabinet has often been held by outstanding labour leaders.[17] Moreover, the government has made it a practice to consult labour leaders in all matters affecting the working conditions and the well-being of the working class. The idea has been to secure the commitment of leaders of organised labour, and through them the parties they represent, to the five year plans and acceptance of the sacrifices that this may entail in their implementation. This required giving unionists opportunities of representation and access to information that goes in policy making, as also higher social status and political support. In this respect, the government has achieved a fair measure of success.

The fourth tenet has been to have political control over the trade union movement without either jeopardising the legal rights of unions or, as far as possible, the personal liberties of union leaders. The reasons for this policy are not far to seek. Indian trade unions, though weak in comparison to their counterparts in the developed countries of the West, have been great foci of potential political power. Their power is bound to grow with industrialisation, legal protection, and political encouragement. It is, therefore, no wonder that the leadership of the Indian National Congress could clearly see that whoever wielded this power would ultimately control the stability and progress of the industrialised sector and through it, eventually, the destiny of the country. The labour wing of the Indian National Congress, supported by some of its powerful leaders, could not take the risk of

---

17. Of the five who have held labour portfolio, V. V. Giri, Khandubhai Desai and Gulzari Lal Nanda were prominent trade unionists prior to joining the government. Jagjivan Ram was actively associated with trade unions in Bihar as the Vice-President of the Provincial Trade Union Congress during 1940-1946. D. Sanjivayya, however, has not been known to have any association with trade union work.

letting this power slip into the hands of communists. It was, therefore, decided at the party level to intervene decisively in the trade union movement and acquire political control over a large section of it. Accordingly, a decision was taken in 1947 to form a separate centre of trade union activity, which was to be known as the Indian National Trade Union Congress (INTUC). In defence of this decision, Khandubhai Desai declared:

> The conclusion was irresistible that there was something inherently wrong in the technique and methods of the trade union congress dominated by communist leadership, drawing its inspiration as is well known, from a foreign country. They also realised that the continued association with the communist leadership in the AITUC was highly undesirable and exceedingly detrimental to the interests of the working class and the country. It was obvious that the working of the trade union movement was entirely due to the disruptive tactics of the communists. It was high time that those interested in building up strong trade unionism dissociate themselves from the communists if for nothing else to demonstrate to the world that whatever prestige and status the movement had was because of the efforts of non-communist trade union workers.
>
> It was also felt by many active trade union men that with the advent of the country's Independence, the trade union movement would have to play its destined and legitimate role of influencing the trends towards the elimination of political, economic and social exploitation. This they thought was impossible as long as the communists, who artificially entrenched themselves in a dominant position in the trade union congress, continued to take their lead and inspiration from a foreign country whose foreign policy was likely to affect the trade union movement in this country, and to the detriment of the real interests of the country and the working class.[18]

18. Khandubhai Desai, "The Indian National Trade Union Congress : Its Role in the Trade Union Movement", *Planning for Labour—A Symposium*, Srirampuram-Bangalore, Labour Publications Trust, 1947, pp. 168-169

The Ideological Factor

It is clear from Khandubhai Desai's declaration that the main purpose of organising the INTUC has been to seize the leadership of the working class from the hands of communists. This policy naturally affected the attitude of governments, probably more in States than at the Centre, in respect of recognising and encouraging the INTUC for fostering its policy of moderation in industrial relations.

It is necessary to remember that political involvement of the Indian National Congress since 1947 in the growth of trade union movement in the country has been determined by a larger purpose. This involvement has led to certain attitudes on vital questions, such as trade union recognition, bargaining rights, territory, etc., which cannot be explained except in terms of continuing concern of the Congress with retaining the control of trade unions in the hands of moderate trade union organisations. This factor accounts for some of the apparently irrational characteristics of trade union movement in India and the ambivalence of authorities on the question of promoting healthy bipartite industrial relations that are generally free from third party interference.[19] In a developing economy it is unavoidable that the government should subordinate its concern for a strong and self-reliant trade union movement to the objective of industrial peace and to seek opportunities for rendering these purposes subservient to a grand strategy of economic development. This is the logical consequence of a consensus that economic development must take place under the aegis of government. This necessitates pyramiding of goals and priorities in planning. In such a hierarchical set-up, the purpose of strengthening bipartite industrial relations at the roots is inevitably sub-

---

19. It is necessary to state that the government could promote bipartism in industrial relations only by taking apparently large risks of industrial conflicts which on balance might have strengthened communists in the trade union movement. Such a risk the government was unwilling to take. This was probably the reason for not implementing the Indian Trade Unions (Amendment) Act, 1947, which had provided for the statutory recognition of the bargaining agent and other measures for strengthening trade unions. See in this connection Chapter 4.

ordinated to more pressing considerations.   Accordingly, the
trade union policy is derived from the dynamic desiderata of
resource mobilisation and effective implementation of plan
projects on the one hand and political balance of power in
the realm of industry on the other.   Then a question arises:
Cannot a government achieve the purpose of its policy better
if the whole or part of the trade union movement is ideologically aligned and politically close to the party in power?   It
is apparent that the answer in the Indian context has been
in the affirmative.

The Alternatives

What are the alternatives to this policy?   One is the
laissez faire policy which would leave trade unions to fend
for themselves against employers many of whom may be
openly hostile to the very idea of workers organising themselves, much less dealing with them fairly.   Such a policy
would be extremely unpopular with trade union leaders of
all shades of opinion and would be inconsistent with the
doctrine of development through planning.   Moreover, the
government would have to adopt a neutral attitude on the
ideological battles among the communists, the socialists, the
followers of Gandhi, and others. On the eve of Independence
communists were a formidable force in the trade union
movement.   Could a government committed to a rival
ideology afford this neutrality?   Clearly not.   The other
alternative is to make trade unions an appendage of the state.
But this being a totalitarian solution is inconceivable under
the Indian Constitution. It, therefore, follows that the policies the government has followed in India are unique to a
developing economy in a framework of parliamentary
democracy.

TRADE UNION LEADERSHIP

In discussing the responses of the trade union movement to
the policies of the government and the stresses of economic
development a distinction should be drawn between the
leaders and the rank and file workers.   It cannot always

be assumed that the interests of both are necessarily the same or that they must speak the same language. The union leader must, of course, protect and promote the interests of his constituents in a large measure if he wishes to retain his position. But, by virtue of his control over the organisation, his greater ability on account of education, intelligence, experience and social connections, he is also in a position to sway the opinion of his followers and persuade them to acquiesce, if not actively support, in his line of action even though the same may not always be in their interest. In this study we are not concerned with this kind of dichotomy of interests, but assume, for the sake of simplicity, that the concern of leaders is generally reflective of the interests of workers. Accordingly, we will be mainly interested in the latter.

The leadership of trade unions has been traditionally supplied by the middle class.[20] The leaders have been either

20. The data on trade union leadership are extremely scanty. In a survey of Agra, which is by no means an industrialised city, it was found that the leadership of 58 trade unions was furnished by 10 persons among whom 7 were outsiders. For the purpose of the survey a worker-leader was defined as one who was in industrial employment at the time of the inquiry. Among the 30 leaders in the sample as many as 21 were workers. The survey suffers from serious limitations. "Leaders" are nowhere defined; the sampling procedure is not spelled out; there are no inklings as to what questions were asked; and it is not always clear whether the opinions expressed are those of the authors or of the respondents. See A. S. Mathur and Raman, "Trade Union Leadership in Agra", *Agra University Journal of Research* (letters), Vol. X, Part I, January 1962, pp. 59-80.

In another recent survey covering the whole of India, but due to low response from other States confined largely to the States of Maharashtra and Gujarat, it has been found that a large majority of leaders (64.1%), defined to include union presidents and general secretaries and, in their absence, vice-presidents, secretaries or assistant secretaries, were educated up to the undergraduate level. This does not necessarily prove that these belong to the middle class but, in view of the widespread illiteracy among workers, such a presumption might not be false. This is further corroborated by the finding that in Greater Bombay as many as 55.1 per cent of leaders use English either alone or in addition to one Indian language, in conducting trade union activities. See S. D. Punekar and S. Madhuri, *Trade Union Leadership in India* : *A Survey* (mimeographed), conducted by the Tata Institute of Social Sciences, Bombay, 1965, Chapter 3 entitled "General Background of the Leaders : Personal Data".

politicians seeking a base for their wider activities or sensitive
men who are greatly moved by the unmitigated misery of
the suffering people.[21]   There have also been working class
leaders mostly at the second and lower ladders who were
caught by the appeal of a militant ideology or the whirlwind
of nationalist movement and were inducted into sustained
trade union activity.   The birth of organised trade unions
coincided with the civil disobedience and non-cooperation
movement and the emergence of communist cadres in the
country.   It is also noteworthy that the trade union movement, suggestive of its outside leadership, was founded as an
all-India organisation much before it had the time to strike
roots.[22]

21. In this context it is instructive to read the memoirs of an ex-trade union
    leader, K. Dwarkadas, who on visiting the residential areas of workers
    in 1920 during a strike, records his feelings in the following words:
        During these visits to the mill area, I came face to face with hard facts
        of life,with human miseries never experienced or dreamt of before. Today
        when I remember some of the sights which I then witnessed I shudder
        with horror and wonder that such things should exist and be permitted
        to exist.   What squalor, what misery, what intolerable suffering, what
        ignorance, what helplessness!   It makes one feel sick when one realises
        that all these were—and are—preventable if decency, sympathy and
        friendliness, consideration, understanding and organised effort prevailed.
    K. Dwarkadas, *Forty-five Years with Labour*, Bombay, Asia Publishing
    House, 1962.
22. The All India Trade Union Congress (AITUC) was inaugurated in Bombay
    on the crest of waves of strikes unprecedented in Bombay Presidency in
    1920.   The first President of the AITUC was Lala Lajpat Rai, one of the
    then foremost nationalist leaders of India.   It is reported by K. Dwarkadas
    that he approached Mahatma Gandhi to join the new organisation and also
    persuade the Ahmedabad Textile Labour Association to do likewise.
    The request was turned down.   *Forty-five Years with Labour*, (op. cit.),
    p. 21.   Also see Ahmad Mukhtar, *Factory Labour in India*, Madras, The
    Annamalai University, 1930, Chapter IX, "The Law and Labour
    Unrest", especially pp. 86-100.
        B. Shiva Rao, one of the founders of trade union movement in south
    India, believes that a combination of several causes including "a radical
    political movement, the enunciation of the doctrine of racial equality,
    rising prices and consequent economic distress, and, finally, the reactions
    of the influenza epidemic, resulting in a shortage of labour" were responsi-
    ble for the emergence of workers' organisations during the post-World
    War I period.   *The Industrial Worker in India*, London, George Allen and
    Unwin Ltd., 1939, p. 19.

Later on, the nationalist leaders continued to support trade unions in return for political backing in their struggle against the British rule. By 1926, the communists had started organising trade unions as part of their political activity. Since then their influence has grown and with it the conflict between them and the moderates. This conflict has been repeatedly witnessed in the splits and the unity moves among the political leaders of the trade union movement since 1929.[23] Due to peculiar historical origins of the trade union movement in India the leadership has, with some outstanding exceptions, remained in the hands of political personalities. This is a fundamental fact of trade union history which has not been altered to this day.

General Effect of Political Disunity on Unionism

What is the significance of political affiliation of trade union leaders to the basic theme of our book? The significance is in three respects. First, political disunity in the trade union movement imparts to it a measure of permanent instability. The instability can take several forms: (i) There may be fluidity in the loyalty of leaders. With a change in the affiliation of a leader the union under his control also acquires a new complexion. (ii) There may be multiple

23. See V. B. Karnik, "The Indian Trade Union Movement", V. M. Tarkinde, "Preserve the Unity of the Trade Union Movement: The Radicals' Approach", and N. G. Ranga, "Broad-based Trade Unionism : Political Trends in Indian Labour Movement", *Planning for Labour*, (op. cit.). These articles were written shortly after the AITUC had been split. Moreover, the authors reflect the dominant political moods in the country. Unfortunately, the official AITUC point of view is not represented in this symposium. It may be noted that in 1947-48 the communist leadership of the AITUC was fully engrossed in defining its position towards the new government. It was generally moving into militant opposition and, therefore, might not even have felt the enormity of change that had taken place. For the purpose of militant action the Communist Party of India would surely have preferred disciplined unity in the ranks of trade unions rather than a solidarity of workers based on a confederation of ideologies. See in this connection K. B. Panikkar, *An Outline of the History of the AITUC*, New Delhi, All India Trade Union Congress, 1959. This 19-page outline gives a bare summary of the events in the history of trade union movement beginning from 1920 up to the date of publication.

unions in the same bargaining territory with the ostensible purpose of organising workers but, in fact, disuniting them. (*iii*) In situations characterised by (*i*) and (*ii*), unions as organisations grow weaker or just do not become robust with the result that they fail to establish viable relationship with either employers or their own constituents. (*iv*) Much of the union energy is consumed in overcoming the tension created by the all-pervasive insecurity and instability such that the basic task of strengthening the organisation is neglected. As a result, unions may not be able to adequately respond on matters vitally affecting workers' interests.

Second, the attitudes of central leadership of the national trade union federations on vital economic issues are generally coloured by ideology rather than determined by the pragmatic concern for attempting to achieve whatever may be feasible under the circumstances. This gets reflected not merely in the resolutions passed at all-India conferences and the memoranda submitted to the government on important matters but at the plant level, too. This affects their methods of settling disputes, the appeals they make to workers and employers, and the degree of reliance placed on the administrative machinery. For instance, if the leadership of a set of unions believes in the inappropriateness of strikes as a method of settling disputes and in reconciling sectional interests of workers with those of the nation as a whole it is likely to put much greater reliance on discussion, negotiation, persuasion and, if necessary, political pressure from outside, than the other that believes in forging unions as an instrument of class warfare.[24]

Third, the diversity in the supply of political leadership is likely to place at the disposal of workers a variety of skills, experience, and policies which may enable the latter to retain the services of most of them at a relatively low price. As individual members of the community they may be expected to behave rationally in committing themselves to no particular brand of leadership but switching support from one to the other depending upon their assessment of the relative effi-

24. See G. Ramanujam, *Industrial Relations, A Point of View*, New Delhi, Indian National Trade Union Congress.

cacy of one as compared to the other. Where issues are such that only militant action can register workers' collective voice, it would be desirable to support the most fiery leadership available on the scene. On the other hand, on routine matters involving disciplinary action it might be prudent to seek the help of a quieter leadership in whom the employers might also have some stake. It is obvious that in such a situation the worker will get the services he desires by paying the least price in terms of fees, time, and organisational loyalty. It is equally obvious that workers, having denied themselves the pains of building an organisation, will have to depend upon the outside leadership more or less on a permanent basis.

Perspectives of Union Leaders

Given the political moorings of a large section of trade unions, their weak membership base, lack of financial viability, inadequate organisational structure supported by regular offices, paid full-time and part-time staff, and widespread unemployment, what could be the strategy of union leadership in an era of planned economic development? In asking this question it is not assumed that union leaders could have foreseen all the developments that have taken place in India since Independence; nor is it supposed that, given the knowledge of the basic problems of the country, all the political centres would think alike. Trade unionists, like political leaders of the country, were probably well versed with the facts of the Indian economy as were known on the eve of planning, but unlike the latter the former could only set limited goals. By the very nature of their occupation, they had to live from day to day with little time left for reflecting over deeper matters of common concern to the entire working class. Nevertheless, trade unions all over the world have voiced demands on such general matters as social security, minimum wages, industrial housing, hours of work, protection of real earnings in the face of rising prices, etc. Most of these demands cannot be adequately met at the level of the firm, particularly so, in a country like India where unions are not only weak but must operate within a social framework of considerable visible unemployment and wide-spread misery.

These circumstances weaken trade unions' capacity to strike a hard bargain in four ways. First, they are faced with employers who are economically much stronger than themselves. The principal weakness of unions is their inability to look after their constituents in the event of unemployment. Second, the economic condition of industrial workers is often superior to the rest of the masses. The knowledge of this fact probably weakens their will to organise and fight for collective interests. The alternative to the job on hand may very well be the return to village and face semi-unemployment and the attendant misfortunes, social disapprobation, and fall in status. Third, the trade union leadership, uncertain of its strength and ability to survive a trial of strength, may be unwilling to take chances with whatever following it may have. The fear of failure may indeed be greater in a union that has acquired some standing but is not yet in a commanding position, than with leaders who are either still fighting preliminary battles of recognition and for a place under the sun, or those who have achieved a pre-eminent position and can afford to take risks. On the basis of common observation and general consensus it can be safely asserted that the bulk of unions in India will fall in the intermediate position. Fourth, the government has been willing to bring its weight down against unions, should it disapprove of their action, just as it is ready to conciliate, arbitrate, and even offer legislated rights for the sake of industrial peace. The knowledge of this circumstance has been of the greatest importance to trade union leaders of practically all shades of political beliefs. While conditioning the scope of manoeuvre at the company level, this has immensely widened the area of negotiations at the national and the industry levels. Its overall effect upon union leaders has been the lifting of sights.

For trade unions democratic India has provided a natural climate of growth. The fundamental rights enshrined in the Constitution gave them as much protection against the arbitrariness of state as the rights legislated by the government had armed them against employers. Fortunately, despite its anxiety for speedy economic development, the government has been committed to democratic values. Moreover, as industries multiply and the economy grows, so will increase the demand for the services of trade unions and their leaders. Free India has, thus, provided trade union leaders with an ever-widening opportunity for natural expansion. This opportunity has been well exploited and, as will be shown in the next chapter, trade unionism in quantitative terms has expanded considerably. Indeed, ever since the movement has been split into conflicting ideological camps, one of the primary concerns of leaders has been to add to their respective following more unions and members. Some of the claims of growth in membership are probably exaggerated—a phenomenon which testifies to the insecurity of leadership on the relative position of one centre in the union movement as a whole. The instinct of survival has probably been the primary impulse behind the leadership's concern for quantitative growth.

The second element in the union strategy is to fight defensive battles for protecting the real earnings of workers. In an expanding economy trade union leadership can conceivably have two choices. One is to use union power for seeking larger gains for workers in the output. This might be accompanied by a ruthless drive for greater control over the decision-making process in enterprises on matters that affect workers' security and welfare. For instance, in the United States it has been repeatedly alleged by leading company executives as well as reputed scholars that trade unions, particularly in the oligopolistic sector, have come to possess a monopoly power during the post-Second World War period which has been persistently and sometimes disastrously used for whittling down management prerogatives, jack up costs, undermine competition and, among other evils, generate secular cost push inflation.[25] These allegations probably

. This has been partly due to the employers' duty to bargain in good faith laid down by the Wagner Act and religiously reinforced by the National Labour Relations Board. As interpreted by the Board, this meant that employers should not only negotiate on the basis of trade union representation but make positive counter-proposals if the same do not lead to agreement. In certain cases the Board decided that good faith bargaining have a measure of truth in them. However, in a country like India unions are no doubt influential but do not have nearly anywhere the power that is supposed to vest in their American counterparts. Collective bargaining, which is the primary source of union power in the USA, is more an exception than a rule in India. There is no Wagner Act that can require the employer to bargain in good faith. Despite economic growth and considerable increase in jobs, full employment is at best a distant goal. Moreover, the economy is highly controlled by the government, which by itself has greatly trimmed the prerogatives of managements to control costs and prices. The process of wage fixation is regulated by the government-instituted authorities, such as wage boards and national tribunals. A large portion of workers' earnings are determined either by law, such as bonus, or by convention, as in the case of dearness allowance. In view of these facts, the logical possibility of an aggressive strategy on the part of unions can be safely excluded.

A realistic policy for unions in Indian conditions would, on the other hand, be confined to adopting a defensive posture in respect of protecting the economic interests of workers. This is indeed essential if unions have to expand

---

required that an employer should refrain from making unilateral concessions to workers, over the head of the union that was seeking to negotiate a contract. See Philip Ross, *The Government as a Source of Union Power. The Role of Public Policy in Collective Bargaining*, Providence, Rhode Island, Brown University Press, 1965, pp. 101-132. The other reasons are (i) the oligopolistic structure of the market in the dominant sectors of the economy, (ii) near-full employment with a built-in inflationary potential (iii) the political commitment of the government to the goal of full employment, (iv) weakness of foreign competition, and (v) barriers to entry into the labour market enforced by union shop and generally supported by both the employers and the government.

There is considerable literature on this subject. See in this connection E. H. Chamberlain, "Labour Union Power and Public Interest", J. W. McKie, "Collective Bargaining and the Maintenance of Market Competition", D. M. Wright, "Regulating Unions", G. Haberler, "Wage Policy and Inflation", and other papers in Philip D. Bradley (ed.), *The Public Stake in Union Power*, Charlottesville, University of Virginia Press, 1959. Also see Arthur M. Ross, *Trade Union Wage Policy*, Berkeley, University of California Press, 1956, pp. 1-44.

their membership base, as has been postulated above. This would involve the leadership in safeguarding earnings against the growing menace of inflation, shielding jobs from technological changes, union interests in the face of victimisation and violence, and demanding improved working and living conditions. Wherever conditions are ripe, unions might also demand a measure of industrial democracy; but this would be fairly low in priorities, and its absence might not even be felt in most instances.

A FRAME OF WORKING HYPOTHESES

In the light of the foregoing discussion, we can set up the working hypotheses which will provide a framework for further analysis. These are expressed as propositions and are presumed to be true under Indian conditions. It is necessary to say this because it is not our intention to claim universality for them. We are discussing social phenomena that are greatly conditioned by culture, traditions, political institutions, laws, and level of economic activity. These not only vary from country to country but often differ in kind. In many respects India is a special case and her conditions are unique. To cite an outstanding instance, India is the only country in the world with extraordinary diversity in cultures, rapidly growing population, and extremely low per capita income, to practise constitutional democracy for nearly two decades. In the underdeveloped world, India is one among the few countries that have a fairly well developed trade union movement that has found it possible to adjust and adapt to the changing problem-mix of a developing economy. Our working hypotheses are:

(i) The multiplicity of union centres is the direct outcome of the desire of political parties to acquire a base among workers on the one hand and the ideological distance among them on the other. The roots of disunity do not lie in the conflict of interests among groups of workers but rather in the goals and the purposes of trade union leaders.

(ii) Trade union rivalry has aided the spread of the movement quantitatively but weakened it qualitatively.

(iii) The spread of trade unionism has been aided by

    (a) the growth in employment by providing larger social base for expansion;

    (b) the threat to job security which may occur either due to introduction of labour saving devices or slackening of demand;

    (c) the threat to real earnings by inflation which induces workers to unite for more dearness allowance, higher bonus, etc.; and

    (d) the growing respectability of unionism as a vocation and lever for social and political advancement.

(iv) The legal framework created by the government has had a net retardation effect upon the natural growth of vitality of trade unions as workers' organisations. It has made the union less self-reliant and weakened the organisational bond between the worker and his institution.[26]

26. See Fred C. Munson and A. C. Nanda, "The Influence of Legal Framework on Labour Leaders and their Unions", *Indian Journal of Industrial Relations*, Vol. 2, No. 1, July 1966, pp. 3-33. The authors carried out a survey of opinions of 40 trade union leaders, mostly in the Delhi region on how the legal system created by the government had influenced the working of trade unions and their leaders. One of their conclusions is that "it has kept unions weak". This is because the legal framework has made it possible for weak unions to stay alive and also strengthened the leaders against the rank and file. In our view the primary cause of union retardation is that the legal framework has made the leader a mere service-providing agent to workers. Moreover, a worker in need of help has the opportunity of choosing among the leaders; according to the latest amendment to the Industrial Disputes Act, 1947, an aggrieved worker does not even need a trade union to move the conciliation machinery. Therefore, it is not so much that the leader has been strengthened against the union members—under Indian conditions a reasonable supply of educated leaders is absolutely required for the continued functioning of an organisation not excluding trade unions—but that the bond of mutual responsibility between them has been weakened.

THE CHAPTER OUTLINE

The working hypotheses stated above are explored in the following chapters. This is done mostly at the aggregate level. It might, however, be instructive to compare the performance of unions in different industries and regions. This has also been attempted to a limited extent as permitted by the available data. It may be added that data on trade unions are quite inadequate. From the point of view of research an acute and almost insoluble difficulty arises due to the shifting rate of submission of returns. There are other difficulties, too, which are brought out at the appropriate places. Mainly due to deficiency in data, it has been necessary to rely on theoretical reasoning to a much greater extent than we would have wished. In studies of this nature it is generally the most preferred course to let facts speak for themselves. But in Indian conditions, and not just in the field of industrial relations, this is hardly possible. The Indian data on agricultural output, national income, capital formation, capital-to-output ratios, indices of consumer prices, and many other related subjects suffer from grave uncertainties. However, these form an inalienable part of the underdeveloped society in which we live and function. The researchers have to do the best they can with the imperfect resources and tools available to them.

This book is divided into eight chapters. The first chapter is the introduction. The second chapter reviews the progress of trade union movement with the aid of published statistics. The analysis has been done at the aggregate as well as the sectoral level. The third chapter analyses the relationship between growth and inflation on the one hand and their effect upon unionism via the differential movement in earnings and productivity and money illusion on the other. The analysis brings out a strong positive correlation between the degree of unionisation and the Consumer Price Index. The fourth chapter is devoted to reviewing the trade union policy of the government. The trade union policy is derived from essential goals; the factors influencing it and its subservience to economic planning are carefully analysed and its effects upon unionism are brought out. In chapter five are analysed the responses of trade unions to the stresses and strains of a developing economy. The negative responses take the form of strikes, occasionally resulting in lockouts, and are revealed in the strange paradox of union leaders involving themselves in no-strike pledges and work-stoppages at the same time and other odd features of unionism in India. Chapter six deals with the relationship of trade unions and the five year plans. It brings out the areas of agreements and disagreements between the government and the unions. The theoretical underpinnings of union arguments are also brought out. In chapter seven the organisational interests of trade unions are analysed. The problems of union recognition, involvement of political parties in trade union movement, and the consequences flowing therefrom and related matters are discussed. In the eighth chapter the entire discussion is summarised and relevant conclusions are drawn on the relationship between the purpose and functioning of trade unions' policy and the behaviour of organised labour. The implications of this study in the making of future policy are also spelled out. The chapter scheme is followed by appendices containing some useful tables and a select bibliography.

CHAPTER 2

PROGRESS OF UNIONISM IN INDIA

TRADE UNIONS : SCOPE AND COVERAGE

TRADE UNIONS ARE GENERALLY UNDERSTOOD AS VOLUNTARY organisations of workers formed for the purpose of defending and advancing the latter's collective interests either mutually or in relation to outside parties, such as employers, government, and other trade unions. In principle, unions of employers, peasants, or any class or classes of people can be formed.[1] However, we are concerned with trade unions of workers only. In this context the term "workers" is understood to include all employees who do not perform supervisory functions. Accordingly, office staff can be regarded as workers and also the highly paid navigators employed by air transport companies.[2]

1. Under the Indian Trade Unions Act, 1926, a trade union is defined as follows:
   "Trade Union" means any combination whether temporary or permanent, formed primarily for the purpose of regulating the relations between workmen and employers or between workmen and workmen, or between employers and employers or for imposing restrictive conditions on the conduct of any trade or business, and includes any federation of two or more trade unions.
   This definition is sufficiently wide to include chambers of commerce and employers' organisations and clearly goes far beyond the territory covered by us. However, the operative clauses of the Act are such that workers' organisations can be registered separately from those of employers.
2. This definition is consistent with that of the Factories Act, 1948. See Chapter 1, section 2(l) of the Act. The definition of "workman" under the Industrial Disputes Act, 1947, explicitly excludes from this category those employed in managerial or administrative capacity and supervisors drawing wages in excess of five hundred rupees per mensem and exercising functions mainly of a managerial nature. See Chapter 1, section 2(s) of the Act. For a discussion of the problems arising out of the conflicting definitions of "worker" and its equivalent terms under different legislations in India, see K. N. Vaid, *State and Labour in India*, Bombay, Asia Publishing House, 1965, pp. 19-23.

Limitations of Data

The Indian Trade Unions Act, 1926, allows for the registration of trade unions and thereby confers upon them certain benefits and privileges but does not require every union to get registered. The registration requires submission of information on objectives, constitution, affiliation, membership, finances, etc. by the applicants. According to the Act, a union desirous of retaining its registration must supply the required information every year and also open its books for inspection. However, not all unions take the trouble of doing this and, as a consequence, sometimes even get their registration cancelled. Under Indian conditions, the lapses on the part of the unions are quite common and by comparison the penalty of deregistration is rather rare. This may not have much effect upon the day-to-day functioning of unions but causes havoc to the data collected by the Registrars of Trade Unions in different States and transmitted to the Labour Bureau, Simla, for processing and publishing. The Labour Bureau in publishing the data states the response rate, *i.e.*, the percentage of unions supplying information to the total registered. The non-response rate is the sum of two causes: (*i*) failure of the unions to supply information; and (*ii*) failure of the Registrars of Trade Unions to classify and transmit the collected information by the due date. Since these two causes vary from year to year, it is not possible to determine their relative contribution in building up the non-response rate.

Considering that submission of returns involves a measure of organisational efficiency, it can be assumed that the unions which submit returns are not only active but also alive to their legal responsibilities. These unions may be interpreted as the core of the trade union movement in India. Those which do not submit returns may or may not be active or possess the organisational set-up required for this purpose. Underlying this statement is the assumption that there is stability among the reporting unions. This may not always be true in practice but, for our purpose, is both reasonable and necessary.

There is also some uncertainty on the accuracy of membership data. The law does not lay down a precise definition of "union membership". But, for purposes of recognition, in undertakings where more than one union exist, the official machinery verifies the membership. However, the verified figure has no legal sanctity behind it. For retaining their registration, unions may or may not report the verified membership. It has often been noted that the claimed membership far exceeds the verified figure. In industries where the problem of inter-union rivalry is particulary marked, the combined claimed membership produces the absurd result of exceeding the figure on the average daily employment. In this study, for making inter-industry comparisons, all such situations have been excluded. However, there is no way of counting them out from the aggregate totals. By comparison, the data on the four recognised centres are verified, and they may be accepted as broadly correct. It should, however, be borne in mind that in relating the latter with the combined all-India total of union membership the proportions are likely to be understated. On the other hand, due to the shifting rate of response, it is possible that the published figures do not fully reflect the actual membership of unions, which may, indeed, be larger. Therefore, for the sake of simplicity, we may assume that the double error of non-reported membership and inflated figures of reported membership mutually cancel out. On this basis rests the premise that the trend revealed by the reported data is broadly accurate and may be relied upon for general purposes.

There is yet another limitation to the data that needs mention. The Labour Bureau publishes data for only four national federations which have been recognised by the Government of India. These are: the Indian National Trade Union Congress (INTUC), the All India Trade Union Congress (AITUC), the Hind Mazdoor Sabha (HMS), and the United Trade Union Congress (UTUC).[3] It cannot, how-

___

3. Among these, the AITUC is the oldest; it was formed in 1920. The INTUC was founded in 1947 by the unions which were formerly affiliated with the Hindustan Mazdoor Sevak Sangh, a Gandhian labour organisation, and others controlled by the labour leaders in the Indian National Congress. The Hind Mazdoor Sabha was created in December 1948 after the Congress Socialists had decided to part with the Indian Nationa

ever, be assumed that trade unions that are not shown as affiliated to any of the four federations are necessarily independent of political parties. Such an assumption would be fatal for two reasons. First, there are at least two other federations controlled by the Jana Sangh and the Samyukta Socialist Party known as the Bharatiya Mazdoor Sangh (BMS) and the Hind Mazdoor Panchayat (HMP) respectively which do not enjoy recognition and hence do not feature in the published statistics. Furthermore, other parties, too, have either formed their labour fronts or are in the process of doing so. It is likely that their members are leading some trade unions and using them for political purposes as in the recognised federations. Second, some leaders, followed by their unions, move in and out of federations. It is thus possible that at any point of time a union may not be affiliated to a national centre, but from this it would not follow that it is apolitical. On the other hand, it is also possible that a trade union affiliated to a national federation may not be led by leaders attached to a party. The HMS and the UTUC were in fact formed with the ostensible purpose of keeping the union movement free from partisanship flowing from party attachments. In other words, though the association of national centres with political parties is quite close, it need not hold good in every case. Similarly, while non-political attachment may be closely associated with the absence of affiliated status (and consequently with its quantitative measure, i.e., the number of unions and members not affiliated to a centre), it may not be invariably true. These limitations of data would prevent us from making sweeping generalisations in these matters. With these limitations in view, the growth of the trade union movement, based on the data collected under the Indian Trade Unions Act, 1926, and other sources, will be analysed.

Congress and join hands with the Indian Federation of Labour—an organisation controlled by the Radical Democrats under the leadership of M. N. Roy. The UTUC was formed in 1949. It consisted of leftists and independents who had left the AITUC in 1947 and 1948, tried to work with the socialists, but finally decided to go their own way. This is the smallest of the four organisations and is generally led by the Revolutionary Socialist Party in association with other splinter parties. See V. B. Karnik, *Indian Trade Unions : A Survey*, (op. cit.), pp. 116-146.

GROWTH IN TRADE UNIONS : 1950-1964

Trade unions have increased enormously both in numbers and membership. The data pertaining to them are set out in Table 1. The table shows that between 1949-50 and 1963-64, over a period of fifteen years, the number of registered trade unions has gone up by 326 per cent. In absolute terms, there were 11,610 unions in 1962-63 and 11,459 in 1963-64. The latter, however, is a provisional figure and will probably be revised upwards when the final returns are received and tabulated. As compared to the previous year's figure, which is more reliable, the growth has been over 329 per cent. It is noteworthy that the response rate has been going up. Between 1949-50 and 1953-54 it fluctuated narrowly in the range of 53-55 per cent, in the next two years it dropped sharply, but since 1957-58 it has been steadily going up. It stood at 61.40 per cent in 1963-64. This can be interpreted as a sign of growing organisational efficiency of the ever-increasing number of unions.

The number of unions submitting returns has increased by 366 per cent during 1949-50 and 1962-63, whereas the total membership has risen by only 201 per cent. It is unlikely that this odd result has been due to greater non-reporting on the part of larger unions. More likely, it shows the direction in which unionism has been expanding. In this period the medium and small-scale firms have increased significantly and might be coming under union influence. It is also possible that multiple unions in the same bargaining territory have been dividing among themselves the union membership. In the absence of data on union registration and membership by size class of firms in various industries it is impossible to be categorical on the relative weight of these causes. It is, however, probable that the first factor has been more important.

Union Membership and Labour Force

How has union membership grown in relation to the increase in labour force? Estimates vary on the latter. According to the Planning Commission, in the decade 1951-1961,

Data on registered trade unions and

Year		No. of Regis-tered Unions	Index No. of Registered Unions (1951=100)	No. of Unions Submitting Returns
1		2	3	4
1949-50	..	3,522	78.18	1,919
1950-51	..	3,766	83.60	2,002
1951-52	..	4,505	100.00	2,509
1952-53	..	4,880	108.32	2,690
1953-54	..	5,919	131.17	3,258
1954-55	..	6,557	145.55	3,517
1955-56	..	8,016	177.94	3,968
1956-57	..	8,477	188.17	4,370
1957-58	..	9,868	219.05	5,460
1958-59	..	10,071	223.55	5,952
1959-60	..	10,656	236.54	6,485
1960-61	..	11,145	247.39	6,708
1961-62	..	11,416	253.41	6,954
1962-63	..	11,610	257.71	7,109
1963-64*	..	11,459	254.36	7,036

*Provisional.
Sources:
  (*i*) For the years 1949-50 to 1950-51, *Indian Labour Year Book*, 1952-53,
  (*ii*) For the years 1951-52 to 1955-56, *Indian Labour Statistics*, 1960,
  (*iii*) For the years 1956-57 to 1960-61, *Indian Labour Statistics*, 1964,
  (*iv*) For the years 1961-62 to 1963-64, *Indian Labour Statistics*, 1966,

1

those submitting returns

Index No. of Unions Submitting Returns (1951=100)	Response Rate (in per cent) Col. (2)÷Col. (4)	Membership of Unions Submitting Returns (in '000)	Index of Union Membership (Base year= 1951=100)
5	6	7	8
76.48	54.49	1,821	91.60
79.79	53.16	1,757	88.38
100.00	55.69	1,988	100.00
107.21	55.12	2,094	105.33
169.78	55.64	2,106	105.93
140.18	53.63	2,167	109.00
158.15	49.50	2,269	114.13
174.17	51.55	2,373	119.36
217.62	55.33	3,006	151.21
237.23	59.10	3,635	182.40
258.47	60.86	3,910	196.68
267.36	60.19	4,000	201.21
277.16	60.91	3,960	199.20
283.34	61.23	3,666	184.41
280.43	61.40	3,899	196.13

p. 50.
pp. 112-113.
pp. 103-104.
pp. 117-118.

the increase was of the order of 21 million.[4] One scholar puts the figure at 17.6 million.[5] In relation to the Planning Commission's estimate, it is further stated that non-agricultural employment increased by about 12 million. Another 5 million may have been employed in the agricultural sector. The remaining joined the growing army of the unemployed, currently estimated at 9-10 million. For the purpose of unionisation the unemployed are obviously unsuitable, and so are those employed in the agricultural sector. The relevant category may be defined as the increase in non-agricultural labour force, net of the additions to the self-employed and other non-unionisable occupations. The "independent workers" and the "employers" comprised 50.9 per cent and 3.3 per cent respectively of the population of self-supporting persons in non-agricultural activities excluding the ones engaged in non-productive occupations.[6] These add up to 54.2 per cent of the total. From this may be excluded another 9.8 per cent on account of health, education, and public administration which though unionisable are occupations subject to severe restraints. Now assuming that employment in these broad occupational categories grew in the same proportion as was revealed by the 1951 census, it is possible to estimate the increase in labour force that could potentially be unionised. This works out to 4.7 million over the decade 1951-1961 if the last category of occupations is excluded. By comparison, the reported union membership has gone up by 2.2 million. Thus, the ratio of increase in union membership to the net addition to the unionisable employed labour force stands at 46.8 per cent. If this is adjusted for the membership of non-reporting unions, the ratio may go well beyond 50 per cent. This is a measure of union dynamism and is suggestive of the expansive phase

---

4. *Fourth Five Year Plan, A Draft Outline*, Part I, Chapter VI, p. 1. (All references are made to the mimeographed copy.)

5. Y. S. Yegnaraman, "On the Comparability of Addition to Working Population During the First and Second Plans—1961 Census and Plan Estimates", *The Asian Economic Review*, Vol. V, No. 3, May 1963, p. 407.

6. *Indian Labour Statistics*, 1964, Table 1.4, pp. 7-8.

through which the union movement has been passing since Independence.

The spread of unionism is sometimes measured through the degree of unionisation defined as the ratio of union membership to average daily employment as expressed in percentage terms. This is an average concept as compared to the marginal concept used above to indicate union dynamism. The degree of unionisation is a good measure of the progress in depth while the marginal concept measures the rate of change and also points to the limit of expansion. It is axiomatic that when the rate of change is going up the average will also rise. Translated in terms of organisational strength, it means that the energy devoted in acquiring new members is not at the expense of the existing ones. In other words, not only new members are being enlisted but the total membership is also growing. Such a combination would clearly suggest both deepening and widening of the trade union movement.

The data on the degree of unionisation in selected sectors are set out in Table 2.[7] These relate to a large portion of manufacturing sector, mining and quarrying, plantations, railways, and posts and telegraphs. They comprise the bulk of the modernised sector that can be unionised, and leave out small-scale industries, unregistered factories, shops and establishments, and several other sectors. It may also be noted that while the data on employment relate to calendar years, those on union membership relate to financial years. The drop in union membership in 1962-63 is probably due to the non-submission of returns traceable to the emergency created by the Chinese aggression on India. But this does not affect the comparability of figures in a time series. Table 2 shows a steady increase in the degree of unionisation and, taken together with the rate of expansion, supports the statement made earlier that the totality of factors operating in India, since Independence, have been favourable to the quantitative growth of the union movement.

7. The degree of unionisation has been calculated only for those sectors for which comparable data, over the period, on average daily employment or near equivalent, and union membership are available. The sectors in which the values are absurdly high have been excluded.

TABLE 2

Trends in the degree of unionisation* in the selected sectors**

Year			Union Membership (in '000)	Average Daily Employment (in '000)	Degree of Unionisation %
1			2	3	4
1951-52	..	..	1,394	5,686	24.5
1952-53	..	..	1,582	5,757	27.5
1953-54	..	..	1,442	5,697	25.3
1954-55	..	..	1,538	5,819	26.4
1955-56	..	..	1,657	6,006	27.6
1956-57	..	..	1,688	5,992	28.2
1957-58	..	..	2,050	6,200	33.1
1958-59	..	..	2,576	6,284	40.1
1959-60	..	..	2,800	6,445	43.4
1960-61	..	..	2,950	6,615	44.6
1961-62	..	..	2,793	7,053	39.6
1962-63	..	..	2,430	7,316	33.2
1963-64	..	..	2,639	6,462	40.8

*$\dfrac{\text{Union Membership}}{\text{Employment}} \times 100$

**Includes Industrial Classification Group No. 0.1; 0.2; 1; 2.0 to 2.2; 2.3; 2.5+2.6; 2.7; 2.8; 2.9; 3.0; 3.1; 3.2+3.3; 3.4+3.5; 3.6+3.7; 3.8; 7.2; and 7.6.

Source: Based on Table 1 in the Appendix.

Regional Variations

The data on registered and reporting unions and the membership of the latter for the eighteen States and political territories in India are laid out in Table 3. The States have been ranked from highest to lowest for the number of unions on the register in 1962-63. The data go back to 1956-57 only. Due to reorganisation of States in that year, the data for the previous years for several States are not on a comparable basis. The table shows that West Bengal has generally retained the top position throughout the period. But apparently due to the unusually low response rate in 1962-63, the union membership in this State has shown a decline. As can be seen in the table, this is completely at variance with the previous years' data and may not be, therefore, relied upon. Surprisingly, Kerala which is much smaller in population and is not particularly industrialised holds the second position. This is due to high literacy rate among the plantation workers and the fact that almost every sector of employment, including small-scale and handicraft industries, is unionised.

The top five States in India are West Bengal, Kerala, Maharashtra, Madras, and Uttar Pradesh. These together account for 49.2 per cent of the total unions on register in 1962-63. Their combined share in 1956-57 was only 14.6 per cent. In terms of reported membership, the share of the top five States has declined from 59.3 per cent in 1956-57 to 55.5 per cent in 1962-63. Part of the reason is that some of the States which had high positions in the ranking by union membership have yielded to others. For instance, Bihar and Uttar Pradesh occupied the second and the third ranks respectively in 1956-57. In 1962-63, both had moved one step down. Surprisingly, West Bengal did not figure among the top five in 1956-57 but moved up to the second position in 1962-63. It appears that for West Bengal this was an year of exceptionally low response; and from this one might conclude that the erratic response has completely distorted the results. However, the results are similar if 1957-58 is compared to 1962-63. Therefore, the explanation might lie elsewhere.

It seems that some of the backward States have marched forward rapidly in unionising their labour force. Delhi and Andhra Pradesh have moved up from eighth to sixth and from tenth to seventh ranks respectively. Other States, such as Mysore and Punjab, have made substantial progress in this respect. The growth of unions in the top five States is pro-

Number of workers' trade unions on register, those submitting

Sl. No.	State			1962-63		
				No. of Unions on Register	No. of Unions Submitting Returns	Membership of Unions (in '000)
1				2	3	4
1	West Bengal	..	..	2,156	950	598
2	Kerala	..	..	1,680	796	220
3	Maharashtra	..	..	1,460	894	638
4	Madras	..	..	1,164	764	289
5	Uttar Pradesh	..	..	1,058	951	291
6	Bihar	..	..	617	537	379
7	Punjab†	..	..	589	418	88
8	Andhra Pradesh	..	..	546	328	245
9	Mysore	..	..	500	293	142
10	Gujarat	..	..	487	346	208
11	Madhya Pradesh	..	..	425	102	44
12	Delhi	..	..	357	300	267
13	Rajasthan	..	..	245	195	47
14	Assam	..	..	138	99	115
15	Orissa	..	..	123	92	81
16	Tripura	..	..	35	16	7
17	Himachal Pradesh	..	..	16	16	4
18	Andaman & Nicobar	..	..	14	12	3

*Includes the number of employers' unions on the register, submittin
†Now reorganised into Haryana and Punjab.

3

returns and membership of the latter by States

	1961-62			1960-61	
No. of Unions on Register	No. of Unions Submitting Returns	Membership of Unions (in '000)	No. of Unions on Register	No. of Unions Submitting Returns	Membership of Unions (in '000)
5	6	7	8	9	10
2,091	1,167	834	1,987	1,250	1,007
1,842	877	262	1,844	878	262
1,397	812	596	1,815	837	256
1,178	836	377	1,107	859	407
961	853	326	1,009	825	326
632	505	387	642*	488*	371*
614	382	83	550	248	63
519	253	129	598	162	125
504	215	104	501	215	104
455	350	199	442	185	90
379	87	37	330	92	31
314	270	239	309	251	210
235	182	49	191	169	43
138	43	250	147	81	227
116	82	76	103	59	53
13	13	7	37	12	7
14	14	3	13	13	2
14	13	2	12	9	2

returns and membership. *Contd.*

TABLE

Sl. No.	1959-60			1958-59		
	No. of Unions on Register	No. of Unions Submitting Returns	Membership of Unions (in '000)	No. of Unions on Register	No. of Unions Submitting Returns	Membership of Unions (in '000)
	1	2	3	4	5	6
1	1,987	1,250	1,007	1,973	867	733
2	1,815	837	256	1,538	909	374
3	1,376	817	577	..	..	..
4	1,107	859	407	943	746	384
5	1,009	825	326	955	652	243
6	642*	408*	371*	565	428	371
7	550	248	63	454	234	57
8	598	162	125	578	262	178
9	442	185	90	403	188	109
10	477	356	203	..	..	..
11	330*	92*	31*	313	84	62
12	309	251	210	302	233	216
13	191	169	43	..	140	40
14	147	81	227	137	89	248
15	103	59	53	138	60	45
16	37	12	7	27	16	8
17	13	13	2	12	12	3
18	12	9	2	9	9	3

Sources: For 1962-63, 1961-62 and 1958-59, *Indian Labour Statistics*, 1966
For 1960-61, *Indian Labour Statistics*, 1965, Table 6.4, p. 119.
For 1959-60, 1958-59, 1957-58 and 1956-57, *Indian Labour Statistics*

3 (Contd.)

	1957-58			1956-57	
No. of Unions on Register	No. of Unions Submitting Returns	Membership of Unions (in '000)	No. of Unions on Register	No. of Unions Submitting Returns	Membership of Unions (in '000)
7	8	9	10	11	12
2,300	780	471	2,033	409	178
1,213	823	355	584	577	241
1,658	1,020	601	1,566	848	480
804	658	315	719	518	235
932	595	259	881	620	277
539	406	318	532	386	309
397	213	61	379	142	37
565	193	106	548	129	82
408	201	108	223	223	114
..	..	..	..	..	..
283	92	45	247	64	29
264	213	187	254	206	141
212	112	24	220	106	23
136	50	73	149	54	175
119	75	71	116	73	48
20	17	7	26	15	6
9	3	4	..	..	..
9	9	4	..	..	..

Table 6.3, p. 118.

1964, Table 6.4, pp. 103-104.

bably indicative of the same trend, *i.e.*, movement from the traditionally unionised sectors to the newly emerging industries mostly in the medium and small-scale sectors. Most of the new unions are probably still having teething troubles and either have low membership on an average or have not yet developed the habit of reporting regularly. It is also probable that the mortality rate among the new unions is still relatively high but this is not fully reflected in the registration data.

The picture as a whole reveals a close relationship between trade union membership and industrialisation. Maharashtra and West Bengal accounted in 1963 for 24.7 per cent of factories and 40.1 per cent of the total average daily employment of all factories registered under the Factories Act, 1948. In the same year, these together had 40.9 per cent of the total membership of workers' unions.[8]   Considering all the limitations of data, this, nevertheless, shows a remarkable association between factory employment and the reported union membership.

Sectoral Variations

The sectoral data on union membership are available for ten major sectors and thirty-one subsectors. These include factories registered under the Factories Act, 1948, as well as the unregistered ones, shops and establishments, plantations, mines, and other places whether or not covered under some legislation. Comparable data on average daily employment for plantations, gins and presses, mining and quarrying, manufacturing, railways, and posts and telegraphs and most subsectors are, however, published by the Labour Bureau. In the manufacturing sector the employment data on clothing, footwear and made-up textile goods do not seem to be comparable to union membership. The sectors on which data appeared to be plausible have been grouped into 17 sectors and subsectors and analysed for the degree of unionisation over a period of 15 years. The relevant statistics are presented in Table 4.   The detailed table on which this is

---

8. *Indian Labour Statistics*, 1966, Table 2.1, pp. 18-19, and Table 6.3, p. 118.

based is included in the Appendix. Table 4 shows that in 1963 leather and leather products (except footwear) had the highest degree of unionisation while gins and presses had the lowest. Next to it, in the ranking order, are the mining and quarrying sector, textiles, basic metals, and manufacture of machinery subsectors. If the first is considered as a class apart from the subsectors, textiles has the second position. It is, however, possible that the degree of unionisation in leather and leather products is overstated. This suspicion arises due to two reasons. First, the variability in its series is too high. It ranges all the way from 100 per cent to 22 per cent. Second, the figure jumps from one year to the next in a manner too dramatic to seem plausible. These variations eliminate the possibility of systematic overstatement of membership. It is, however, likely that the variability in the degree of unionisation is the result of two unpredictable factors, *viz.*, (*i*) the membership might include production units and other establishments not included in the Factories Act, 1948, and (*ii*) the response rate of unions might vary from year to year. In view of these uncertainties it might not be safe to accord this industry the pride of place in the ranking of industries.

The most unionised industry in the manufacturing sector is probably textiles. This is not accidental. In terms of employment, it is the biggest industry in India. Trade unions were born in this industry and have retained their traditional stronghold in the various centres where it happens to be well organised. The basic metals industry has been another stronghold of trade unions in India. The industry has been growing at a rapid rate and it appears that unionisation of labour has been keeping pace with it. The machinery manufacture is a new industry in India and has grown rapidly since the high priority accorded to it in the Second Plan. It is important to note that all of these are large-scale industries working on a highly centralised basis.

The inter-sectoral distribution of ranks over the years shows interesting variations. The ranking variation is defined as the difference between the highest and the lowest ranks reached by a sector or a subsector during 1951-1963. This is a measure of relative stability though, in view of the non-

TABLE

Degree of unionisation

Code No. of Industry	Industry		Year			
			1963	1962	1961	1960
1	2		3	4	5	6
0.1	Plantations	.. .. ..	..	13.4 (15)	28.8 (13)	39.7 (11)
0.2	Gins & Presses	.. ..	1.9 (16)	..	0.6 (17)	0.6 (17)
1	Mining & Quarrying	..	51.6 (2)	51.9 (3)	45.9 (8)	48.0 (9)
2.0 to 2.2	Food, Beverages & Tobacco	..	43.1 (9)	42.0 (10)	37.6 (10)	56.2 (4)
2.3	Textiles ..	.. .. ..	49.4 (5)	47.6 (4)	49.5 (5)	58.1 (3)
2.5+ 2.6	Wood, Cork: Furniture & Fixtures		11.5 (15)	18.7 (14)	21.7 (14)	26.9 (14)
2.7	Paper & Paper Products	..	42.9 (10)	46.8 (6)	52.4 (3)	51.3 (7)
2.8	Printing, Publishing & Allied Industries		39.1 (11)	45.9 (7)	43.1 (9)	53.3 (5)
2.9	Leather & Leather Products (except Footwear)		96.1 (1)	68.2 (1)	85.0 (1)	84.2 (1)
3.0	Rubber & Rubber Products	..	50.0 (3)	45.5 (8)	30.8 (12)	34.3 (13)
3.1	Chemical & Chemical Products		43.2 (8)	43.3 (9)	50.7 (4)	52.8 (6)
3.2+ 3.3	Non-metallic Mineral Products (including Products of Petroleum & Coal)		43.9 (7)	47.3 (5)	48.8 (6)	50.5 (8)
3.4+ 3.5	Basic Metal Industries (including manufacture of Metal Products)		49.5 (4)	53.9 (2)	70.0 (2)	76.1 (2)
3.6+ 3.7	Manufacture of Machinery (including Electrical Machinery)		44.7 (6)	33.6 (11)	31.8 (11)	36.0 (12)
3.8	Transport Equipment	.. ..	12.9 (13)	23.9 (12)	16.2 (15)	11.0 (16)
7.2	Railways	.. ..	34.9 (12)	23.8 (13)	48.2 (9)	45.4 (10)
7.6	Posts & Telegraphs	.. ..	12.2 (14)	11.9 (16)	9.9 (16)	11.9 (15)

Note : Figures in parentheses indicate the ranks.
Source: Based on Table 1 in the Appendix.

4

in selected industries

				Year				
1959	1958	1957	1956	1955	1954	1953	1952	1951
7	8	9	10	11	12	13	14	15
38.6 (12)	39.4 (10)	21.9 (14)	20.6 (12)	24.9 (10)	19.5 (13)	16.5 (15)	13.3 (14)	9.1 (14)
0.6 (17)	0.8 (17)	0.6 (17)	0.9 (17)	0.7 (17)	0.7 (17)	..	0.8 (17)	0.8 (16)
50.5 (7)	47.5 (7)	36.9 (10)	40.9 (7)	33.5 (7)	36.1 (6)	31.6 (8)	26.3 (10)	24.2 (8)
52.0 (6)	57.3 (4)	52.1 (5)	49.2 (3)	35.8 (5)	34.8 (7)	30.4 (9)	27.7 (9)	20.9 (11)
68.7 (3)	58.6 (3)	46.7 (7)	38.9 (8)	35.5 (6)	38.8 (4)	37.9 (6)	39.8 (3)	31.2 (6)
28.0 (14)	35.6 (12)	30.0 (11)	23.3 (11)	16.7 (13)	12.8 (14)	13.5 (16)	9.8 (15)	8.1 (15)
54.3 (5)	54.3 (5)	55.2 (3)	32.1 (9)	26.7 (9)	27.6 (10)	42.3 (4)	28.6 (8)	25.9 (7)
57.5 (4)	54.0 (6)	54.3 (4)	57.1 (1)	41.5 (3)	32.5 (9)	36.5 (7)	34.2 (6)	38.0 (3)
100.0 (1)	83.3 (1)	42.1 (8)	50.0 (2)	60.0 (1)	45.0 (2)	42.9 (3)	44.4 (1)	22.2 (9)
38.7 (11)	23.3 (14)	41.4 (9)	11.5 (15)	14.8 (14)	34.6 (8)	29.2 (10)	25.0 (11)	20.8 (10)
48.3 (8)	42.2 (8)	56.4 (2)	46.0 (5)	34.3 (8)	39.4 (3)	48.9 (1)	42.7 (2)	34.4 (4)
46.2 (9)	40.7 (9)	46.9 (6)	43.8 (6)	38.1 (4)	37.1 (5)	24.8 (12)	23.4 (12)	14.2 (12)
90.1 (2)	60.4 (2)	69.7 (1)	47.4 (4)	51.5 (2)	49.0 (1)	44.7 (2)	39.5 (4)	54.4 (1)
41.3 (10)	39.2 (11)	23.8 (13)	30.4 (10)	21.3 (11)	19.8 (11)	18.2 (13)	14.2 (13)	10.1 (13)
6.4 (16)	5.8 (16)	4.0 (16)	3.9 (16)	3.3 (16)	1.7 (15)	0.9 (17)	3.1 (16)	0.5 (17)
28.4 (13)	29.8 (13)	24.8 (12)	11.9 (14)	20.7 (12)	19.7 (12)	17.1 (14)	39.3 (5)	44.1 (2)
16.5 (15)	11.0 (15)	13.9 (15)	17.7 (13)	13.4 (15)	1.2 (16)	27.1 (11)	30.2 (7)	33.2 (5)

random nature of non-response, it has to be interpreted with caution. One can hypothesise that the rank variability will be the least in those industries that are highly unionisable because of the scale of operations, the character of market, the skill content in their labour force, and historical factors. We may expect a nonlinear positive relationship between the explaining and the dependent variables. These will result in early unionisation but, once unions are established and feel secure, the degree of unionisation will begin to rise slowly; it may even fall after the point of saturation has been reached. This is already happening in the oligopolistic sectors in the advanced countries of the West. For similar reasons it would appear that the weakness of these variables will keep unions in industries at the other extreme at very low levels of operation. Between these limits are the intermediate industries which are either coming into existence, or may be in the early stages of growth, or actually fading out. These may be in part large-scale manufacturing units and in part small-scale and decentralised. This vast stratum is likely to show varying degrees of instability depending upon the individual characteristics of each industry.

These propositions are generally supported by the data on rank variations for the sectors included in Table 4. Among the high ranks the basic metals industry shows the least variation, viz., three points. Textiles has the second position showing the variability of five points. In the lowest rank, gins and presses reveal the greatest stability for all the sectors, viz., one point only. The woods and fixtures industries show a variability of four points. It is obvious that the latter two are also the least unionisable. It is equally evident that the first two have a high unionising potential. Among the remainders the greatest variability is shown by the railways and the machinery manufacturing industries followed closely by the printing, publishing and allied industries. The first two show rank variations of twelve points each while the third of eleven points. For the railways this is, indeed, an extraordinary showing. It was unionised as early as the twenties, if not earlier, and had achieved 44.1 per cent of unionisation in 1951 when its rank was second. But either due to slackening of pace, or under the impact of general disruption resulting from political rivalry, or as a result of erratic reporting response, its relative position has moved about greatly. In the case of printing industry, the last factor appears to be responsible for causing the greatest disturbance. Also, occasional overreporting of membership followed by natural slumps might be behind the curious swings in its degree of unionisation. The case of machinery industry is different; this seems to be steadily moving in the direction of greater unionisation. Its low position in the early years is reflective of its relative importance in the industrial structure of the country. The variability in this case is indicative of a steady advance over the years.

It may be added that the rank stability, or its absence, of an individual industry is greatly affected by the extremes. If in any year unions in several firms fail in reporting their membership, the rank will be severely displaced. Since erratic response has been the endemic feature of trade unions in India, in practice the rank instability for several industries might not be as much as has been shown in Table 4. In view of this uncertainty, the conclusions derived in this respect should be treated as of a tentative nature. These may be verified either by intensive industry studies or whenever more reliable data are available.

POLITICAL RIVALRY IN THE TRADE UNION MOVEMENT

The Historical Legacy

The organised trade union movement in India can be traced to 1920. In the 45 years that elapsed between that year and 1965 it had passed through cataclysmic changes. In the modern history of India this period had witnessed the majestic sweep of the nationalist mass movement, the emergence of all-India communist and socialist parties, the Great Depression, the Second World War, and the partition of the country accompanied by some of the greatest upheavals. It would have been surprising if these events had not left their political imprint on the trade union movement. Moreover, since the twenties, trade unions have been the arena of repeated clashes of ideologies and their spokesmen. The issues on which the All India Trade Union Congress had been split have had practically nothing to do with the lives of workers, or the ordinary union members, but mattered a great deal to the leaders. The first great split occurred in 1929 and the circumstances are narrated by Karnik in the following words :

> Under the influence of the communists, the All India Trade Union Congress decided to boycott the Royal Commission on Labour, the Whitley Commission, to affiliate itself to the League against Imperialism and the Pan-Pacific Trade Union Secretariat, and to appoint the Workers' Welfare League as its agent in the United Kingdom. All the three organisations mentioned above were communist organisations. The Congress also decided to denounce the Asiatic Labour Conference and the Round Table Conference. It further decided to reject the Nehru Report and not to participate in the Conferences of the International Labour Organisation. All these resolutions were adopted in the teeth of the opposition of the moderate group. N. M. Joshi and D. Chamanlal had been appointed members of the Whitley Commission. Joshi had been also invited to the Round Table Conference. Besides, he and his group did not believe in the policy of boycott. They were equally opposed to affiliation with communist international organisations and to the decision not to send representatives to the Conferences of the International Labour Organisation. All these decisions were against the policies that they had followed so long and also against the principles which guided their activities. They could not be expected to accept those resolutions and implement them. The communists knew this very well. As a matter of fact, the resolutions were passed with a view to drive them out of the Congress. The programme of their party had asked the communists to expose and isolate the "reformist" leaders and to convert the Congress into a revolutionary class organisation.[9]

9. V. B. Karnik, *Indian Trade Unions: A Survey*, (op. cit), p. 49. Also see K. B. Panikkar, *An Outline of the History of the AITUC*, (op. cit) pp. 7-8.

The trade union movement could not be reunited until 1940, and the unity achieved could not last for more than 15 months. It was again split on the issue of defining the attitude of the AITUC towards the Second World War. Since December 1941 unity has been evading the Indian trade union movement.

The position taken in this book is that disunity is a function of three variables. First, and the most important, is the political distance among the groups of trade union leaders. The distance is determined to some extent by ideology but more by the differences in policies that are considered suitable for reaching the ideology-determined goals. It is, thus, possible that leaders may profess the same ideology and yet differ on policies. Second, disunity is caused by the subordination of purely trade union interests to the goals of trade union movement as perceived by leaders. It is possible that leaders may take opposite positions on "bread and butter" issues, because they may represent conflicting interests of groups of workers. But these can be overcome, as has been shown in the United States. It is not even necessary for an organisation to split on these questions as has been demonstrated by the British Trade Union Congress, by the HMS, and by the present-day AITUC in India. An organisation can remain intact, *cateris paribus*, as long as ideological and policy questions are subordinated to a concern for promoting the immediate interests of unions and workers and the functioning of internal democracy permits the airing of conflicting viewpoints. Third, disunity is likely to be caused and perpetuated where it already exists, if a sufficiently large number of employers with either the active support or passive consent of authorities acquire a vested interest in it. In other words, a trade union movement has a better chance of remaining united or, when split, of reuniting if the government and the employers acquire an interest in a strong and united trade union movement. In India, neither the authorities nor the employers have shown a strong inclination in this direction. Considering that trade unions always have germs of disruption because of conflicting interests, differences in the perception of the real needs of workers, personal ambitions, competing political affiliations of leaders, and ideological clashes, to cite only the most important causes, keeping them united is not an easy task. It is rendered easier if the other two parties either collaborate with leaders, or remain neutral on preserving trade union unity.

In India, since trade union leadership has been traditionally supplied by political parties, the ideological clashes among the latter have caused and maintained rival camps in the union movement from the beginning. This holds true even today. Formerly it was a triangular clash among the moderates, the communists, and the Royists. Since Independence the conflict has been widened, and now it includes the nationalists, the communists (now split into the left and the right parties), the socialists (divided into two camps), the assorted leftists, and several others. Prominent among these are the four centres *viz.*, the INTUC, the AITUC, the HMS, and the UTUC. These represent conflicting ideologies, diverse political programmes, clashing party and personal interests, and sometimes closely tied up with regional and caste loyalties. In contemporary India these are inevitable and will probably last for a long time. Although the ideological and political distance among trade union leaders is the most important cause of disunity in the movement, it is not all pervasive. There are sectors, such as posts and telegraphs, commercial banks, insurance, and several industries, where trade unions have been united and are relatively strong. This reflects in part a will on the part of leaders to preserve unity and partly the cooperative attitude of employers. On the national scene, however, these remain mere islands of solidarity and are probably the outcome of an unusual constellation of forces favouring unity.

The four centres form a shapeless quadrangle rather than a straight line continuum. It is not that the INTUC and the AITUC stand at the opposite extremes with the HMS and the UTUC occupying middle positions. Had it been so the INTUC and the HMS would have been drawn toward each other, while the UTUC would have approached the AITUC more closely. Such a tendency is nowhere observable despite fleeting alliances on local issues and the realisation on the part of the leadership of both the HMS and th

UTUC that these have been stagnating. The main reason why the latter two have neither been advancing nor moving towards each other is that the political parties of which these form props, and from which they seek the principal support, have themselves been in a state of doldrums. Instead of seeking strength in unity, these, to all appearances, have been more concerned with retaining their organisational independence and the political advantages that go with it.

To carry the analogy further, the four centres may be viewed as occupying four corners separated by varying distances in the trade union "space" with the INTUC and the AITUC placed at the diagonally opposite extremes at the farthest distance. The other two poles, signifying the positions of the HMS and the UTUC, are not rigidly defined. These gravitate occasionally towards one another but mostly towards the AITUC on all matters involving the use of the strike weapon. On broader ideological and policy questions, the HMS may gravitate towards the INTUC.

The leaders of both the INTUC and the HMS profess faith in democratic socialism and economic planning. Both are hostile to communism, although the HMS leaders have not yet gone that far as the INTUC in demanding a ban on the Communist Party of India and its fronts. On policy matters, there are differences in accent and on emphasis. For instance, the HMS leaders believe in collective bargaining to a greater extent than the INTUC's. The former, unlike the latter, have no inhibitions in criticising the government. There have been even suggestions of unity between the two, but they have not so far yielded any tangible results. As a result of weaknesses, generally characterising the HMS and the UTUC, the two have been forced to seek alliances with powerful parties and, as a consequence, have been losing members. All the four centres have zealously guarded their organisational identity and independence of action. Indirectly, but assuredly, the government, too, has been lending a measure of moral and political support to enable them to continue as separate organisations.

These four centres together occupy more than half of the total "space" defined by the reported trade union membership. Of the remaining "space", less than half a portion is occupied by smaller political centres such as the Hind Mazdoor Panchayat (HMP), the Bharatiya Mazdoor Sangh (BMS), the Indian Federation of Independent Trade Unions (IFITU), etc. Whatever is left out may be classified, for want of a suitable term, as independent unionism. For the sake of convenience, unions controlled by non-recognised political centres will also be considered independent. It is noteworthy that this subset has grown significantly during 1952-53 and 1962-63. The relative increase of independents has been from 22.2 per cent of the total reported membership in 1952-53 to 39.8 per cent in 1962-63. Despite this trend, these have not been able to make any impact on the hard core of political unionism. Nevertheless, the trend is revealing and might be indicative of the likely direction in which the increasing number of unions will move. This possibility will be strengthened with the emergence of a class of professional, full-time trade union leaders. In fact, this possibility can be realised only if, in the near future, such a cadre of union functionaries comes into existence and makes its presence felt. However, whether or not the independents are the wave of the future, it seems clear that during the past decade these, like the ballast in a ship, have been a powerful factor of stability.

Relative Growth of Trade Union Centres

The data on the number of unions affiliated to the four centres and their reported membership as verified by the Chief Labour Commissioner's office are published by the Labour Bureau. These are set out in Table 5.[10]

10. There are considerable differences between the claimed and the verified unions and their memberships. The verification procedure is complicated and time-consuming, but so far it has been accepted by the centres concerned. For a description of the procedure and its working, see S. B. Kale, "Verification of Membership of Trade Unions—Procedures and Practice", *Indian Journal of Industrial Relations*, Vol. 2, No. 1, July 1966, pp. 50-69. It should also be remembered that the AITUC, as a matter of policy, has refrained from seeking unions' affiliation in railways, banking, insurance, and several public sector enterprises. It is, however, widely known that the political influence of the AITUC in these sectors is not inconsiderable.

The data show that while the INTUC and the AITUC have gained in membership over the decade, the other two organisations have lost the ground. Comparing 1962-63 with 1952-53, the AITUC has recorded an increase of 137.4 per cent, while in the case of the INTUC this has been only 37.9 per cent. The HMS and the UTUC have shown a decline of 11.5 per cent and 15.5 per cent respectively. It is, however, possible that the negative rates of growth have been exaggerated by non-response due to organisational inadequacies. Even allowing for this factor, there can be no doubt that these two organisations have been stagnating.[11]

Table 5 also shows that the relative position of the four centres in respect of each other has not undergone radical changes. The INTUC continues to control more than half of the combined total of the reported membership of the four centres. In the case of the AITUC there was a steady improvement up to 1957-58, but thereafter it has been slipping downwards. The HMS started in a big way but fell disastrously until 1958-59 when it began to rise again. The relative position of the UTUC has been going down the hill without any significant reversal. These trends should be viewed in the context of the 74.6 per cent increase in the reported union membership over the same period. In a broader perspective it appears that among the four centres only the AITUC has done well although it has also been on the backslide.

HAS THE MOVEMENT IMPROVED IN QUALITY?

As has been seen in the previous two sections, the trade union movement has expanded in size, and acquired a greater depth in several sectors, while the political core, to all

11. In the case of the UTUC, this point has been conceded in the General Secretary's report to the 5th All-India Sessions held at Bombay in 1964. The Secretary complained that the decline in the membership of the UTUC "has not been so much on account of any diminution of UTUC influence but mostly on account of the fact that our union leaders have been sadly remiss in maintaining union records and papers properly." *United Trade Union Congress*, Report presented by Sudha Roy, General Secretary, pp. 21-22.

Trends in the relative positions of

Year	INTUC		AITUC	
	Member-ship ('000)	Percentage of the Total	Member-ship ('000)	Percentage of the Total
1	2	3	4	5
1952-53	919	56.29	211	12.92
1953-54	888	..	..	..
1954-55	931	56.61	307	18.67
1955-56	972	55.29	423	24.06
1956-57	934	..	..	..
1957-58	910	52.84	538	31.20
1958-59	1,023	54.92	508	27.25
1959-60	1,053	53.78	509	25.99
1960-61	..	..	..	..
1961-62	..	..	..	..
1962-63	1,268	57.18	501	22.58

Notes: For 1960-61 and 1961-62 the Chief Labour Commissioner did not verify the membership because of the general election and the declaration of emergency respectively. Blank entries in other years denote absence of verification.

5

the INTUC, AITUC, HMS, and UTUC

HMS		UTUC		Total	
Member-ship ('000)	Percen-tage of the Total	Member-ship ('000)	Percen-tage of the Total	Member-ship ('000) (2+4+6+8)	Total (3+5+7+9)
6	7	8	9	10	11
373	22.87	129	7.94	1,632	100
..	..	164	..	..	..
211	12.85	195	11.87	1,644	100
204	11.60	159	9.05	1,758	100
234	..	..	..	..	..
193	11.20	82	4.76	1,723	100
242	12.97	91	4.86	1,864	100
286	14.61	110	5.61	1,958	100
..	..	..	..	..	..
..	..	..	..	..	..
330	14.87	109	4.91	2,208	100

Sources: Labour Bureau, *Trade Unions in India*, various issues pertaining to 1954-55, 1955-56, and 1960-61. For 1962-63, see K. N. Vaid, *Trade Unions in India*, Industrial Relations Statistical Series IV, New Delhi, Shri Ram Centre Press, 1965, pp. 6-7.

outward manifestations, has lagged behind. But, has the
trade union movement become more viable, self-reliant, and
purposive? These are the qualities that are generally associated with trade unions in matured countries. These create
an image of strength, autonomy, and social respectability.
A rational leadership would strive towards these goals, and
the organisational compulsions ought to be such that would
propel it steadily forward—provided the leaders and the rank
and file have organic bonds and the same are inextricably
embedded in the union's organisational structure. Where
the leader emerges from among the people and is steeled
in the fires of union battles, the bonds are close and the
leader responds to the dominant sentiments of the workers. He can stay in power only as long as he can renew
the members' trust through faithful implementation of their
collective will. Workers join the union in their self-interest
and wield it for the same purpose. In these situations the
leader is an inalienable part of the society that comprises
workers. He leads by virtue of superior leadership abilities
which often require the transmuting of the generally shared
sentiments into a common will, maintaining unity in the
organisation, and retaining the following during periods of
acute stresses and crises. In the process of doing this, a
powerful leader can often succeed in winning the allegiance of his constituents to himself rather than to the union
and also in securing their acceptance of his personal values
and goals.[12]

In Indian circumstances, however, the situation can be
expected to be different. Quite often workers are persuaded
into forming a union by leaders who do not belong to them

12. Because of these attributes, a union is sometimes described as a political
institution which is primarily concerned with survival against the threats
of hostile employers, apathetic workers, and indifferent state. The principal function of a union leader is to ward off these threats and ensure
(i) the survival, and thereafter (ii) the growth of the union by adding to its
functions and thereby increase its utility to the members. For a lucid
discussion of this point of view, see Arthur M. Ross, *Trade Union Wage
Policy*, (op. cit.)., pp. 21-44. Also see Albert Rees, *The Economics of
Trade Unions*, (op.cit.), Chapter X entitled "The Union as a Political
Institution", pp. 170-186.

socially. Once the union is formed and workers have realised its utility they give natural allegiance to the leader that showed the path. But gratitude alone cannot ensure the continuance of outside leaders in trade unions. Outside leaders stay on because of the services rendered which often require competence in written and spoken English, social connections, ability to raise funds and help individual workers in the hours of need. In view of these aspects of leadership, it would not be correct to look for trends in the share of outside leaders in the trade union movement as yet another indicator of its growing viability. The union movement may not grow in strength just by dropping outside leaders. The real question is whether the latter have shed their alienation and have gradually identified themselves with union members to a point when this label ceases to be meaningful. Furthermore, a union may be said to have grown in strength if it enjoys the continuous allegiance of the majority of its members in periods of stress as well as ease and can discipline both the leaders and the followers in subservience of a common purpose. Clearly the social origin of leaders is not particularly relevant to this consideration; rather the concern should be with the distance the union has travelled since its inception and its record of performance.[13] Unfortunately, information of this nature is neither available nor can be expected from government sources. This can be collected only through carefully planned case studies of a wide cross-section of trade unions spread all over the country.

From the published data certain broad characteristics can nevertheless be discerned which can be interpreted as indicative of an increase in the viability or its opposite in the

13. In Indian conditions of widespread illiteracy, one of the primary functions of union leaders is to make workers aware of their legal rights. According to a recent report on the subject, 87.21 per cent of workers employed in the sample units in tea plantations were illiterate, while the figure was 89.86 per cent in coal mining, 81.79 per cent in jute textiles, 60.49 per cent in cotton textiles, and 51.3 per cent in iron and steel industries. Government of India, Planning Commission, Committee on Plan Projects, *Report on Literacy among Industrial Workers*, New Delhi, November 1964, Appendix III, pp. 47-49.

trade union movement. Three indicators have been selected for this purpose. These are : (*i*) trend in the frequency distribution of unions by the size groups of membership, (*ii*) trend in the average membership for unions, and (*iii*) trend in the average income and expenditure of all reporting unions and those in the Central and State spheres. It is supposed that the trade union movement in the aggregate has gained in viability if (*i*) indicates the relative growth of larger unions, and indices in (*ii*) and (*iii*) show rising trends. The opposite tendencies will be taken to mean that there has been some diminution in its viability. Data pertaining to these are set out in Tables 6, 7, and 8 respectively.

Table 6 shows that in 1951-52 the small unions, each having less than 100 members, accounted for 32.8 per cent of all reporting unions but only for 2.2 per cent of total membership. In 1960-61, the situation was not much different. This group claimed 42.9 per cent of the total unions and a mere 3.8 per cent of their membership. On the other extreme, the large unions each having a membership of 1,000 or more had in 1951-52 in their group 12.8 per cent of the unions but 74.2 per cent of the total membership. But, in 1960-61 their share in unions had dropped to 9.2 per cent and in membership to 70.1 per cent. From the data it appears that 1960-61 is not an unusual year because there is a systematic fall in both the series. By comparison, in the medium-sized unions, each having between 100 and 999 members, the situation remained unclear. The share of this size class in the aggregate of unions fell from 54.4 per cent in 1951-52 to 47.9 per cent in 1960-61 while in membership it rose from 23.6 per cent to 26.1 per cent. Both the series show variability rather than systematic trends. This may be partly due to the fact that some unions which should really belong to the lower class have been included in it and have a higher than average proneness to not submitting returns regularly or due to other chance factors. On the other hand, it is more probable that while unions have multiplied faster at the lower end of the membership scale, those in the medium class have acquired new members at a faster than average pace. While this pace would naturally vary from year to year, in the long run

TABLE 6

Frequency distribution of trade unions submitting returns according to membership

Year	Small Size (1-99)				Medium Size (100-999)				Large Size (1000-above)			
	No. of Unions	% to Total	Total Member-ship	% to Total	No. of Unions	% to Total	Total Member-ship	% to Total	No. of Unions	% to Total	Total Member-ship	% to Total
1	2	3	4	5	6	7	8	9	10	11	12	13
1951-52	839	32.8	44,280	2.2	1,390	54.4	471,299	23.6	326	12.8	1,480,702	74.2
1952-53	950	35.2	48,696	2.4	1,400	52.0	479,822	23.2	343	12.8	1,536,414	74.4
1953-54	1,237	37.5	61,905	3.0	1,694	51.5	586,193	27.7	364	11.0	1,464,597	69.3
1954-55	1,426	40.2	67,391	3.1	1,737	49.0	538,569	24.8	382	10.8	1,564,490	72.1
1955-56	1,318	40.3	67,623	3.5	1,605	49.1	576,664	29.2	346	10.6	1,329,085	67.3
1956-57	1,714	38.9	85,323	3.6	2,273	51.6	692,354	29.1	412	9.5	1,599,085	67.3
1957-58	2,271	42.7	111,802	3.9	2,556	48.8	826,933	28.4	492	9.3	1,968,708	67.7
1958-59	2,535	41.9	126,046	3.3	2,944	48.7	924,854	25.4	561	9.4	2,596,248	71.2
1959-60	2,850	43.3	140,708	3.6	3,158	47.9	1,011,182	25.8	580	8.8	2,771,455	70.6
1960-61	2,921	42.9	152,798	3.8	3,266	47.9	1,017,197	26.1	626	9.2	2,814,154	70.1

Note: The union membership figures have been rounded off.

Source: (i) For the years 1951-52 to 1953-54, *Indian Labour Year Book* of the respective years.

(ii) For the years 1954-55 to 1960-61, *Trade Unions in India* of the respective years.

TABLE 7

Average size of membership of Central unions, State unions, and all-workers' unions

Year			Central Unions	State Unions	All-Workers' Unions
1			2	3	4
1951-52	..	..	4,951	628	781
1952-53	..	..	5,774	629	767
1953-54	..	..	2,719	584	641
1954-55	..	..	1,688	583	616
1955-56	..	..	1,573	583	609
1956-57	..	..	1,836	512	543
1957-58	..	..	2,289	529	570
1958-59	..	..	1,833	576	611
1959-60	..	..	1,839	562	603
1960-61	..	..	2,574	545	596

Sources: (i) For 1951-52 to 1953-54 and 1957-58, *Indian Labour Year Book*, 1952-53 and 1953-54, 1954-55, 1958.

(ii) For 1953-54 to 1960-61, *Trade Unions in India* of the respective years.

it would reveal a rising trend. A further breakdown in the data is suggestive of this reasoning.

Table 7 shows trends in the average membership of unions within the State and the Central spheres and their combined totals. The former unions are those which are limited in their membership to the States of their registration while the latter denote location of membership in more than one State. The table also shows that the average membership of unions in each of the three categories has been going down. In fact, this trend is perceptible over a longer period. The average membership for undivided India for all-workers' unions during 1937-1942 was 1,124. It rose to 1,418 in

TABLE 8

Average income and expenditure per Central union, State union, and all-workers' union

(in rupees)

Year	Central Union		State Union		All-Workers' Union	
	Income	Expenditure	Income	Expenditure	Income	Expenditure
1	2	3	4	5	6	7
1951-52	8,905	8,282	2,215	2,089	2,158	1,937
1952-53	9,272	7,911	1,707	1,536	1,906	1,704
1953-54	4,624	4,235	1,766	1,536	1,845	1,611
1954-55	4,724	4,131	1,789	1,541	1,876	1,618
1955-56	4,939	4,647	2,215	1,687	2,288	1,767
1956-57	6,212	5,283	1,721	1,548	1,826	1,636
1957-58	7,051	6,094	1,787	1,640	1,926	1,733
1958-59	6,689	5,661	1,979	1,862	2,102	1,961
1959-60	7,860	6,256	2,192	1,936	2,372	2,073
1960-61	8,041	7,528	2,127	1,933	2,279	2,078

Sources: (*i*) For 1951-52 to 1953-54 and 1957-58, *Indian Labour Year Book*, 1952-53, 1953-54, 1958.

(*ii*) For 1954-55 to 1956-57 and 1958-59 to 1960-61, *Trade Unions in India* of the respective years.

1942-1947 and fell to 1,061 in 1948-49, to 781 in 1951-52, and thereafter, with occasional reversals, to 596 in 1960-61.[14] The steady decline in membership, it may be remembered, has been accompanied by a sustained increase in the number of unions. This is fully consistent with the higher than average rate of growth of unions of small size and the oppo-

4. See *Indian Labour Year Book*, 1954-55, p. 149.

site tendency revealed by large unions. This may be compared to the effect of rapid increase in the population of the poor in a low income economy. Such a growth in numbers cannot but be a drag on the country's progress. Similar is the effect of a vast increase in the number of tiny unions. These do not lend strength to the trade union movement any more than adding up many zeros and near equivalents will do to a sum. The oversized trade union movement is in danger of becoming a menace to its health which was never known for much inherent strength.

It may be said that the relatively faster growth in the number of small unions is the result of two unrelated tendencies. One is the fragmentation of membership due to the formation of rival unions in the same bargaining territory. The other is the creation of plant unions particularly in the medium and small-scale enterprises. These tendencies operate differently from industry to industry and even from State to State. For instance, in the engineering industry the trend has been to form plant-wise unions while in mining and plantations unions have developed on a regional basis. In the cotton textile and jute industries, too, unions have been formed on an industry-cum-region basis. This shows that there is considerable diversity in actual life which average statistics cannot fully reveal. Nevertheless, the fact remains that the trend towards declining average membership is unmistakably present in unions whose jurisdiction cuts across State boundaries and also others that are confined to the States of registration. Despite all the variegated patterns that the trade union movement has developed in the country, there is no doubt that the central tendency is for the average union to become weaker.

This conclusion is further supported by data on income and expenditure per union as given in Table 8. It shows that income and expenditure have generally remained the same. This cannot be explained by either the non-response or the other chance factors. The growth in the number of unions has not added to their financial soundness. It may be noted that during this period the per capita income at current prices rose by 18.7 per cent while the money earnings of factory workers and mining workers went up by 30.6 per

cent and 89.6 per cent respectively.[15] The increase in the
financial ability of workers is nowhere reflected in the
reported financial position of average unions. In fact, with
static income and rising prices, the trade union movement
has become poorer and its overall effectiveness must have
been correspondingly reduced.

It may be asserted that unions are prone to understating
their income and expenditure. But this cannot fully explain
why the average of an ever-increasing number should produce stagnant financial position year after year. This cannot be either accidental or attributed to a vast social conspiracy of duping the public. Nor can it be due to the fact
that the problems of maintaining accounts and keeping track
of *ad hoc* collections have grown with the time. These
features of trade union finances have been present all along
and can be treated as constants that do not affect the trend.

Taking into account the entire discussion in this and the
preceding sections, the conclusion is inevitable that while
in independent, democratic India the population of trade
unions has grown enormously, the acquisition of membership has lagged behind. The overall effect has been an expansion by size and in space but a general weakening of
quality. This should not be taken to mean that some unions
may not have gained in strength. In fact, there is a general
impression that within an expanding and diffuse trade union
movement there is a core of strong and viable trade unions
that is also growing. These, however, do not show up in
statistics. As far as is known, most of the well-organised
unions are affiliated to political centres. The drop in the
combined share of political centres should be viewed in this
general context.

It appears that the trade union movement has grown too
diffuse to be properly controlled by political centres some of
which might themselves be suffering from debility of leadership and poor organisational health. Moreover, factionalism
within these centres has adversely affected their public image.
These factors tend to weaken or slow down the growth of
any organisation, and the trade union centres are no excep-

See *Indian Labour Statistics*, 1966, Tables 12.4 and 12.7.

tion. On the other hand, it is also possible that the leadership of political centres may not consider it worthwhile to affiliate unions that, on balance, are deemed more of a liability than of an asset. If the latter factor is significant at all, it would signify that the decline in the combined share of the four political centres is not indicative of proportionate decrease in their power. The data on work-stoppages, as analysed in Chapter 5, in fact show that it is substantially more than revealed by the membership data. The relationship between conflicts and union membership shows a probability that unions in India have been adding to their membership and influence through conflicts. The empirical and theoretical bases of this phenomenon are brought out in Chapter 3, where the combined effect of growth and inflation on unionism is analysed.

UNIONISM, EARNINGS, EMPLOYMENT, AND PRODUCTIVITY

TRENDS IN INVESTMENT, OUTPUT, AND PRICES

IT HAS BEEN SAID IN CHAPTER 1 THAT INDIA HAS ADDED MORE to its national output in the 15-year period since 1950 than over the entire half a century that preceded the commencement of the planning era. Let us now see what efforts it involved and the manner in which it affected workers and their unions.

Growth in Investment and Output

In simple terms, the rate of growth of output is determined by the rate of capital formation and the investment-to-output ratio. If the latter is taken as given (being determined by the state of technology, the skills of people, the quality of organisation, etc., which are fixed in the short period), the growth rate of output can be taken as a function of investment. On the eve of the First Five Year Plan, the ratio of investment to national income was estimated at 5.6 per cent. In 1955-56 it had gone up to 7.0 per cent. At the end of the Second Five Year Plan (1960-61), it stood at 10-11 per cent and in 1964-65 it might have risen to 14-15 per cent.[1]

---

1. There is some uncertainty about these figures. The unofficial estimates are systematically higher over the entire period. Conversely, the official estimates indicate a higher pace of increase in investment than the unofficial estimates. Since both the sourses rely on the official estimates of national income, the difference between them is solely due to the methods of estimating savings and investment. For the data cited in the text, see *Third Five Year Plan*, p. 32 and p. 35, and *Fourth Five Year Plan* : *A draft outline*, Part I—Approach and Policy, pp. I-19-20 and II-1-5. A non-official estimate for the period 1950-51 to 1961-62 has been prepared by the National Council of Applied Economic Research : See *Savings in India*, July 1965, Table 1, p. 97, and Table 5, p. 103.

In absolute magnitudes investment increased from 5 billion rupees in 1950-51 to 8.5 billion rupees in 1955-56, to 16 billion rupees in 1960-61, and to over 22 billion rupees in 1965-66. As a result, the national income, in real terms, has risen by 42 per cent in the decade 1950-51 to 1960-61, and by 16.7 per cent in the first four years of the Third Plan. In 1965-66, due to bad harvests and other reasons, the national income actually fell by 4.2 per cent.[2] Much of this increase in income has been wiped out by the growth in population. Accordingly, the per capita income has gone up by mere 55 rupees between 1950-51 and 1965-66.

The most significant changes have taken place in the structure of the manufacturing industries. These are brought out by Table 9. In this table the entire output, measured in terms of value added, has been grouped into four convenient

TABLE 9

Shares of subsectors in the aggregate value added in manufacturing industries
(at 1960-61 prices)

(in percentages)

Subsectors	1950-51	1960-61	1965-66
1	2	3	4
1 Consumer goods	68.4	45.5	33.9
2 Intermediate goods	23.4	37.3	43.2
3 Machinery	7.8	16.2	21.9
4 Others	0.7	0.1	0.6
5 Total	100	100	100
6 Total value added (in billion rupees)	3.8	9.3	14.3

Note: Percentages may not add up to 100 because of rounding.
Source: *Fourth Five Year Plan : A draft outline*, Part I, pp. I-13-14.

2. *Fourth Five Year Plan*, (op.cit.), p. I-4-9. It may be noted that since the commencement of economic planning, national income has declined in two years only. In 1957-58, the fall was 1.7 per cent as compared to an estimated 4.2 per cent in 1965-66. The latter was, therefore, an exceptionally bad year.

subsectors. The changes in their proportion indicate the extent of structural transformation that has occurred under the impact of planning. The table shows that in 1965-66 the machinery and intermediate goods producing industries together accounted for 71.1 per cent of the total value added, whereas in 1950-51 their share was only 31.2 per cent. On the other hand, the importance of consumer goods producing industries has been severely reduced. These dramatic changes have occurred mainly due to the shift in priorities to producer goods industries in the Second Plan, which has continued in the Third Plan.

Although the structure of output in the manufacturing sector has changed completely, it is not reflected in the relative position of industries in the economy as a whole. Between 1950-51 and 1963-64, the share of factory establishments in the generation of net domestic output, at current prices, rose from 5.8 per cent to 11.1 per cent, but this was partly offset by the decline of small enterprises from 9.6 per cent to 7.3 per cent. Accordingly, their combined share rose from 15.4 per cent in 1950-51 to 18.4 per cent only in 1963-64.[3]

The summary statistics given above indicate the magnitude of effort that the country has undertaken to develop itself. However, this has not been an easy task and has shown up in severe strains in the economy, particularly in the persistent balance of payments crisis that has recently culminated in the devaluation of the rupee and the threat of inflation that has grown ever more ominous. In this book we will ignore the former and be concerned mostly with the latter.

Trends in Prices

The data on prices, measured by the Wholesale Price Index (WPI) and the Consumer Price Index (CPI) and related variables are set out in Table 10. It will be seen that the WPI and the CPI have moved together and show magnitudes of price increases which are remarkably close. This is not surprising because the food items have been assigned

3. See *Estimates of National Income*, 1963-64, (op.cit.), p. 3.

TABLE 10

Trends in prices and related variables in India

Year	Whole-sale Price index (1952-53 =100)	Consu-mers' Price Index (1949= 100)	Index of Food Produc-tion (1949-50 =100)	Money Supply (in billion rupees)	Income Velocity of Money	Budge-tary Deficits (—) Surplus-es (+) (in billion rupees)
1	2	3	4	5	6	7
1950-51	107.6	102.0	90.5	19.66	4.8	—0.12
1951-52	118.0	105.0	91.1	18.03	5.5	—0.1
1952-53	100.0	104.0	101.1	17.65	5.6	—0.53
1953-54	104.6	107.1	119.1	17.94	5.8	—0.63
1954-55	97.4	102.0	115.0	19.21	5.0	+0.08
1955-56	92.5	96.2	115.3	22.17	4.6	—1.59
1956-57	105.3	107.2	120.8	23.42	4.8	—2.95
1957-58	108.4	111.7	107.9	24.13	4.7	—4.78
1958-59	112.9	118.0	130.1	25.26	5.0	—1.69
1959-60	117.1	122.2	124.3	27.20	4.7	—1.58
1960-61	124.9	125.2	135.76	28.69	4.9	+0.68
1961-62	125.1	127.3	137.5	30.46	4.8	—1.52
1962-63	127.9	131.0	130.4	33.10	4.6	—1.28
1963-64	135.3	137.0	134.9	37.52	4.6	—1.72
1964-65	152.7	157.0	..	40.80	4.9	—1.20

Notes:　Money supply is as on the last Friday of the year. The income velocity of money is derived by dividing the national income at current prices by the stock of money. The budgetary deficits/surpluses are for the Centre and the States combined. The figure for 1964-65 is based on the revised estimates while the data for previous years are based on accounts.

Source:　Reserve Bank of India, *Report on Currency and Finance*, various issues.

heavy weights in both of them. Thus, the same factor gene-rates similar movements in both the indices. In view of their importance the indices on food production are included in the table. Considering the widely shared belief that money supply is an important determinant of prices, the data on the same are also set out in Table 10. An indicator of excess monetary demand is the behaviour of the income velocity of money. This, too, is included. The principal source of excess money demand in the economy is the state of balance in the budgets of the Central and the State Governments. The consolidated budgetary deficits or surpluses are set out in column 7 of the table.

It can be readily seen in Table 10 that the WPI has shown greater variability than the CPI. This is not unusual. The wholesale prices are generally more sensitive to fluctuations in demand and supply than the retail prices. Their index responds to changes not only in the domestic economy but also in the international market. Moreover, changes in the fiscal policy, interest rates, and the inventory policies of traders and producers are quickly registered by the WPI but only gradually and often to a lesser extent by the CPI. Furthermore, due to its comprehensiveness, the WPI is a more reliable indicator of the economic health of the country than any other comparable series. For these reasons, it is preferable to analyse the process of inflation in India in terms of wholesale prices. However, our concern is primarily with workers and their unions whose interests are tied up with the movements in the CPI. The dearness allowance, in one way or the other, is linked with the CPI. The behaviour of this index number is, therefore, a matter of great importance to this study. But it has many limitations. Its coverage is limited, and the representative character of most of the series on the basis of which the all-India index has been constructed is in doubt. It has been a subject of union agitation and consequently of several governmental inquiries. In fact, the Labour Bureau has already started publishing a new series with 1960 as the base year. But, despite these limitations, the old series of the CPI is of relevance for our analysis.

As Table 10 shows, the wholesale and the consumer prices have been steadily rising since 1956-57. This coincides with the commencement of the Second Five Year Plan which was not only much bigger than its predecessor but was also financed to a much larger extent through budgetary deficits. Moreover, the Second Plan was aimed at capacity creation, particularly in the heavy goods sector, rather than capacity utilisation as in the First Plan. Due to these features of the

Second Plan, it was expected by the planners that the relative prices would undergo significant changes and some inflation would also occur. By contrast, the First Plan was modest in size and aimed at the restoration of the economy to the pre-war level. It, therefore, did not strain the economy in any way. Actually, the price level had fallen and the reserves in foreign exchange had gone up.[4]

Between 1951 and 1956 the WPI fell by 18.1 per cent while the CPI declined by only 6.0 per cent. This trend was reversed in the Second Plan when the WPI and the CPI rose by 35.0 per cent and 30.1 per cent respectively. The inflationary pressure did not abate in the Third Plan and, excepting the relative stability of 1961-1963, prices had risen throughout.

During 1961-1965 the WPI moved by 22.2 per cent while the CPI rose by 25.3 per cent. Over the fifteen-year period, the WPI and the CPI have gone up by 41.9 per cent and 53.9 per cent respectively. If 1952-53 is taken as the normal year for judging the extent of inflation in India, for both the WPI and the CPI the price increases have been 52.7 per cent and 50.9 per cent respectively. Both the series reveal an average rate of price advance at over four per cent. For a poor economy like that of India where the large majority of people live at a subsistence level, this has no doubt been a substantial dose of inflation. It has eroded the real earnings of workers in many industries, caused industrial unrest, upset the rational basis of cost estimation and, consequently, project planning, fed speculation, and reached a stage where it may pose a serious threat to social and political stability. The evil effects of inflation are widely recognised, and it is generally agreed that the government must act to slow it down, if not to stop it

---

4. The total investment in the First Plan (1951-56) was 3.36 billion rupees In the Second Plan (1956-61) it had gone up to 6.75 billion rupees. Th shift in the resource allocation from the First to the Second Plan is indi cated by the fact that 31 per cent of the total outlay in the former wa spent on agriculture and irrigation as compared to 20 per cent in the latte The share of industries and minerals in the First Plan was 4 per cent a compared to 20 per cent in the Second Plan. For these and other detail see *Third Five Year Plan*, Chapter III entitled "Ten Years of Planning' pp. 31-47.

ltogether.   Trade union leaders, too, have been demanding
n effective government policy to counter and overcome the
menace.

Considering the seriousness of the problem, it is necessary
o define it in unambiguous and measurable terms and determine its origin in the economic system.   Having done that,
e will proceed to assess its impact on workers' earnings and
fectiveness of unions' response to counter its baneful effect.

Inflation is defined as a general increase in prices which
ontinues over time. It should be distinguished from a change
in the relative prices and once-over changes in the price
vel.   Changes in the price structure occur all the time in
esponse to shifts in relative demand and supply of commodi-
es and generally tend to cancel each other out producing
ttle or no effect upon the price level.   These may be com-
ared to the waves in the ocean which keep the latter in a
ate of ceaseless motion without affecting its level. The once-
ver changes in price level may occur for a variety of causes,
ich as climatic factors, an unbalanced budget, a sudden
se or fall in the monetary value of foreign trade, etc. But
ese will happen only once, and the economic system will
adually adjust to the new price level.

Inflation, however, occurs when prices continually rise, at
owsoever a small rate, and are embedded in the expectations
' people. Thus, the previous price increases generate expec-
tions of future rises and so condition the behaviour of
eople that the anticipations broadly come true. This pro-
ss can be kept going only under two possible conditions.
ne is that the government should go on supplying as much
oney as may be required to finance rising prices.   This can
ke the form of either budgetary deficits, or easier bank
edit, or both.   The other is that trade unions should gene-
te a relentless upward pressure on wages, costs, and prices
d thereby cause inflation. The two are not mutually
clusive, and it is indeed possible to assert that even under
e latter condition, inflation can become a mandatory
enomenon only if monetary authorities let the money
pply increase sufficiently to validate each round of cost-
ice increases. Under Indian conditions, the hypothesis
' cost-push inflation must be excluded as either generally

irrelevant or non-plausible. This is not to deny that wage and costs have imparted a successively rising floor for up ward adjustments in prices. Every time a wage hike take place, costs go up and prices rise correspondingly. How ever, in India, the principal escalating factor is the dearnes allowance which is linked to the CPI.

The explanation for the rise in the cost of living index i to be sought not so much in higher wage incomes create by the increase in earnings as in the factors operating to rais the level of aggregate demand in excess of the growth in rea output. The key variable is the gap between planned inves ment and savings which has been met partly by deficit finan cing and in part by the net inflow of foreign capital. It is no that the government alone has sought to acquire comman over real resources through new money creation; the privat corporate sector, too, has done the same by relying more an more on bank credit and other forms of loan finance. Th dominant factor operating on the money supply is, howeve the budgetary deficits.

It may be noted that the government, particularly th Planning Commission, is inclined to attribute the risin prices to the retardation in agricultural production rathe than budget-induced expansion in monetary demand. It i needless to say that both supply and demand interact i determining the trend in prices. However, in India, the lat ter has increased far more than can be justified by reasonabl assumptions on the potential growth rate of real output. Th latter is crucially dependent upon agricultural productio which is conditioned, as before, by weather and, besides has suffered from relative neglect of authorities. The retard ed flow of farm output, in the context of rising demand, ha affected the behaviour of the CPI both directly and indirectl The direct effect is the rising trend of foodgrains prices whil the indirect effect is through the raw material prices which rais the cost of production of consumer goods that are enterin into the family budgets of workers. Given the pattern c consumption of most industrial workers, the indirect effec has been quite small.

The data as set out in Table 10 show that over the fifteen year period the budgetary deficits have aggregated to a ne total of over 19 billion rupees. In the same period, the monetary stock expanded by 21.14 billion rupees. It is noteworthy that while in the six-year period (1950-1956) the money supply increased by 2.51 billion rupees, in the five-year period (1961-1965) the increase has been of the order of 12.11 billion rupees. Such an enormous increase in the monetary stock could not be absorbed by the real economy and has resulted in higher prices. A rough indicator of the inflationary gap is the difference between the national income at current prices and its deflated estimate at constant prices. Between 1950-51 and 1955-56, the national income at current prices fell by 4.5 billion rupees while the real output rose by 16.3 billion rupees. Thus, the First Five Year Plan not only wiped out the inflationary gap that had formerly existed but probably created some deflationary gap in the economy. At the end of the Second Plan, the national income at current prices had gone up by 41.6 billion rupees while the real output had risen by 22.5 billion rupees only. It is possible that a part of the gap of 19.1 billion rupees was just a corrective to the deflationary gap that had existed earlier. Nevertheless, a sizable inflationary factor had been built into the economy. In the first four years of the Third Plan, for which complete data are available, the inflationary gap had widened substantially. This is indicated by the fact that while real output had gone up by 23.2 billion rupees only the aggregate net monetary outlay on goods and services had risen by 58.7 billion rupees. In 1964-65 alone the people and the governments in India spent an excess of 49.6 billion rupees over the amount justified by the output of real goods and services. This has naturally shown up in the escalating prices.[5] Indeed, the trend in income velocity of money shows that the expansion in money supply has been in excess of even the growth of aggregate outlays. The decrease in velo-

---

5. For the latest estimates of national income, see "National Income of India, 1964-65", *Reserve Bank of India Bulletin*, April 1966, pp. 394-396. For a fuller analysis of inflation and related matters, see C.K. Johri, *Monetary Policy in a Developing Economy*, Calcutta, The World Press (P) Ltd., 1965, Chapter 2 and Appendix I. Also see in this connection, National Council of Applied Economic Research, *Growth Without Inflation*, New Delhi, February 1965.

city indicates that people have been adding to their cash balances. This may be partly due to the gradual monetisation of the non-monetised sector, or, to put it differently, the extension of the market nexus to the barter economy, and for the remaining part the accumulation of cash in the hands of people. The latter factor is suggestive of the diminishing opportunities for spending money which, unless corrected, may be built up to a disastrously explosive potential.

As the foregoing analysis shows, inflation in India has its origin in the five year plans which have been framed on the assumption that an underdeveloped economy cannot be speedily developed unless resources are diverted from current consumption to investment through overt and covert forms of deficit financing. Some measure of price rise is thereby assumed to be inevitable, although it may well be that the actual inflation has far exceeded the planned expectations. The principal reasons for the unanticipated spurt in prices are two. First, the food production has not increased according to plan targets; in fact, it has fallen grievously in 1965-66. Second, the rapid mounting of defence expenditure since 1962 has been wholly outside and in addition to the provisions of the Third Plan, and has aggravated the inflationary situation.

EMPLOYMENT, EARNINGS, AND REAL WAGES

Trends in Employment

In a developing economy both employment and earnings are expected to rise. Table 11 shows that the total employment during 1951-1964 has gone up. The table also gives the sectoral trends for factories, mines, plantations, railways, posts and telegraphs, and shops and establishments. The employment data on these sectors are collected under the Factories Act, 1948, the Mines Act, 1952, by the Tea Board, the Coffee Board, the Ministry of Food and Agriculture, the Railway Board, and the Director General of Posts and Telegraphs and under the Shops and Establishments Acts of the various States respectively. In view of the differences in the

TABLE 11

Trends in employment in the selected sectors, 1951-1964

(in millions)

Year	Fac-tories	Mines	Planta-tions	Rail-ways and Posts and Tele-graphs	Shops and Com-mercial Establ-ish-ments	Total
1	2	3	4	5	6	7
1951	2.91	0.55	1.24	1.12	0.93	6.75
1952	3.02	0.56	1.24	1.14	1.09	7.05
1953	2.97	0.59	1.17	1.17	1.09	6.99
1954	3.04	0.57	1.21	1.21	1.03	7.06
1955	3.11	0.59	1.25	1.25	1.17	7.37
1956	3.44	0.63	1.29	1.31	1.53	8.19
1957	3.54	0.65	1.27	1.35	1.58	8.39
1958	3.60	0.65	1.26	1.42	1.70	8.63
1959	3.64	0.62	1.27	1.48	1.63	8.64
1960	3.77	0.65	1.22	1.51	1.86	9.01
1961	3.93	0.67	1.21	1.53	2.07	9.41
1962	4.12	0.68	1.18	1.57	2.03	9.58
1963	4.38	0.70		1.64	2.03	
1964	4.58	0.69		1.73	2.20	
1951-1956 increase in %	17.8	14.5	4.0	16.0	64.5	21.3
1956-1961 increase in %	14.5	6.3	—6.6	15.2	31.3	16.9
1961-1964 increase in %	16.5	9.5	..	13.0	6.2	
1951-1964 increase in %	57.3	25.4	..	54.4	136.5	

Source: *Indian Labour Statistics* and *Digest of Indian Labour Statistics*, various issues.

coverage of the relevant legislation and the administrative requirements of the government, there is no uniformity of concepts in the enumeration of the employed. Moreover, though the data are collected through the census method, the actual returns generally disclose varying rates of non-response from year to year.   The Labour Bureau, however, makes adjustments for the non-response wherever possible, particularly in the employment data collected under the Factories Act.   It is, therefore, hoped that the data in the aggregate are on the whole reliable.   Nevertheless, the lack of uniformity in coverage poses serious problems.   The data do not necessarily relate to workers.   In some cases these include clerks, supervisors, officers, and even apprentices. However, on the assumptions that in most establishments workers comprise the bulk of employees and the ratio of workers to non-workers does not change over time,   the various series set out in Table 11 may be comparable as indicative of the trends in broad magnitudes.

Table 11 shows that, except in plantations, average daily employments have grown in all sectors.   The greatest increase in employment has been shown by shops and establishments, and the least by mines.   In the case of the former, the trend shows a steep decline from 1956 onwards.   This suggests that the growth in employment in the First Plan may be partly fictitious. It was probably due to improvement in the coverage of the Shops Act in various States and better collection of data under the same.   To some extent the increase in employment in shops is indicative of the combined effect of the development-induced   growth   in   urbanisation,   diversification in the economy, change in spending patterns, etc. The railways and posts and telegraphs have shown a steady increase   in   employment   throughout   this   period.   On the   other   hand,   in   factories   and   mines   the   rates   of employment fall in the Second Plan and rise in the Third Plan.   These trends have been produced by two causes. At the beginning of the First Five Year Plan there was a varying extent of slack in both these sectors.   But by 1956, these were operating at either full or near-full capacity.   As the rate of utilisation of productive capacity increased, so the employment in factories and mines also grew.   By the time the Second Plan got into motion, this impulse had petered out. The Second Plan had laid greater emphasis on the creation of new capacity.   Accordingly, more jobs had been created at the construction rather than the factory employment levels. However, as new factories were commissioned, the total of average daily employed workers also began to rise. The full impact of the new capacity created in the Second Plan was felt only during the Third Plan. The same explanation, although to a lesser extent, may also hold good for the mining sector.[6]

Employment Lags Behind Output

The increase in employment has fallen behind not only investment but also output. The trends in production and employment for the manufacturing, mining, and plantations sectors are set out in Table 12. This table shows that in the manufacturing sector production increased by 133.5 per cent while employment rose by 57.3 per cent only in the period 1951-1964. In mining, the increases in production and employment during 1951-1963 had been 157.8 per cent and 27.1 per cent respectively. In plantations, during 1951-1962 while output went up by 28.1 per cent, employment actually fell by 4.3 per cent. These trends raise questions in which the unions are as much interested as the government and the employers. Why has employment systematically lagged behind production? The answer to this question is to be sought in the gradual shift in the technological condition of the Indian industries. This shift, paradoxically, is from capital saving to labour saving techniques. The paradox lies in that, in a labour surplus economy the shift could have been in the opposite direction. The general effect of the technological change is seen not only in the new industries but to some extent even in the older industries. Some industries, such as iron and steel, heavy and fine chemicals, petroleum refineries, heavy engineering, and electricals are, of course, by their very nature labour saving and capital consuming industries. Since the designing of these factories and their technological requirements are generally determined by the foreign collaborators, there is often no choice in the selection of machinery.

6. See in this connection, *Third Five Year Plan*, Chapter X and Appendix C, and K. N. Raj's paper on India in I.L.O., *Employment Objectives in Economic Development*, Geneva, 1951, pp. 159-169.

TABLE 12

Index numbers of employment and output in manufacturing, mining and plantations sectors

(1951=100)

Year	Manufacturing		Mining		Plantations	
	Index Nos, of Production	Index Nos. of Employment	Index Nos. of Production	Index Nos. of Employment	Index Nos. of Physical Production (1951-52 =100)	Index Nos. of Employment
1	2	3	4	5	6	7
1951	100.0	100.0	100.0	100.0	100.0	100.0
1952	103.0	103.7	105.6	101.8	105.6	100.7
1953	105.8	102.1	104.6	108.2	95.1	95.1
1954	113.2	104.2	107.1	103.5	103.5	98.3
1955	125.6	106.9	111.6	107.6	103.5	101.1
1956	137.2	117.8	114.9	114.6	112.4	104.7
1957	141.7	121.6	126.0	119.4	112.2	103.1
1958	145.7	123.4	133.3	118.3	116.4	101.9
1959	157.7	125.1	141.0	112.6	120.0	102.7
1960	175.3	129.5	157.7	118.8	124.1	98.9
1961	185.0	134.8	169.3	122.2	128.5	97.9
1962	201.1	141.4	185.4	124.6	128.1	95.7
1963	216.2	150.2	202.2	127.1	N.A.	N.A.
1964	233.5	157.3(P)	194.4	125.0	N.A.	N.A.

Sources: (*i*) Index Nos. of Production: See, *Indian Labour Statistics*, 1966, p. 198.

(*ii*) Index Nos. of Employment: (*a*) *Ibid.*, pp. 36 and 37; (*b*) *Statistical Abstract of India*, 1963 and 1964, p. 526.

In the older industries, too, the pressure of domestic and foreign competition has produced similar results. These pressures take several forms. First, in many firms the machinery had grown over-aged and was no longer considered serviceable. In the older factories, the replacement was already overdue at the termination of the Second World War. The new machinery was not only more modern but could make products cheaper and better. The cotton textile and the sugar industries are the foremost examples of this kind of switch-over. Indeed, the diversification of products in the textile industry would not have been possible but for this change. Second, labour is no longer as cheap a factor of production as it used to be in the thirties and the forties. The labour cost has not only risen directly through higher earnings, but also indirectly through increased social security legislation and the retention of surplus labour force in many industries.[7]   Ordinarily, employers would prefer to retrench workers that, in their judgement, are surplus, but in India this has been made extremely difficult by the Industrial Disputes Act, and the attitudes of the government and the unions. Wherever possible, particularly in the growing enterprises, this problem has been solved by the process of absorption of surplus labour in new plants and natural wastage. Over a period of time, these policies have shown up in the employment lags as disclosed by Table 12. Third, the government policy has contributed not only to make labour costlier but also to render capital a relatively cheaper factor of production. This has been done by keeping the long-term

7. The effect of social security and other legislation on the cost of labour cannot be directly estimated. If comparable data on physical production, labour employed, wages, legislated and fringe benefits had been available, it would have been possible to estimate the increase in cost per unit of physical output on employed labour resulting from the legislated and other social security benefits. Since these data are not available, such estimates cannot be prepared. The CIM and the ASI data show that the ratio of total wages to value added has been falling. For the entire manufacturing sector, during 1950-1962, the three-year average of this ratio stood at 0.479 for 1950-1952, 0.457 for 1953-1955, 0.412 for 1956-1958, and 0.396 for 1959-1962. In the ASI period, 1959-1962, the figure was unchanging. In interpreting this trend it should be borne in mind that value added includes profit that is a residual and may be expected to rise in an inflationary economy. Moreover, this ratio is the final outcome, from the supply side, of a variety of management decisions on factor substitutions that are actuated by changes in the relative factor prices. Managements may economise on labour as this factor becomes relatively more costly to a point that the proportion of labour costs itself may begin to fall. This has happened in the advanced capitalist countries where even though the cost of hiring labour has been going up the labour cost per unit of output has not, and may have even declined. The effect of this process should be seen in the growth in employment. As the data for India clearly reveal, it has tended to lag behind both investment and output.

interest rate as low and credit conditions as easy as are feasible under the circumstances. The same purpose is served
by pegging the rupee exchange rate at an abnormally high
level.

The government, no doubt, has been forced by circumstances to drastically alter these policies so that interest rates
are raised, credit is tight, and the rupee is devalued. But, over
the period under review, the policies described above held
sway. These policies, though reversed now, have served
the cause of industrialisation in a most significant manner.
The government succeeded in reducing the social cost of
industrialisation by increasing the remuneration of workers
and preventing retrenchment. The economic cost to employers that this policy entailed was partly, if not wholly, offset
by enabling them to modernise and expand production facilities at a lower price for capital than would be possible otherwise. Moreover, rising product prices in a protected market
have in any case generally reimbursed the employers of the
additional labour costs that the government policies have
created. Thus, in the economic sense, the employers as a class
have lost nothing while the workers have gained new rights
and some apparent prosperity. The real opportunity cost
of these policies has not been any less significant. The ab-
normal rise in prices, the stagnation in exports, the mounting
burden of foreign debt, and the economic wastage resulting
from an artificial cheapening of a scarce resource are by now
only too apparent to need further elaboration.

Trends in Earnings

An important consequence of this policy has been that
workers' earnings have been steadily rising. The data on
earnings of workers employed in factories and mines for the
period 1951-1964 are set out in Table 13. These are
collected under the Payment of Wages Act, 1936, and by the
Chief Inspector of Mines under the Mines Act, 1952, respectively. In the case of factories, only workers earning less
than 200 rupees per month are included. Since 1958, the
Labour Bureau has also been publishing earnings data for
workers getting less than 400 rupees per month. However,

TABLE 13

Trends in earnings in manufacturing and mining and per capita income, 1951-1964

Year	Index Nos. of Earnings of Factory Workers (1951 = 100)	Index Nos. of Earnings of Mining Workers (1951 = 100)	Average Annual Earnings of Factory Workers (in rupees)	Per Capita Income (in rupees)	The Ratio of Col. (4) to Col. (5)
1	2	3	4	5	6
1951	100.0	100.0	1,036	274.2	3.7:1
1952	107.1	105.7	1,112	265.4	4.1:1
1953	107.7	105.6	1,111	278.1	3.9:1
1954	107.7	107.8	1,111	205.3	4.4:1
1955	113.1	109.9	1,173	255.0	4.6:1
1956	115.4	143.6	1,187	283.3	4.1:1
1957	120.8	159.9	1,234	279.6	4.4:1
1958	122.3	170.7	1,251	303.0	4.1:1
1959	126.4	183.1	1,310	304.8	4.2:1
1960	134.4	189.6	1,375	325.7	4.2:1
1961	138.6	198.0	1,408	333.6	4.2:1
1962	144.0	204.9	1,465	339.4	4.2:1
1963	145.2	218.7	1,479	370.9	3.9:1
1964	148.7	220.8	1,528	421.5	3.6:1

Sources: (*i*) For Columns (2), (3) and (4): *Indian Labour Statistics*, 1964 and 1966.

(*ii*) For Column (5), *Reserve Bank of India Bulletin*, April 1966, p. 395.

he former has been preferred due to its larger coverage. t may be noted that, although the average earnings in the atter class are naturally higher than the former, the two have noved at about the same pace.

Table 13 shows that factory workers' earnings have risen by 48.7 per cent between 1951 and 1964, *i.e.*, at an average annual rate of 3.7 per cent. The increase in mining workers' earnings has, however, been more substantial. These have isen at an average annual rate of 9.3 per cent. It may be noted that, during the same period, the per capita income at current prices has gone up at an average yearly rate of 4.1

per cent. From this it may be concluded that factory workers' earnings have lagged behind the per capita income.
However, a careful look at the table will reveal that this
has happened only in the last two years.

Column 6 in Table 13 shows that workers in India enjoy
a privileged position as compared to an average citizen.
This probably reflects the higher productivity of labour in
industry as compared to agriculture and the ability of the
organised labour movement to retain its relative advantage
in a developing economy. The data for 1963 and 1964,
however, show that the differential of earnings over per capita
income is on the decline. This is probably due to the lag
in earnings with respect to prices. Such variations in the
differential had occurred in earlier years, too, but were cancelled out by opposite changes in the subsequent years. It is,
thus, possible that the drop in the relative position of workers
in these years is no more than a passing phase.

Though average earnings of industrial workers have been
rising, the inter-industry wage structure shows considerable
variations. The data for four key years, viz., 1951, 1956,
1961, and 1964, on 16 industries are set out in Table 14.
The table shows that in 1951 workers in seven industries had above average earnings. In 1956 the position was un-
changed, but in 1961, though the number remained the same.
one industry, viz. printing, dropped out of the list while
chemicals moved up. In 1964, two more industries, viz.
rubber and basic metals products, fell behind leaving only
five industries, among which four were originally paying
above the average earnings.[8]

What are the implications of rising average earnings for the
bulk of industrial workers? One gets the impression that
the majority of workers are doing as well, as the average
indicates. But, not quite so. A further analysis of the data
shows that the proportion of workers who on an average

8. For a complete analysis of this problem, see C. K. Johri and N. C
   Agarwal, "Inter-Industry Wage Structure in India, 1950-1961—An Ana
   lysis", *Indian Journal of Industrial Relations*, Vol. 1, No. 4, April 196(
   pp. 377-414. Also see H. B. Shivamaggi, "Trends in Money and Re:
   Wages in India; 1951-61," *Reserve Bank of India Bulletin*, April 196(
   pp. 421-439.

TABLE 14

Average annual earnings of factory workers earning less than Rs. 200 per month by selected industries

Industry	Average Annual Earnings for all Industries			
	1951 Rs. 1036	1956 Rs. 1187	1961 Rs. 1417	1964 Rs. 1528
1	2	3	4	5
1 Gins and Presses	..	211	227	278
2 Food, Beverages & Tobacco	..	652	876	808
3 Textiles	1,044	1,306	1,491	1,669
4 Wood, Cork & Furniture & Fixtures	797	739	996	1,157
5 Paper & Paper Products	958	1,036	1,254	1,620
6 Printing, Publishing & Allied Industries	1,053	1,189	1,326	1,347
7 Leather & Leather Products	752	757	1,180	1,470
8 Rubber & Rubber Products	1,325	1,502	1,542	1,517
9 Chemicals & Chemical Products	868	981	1,449	1,590
0 Products of Petroleum & Coal	1,132	1,686	1,855	1,767
1 Non-metallic Mineral Products (Excluding Products of Petroleum & Coal)	699	833	1,020	1,077
2 Basic Metal Industries	1,368	1,483	1,814	1,445
3 Metal Products (Excluding Machinery & Transport Equipment)	917	1,120	1,323	1,335
4 Machinery (Excluding Electrical)	998	1,136	1,330	1,401
5 Electrical Machinery, Appliances, Apparatus, etc.	1,238	1,314	1,496	1,452
6 Transport Equipment	1,171	1,473	1,547	1,674

Sources: For 1951, *Statistical Abstract of India*, 1952-53.
For others, *Indian Labour Statistics*, 1965 and 1966.

re getting more than the average has been gradually falling.
he share of workers employed in the industries paying above
verage earnings has declined from 54.0 per cent in 1951 to
7.5 per cent in 1956, to 47.3 per cent in 1961, and to 43.8

per cent in 1964.[9] This indicates that the income distribution among industrial workers has become progressively inequitous to the detriment of a large number of workers.

It has been noted above that the leaders in earnings, defined as industries that paid above average earnings to workers had changed position though a few among them retained their position throughout the period.   These were not necessarily the industries wherein earnings had risen the fastest.   In a group of twenty-one industries, the top seven positions, ranked by the highest increase in the index number of earnings with 1951 as the base year, has been occupied by (i) leather and leather products, (ii) furniture and fixtures, (iii) textiles (iv) chemicals and chemical products, (v) wood and cork (vi) non-metallic mineral products, and (vii) printing, publishing and allied industries respectively.   (See Table 3 in the Appendix.)   Among these, only textiles has been a leader throughout 1951-1964.   Chemicals and printing, too, have been leaders and are generally high earnings industries.   All others were low wage industries in 1951, but moved up with great speed.   It is indicative of their backwardness, that despite this advance, in 1964 the number (iv) was paying less than the average of all industries of 1951, while the number (vi) was paying a little over the average of 1951 but were below that of 1956.

It has been seen that while average earnings have generally kept pace with per capita income, those of the majority of workers have steadily fallen behind.   From this it follows that an increasing proportion of workers have not only failed in directly sharing the fruits of economic development but are probably relatively worse off.   Even among the industries

9. These figures are derived by applying the data on average daily workers employed in industries paying above average earnings as reported under the Payment of Wages Act to the employment data reported under the Factories Act.   This is on the assumption that the two series bear a stable relationship over time.   The necessity for using the Factories Act data has arisen due to the non-availability of employment data under the Payment of Wages Act over the comparable period.   It may be noted that a similar finding was reported by C. K. Johri and N. C. Agarwal (op. cit.) in a study of inter-industry wage structure based on the CIM and the ASI data. The similarity of results based on two sets of data collected independently by different agencies has greatly strengthened our confidence in them.

that have moved faster than the average, the real gain is probably limited to a small proportion of workers who may have been in a privileged position owing to higher skills or seniority, or both, or may be employed in prosperous concerns. The latter factor may be of great importance because the level of earnings is determined to a significant extent by the amount of bonus.   There are no data on the composition of earnings by industries, but the Labour Bureau has published data on the same by States.   These data show that the share of bonus in the total earnings has varied from year to year, but generally it is in the range of four to five per cent for all-India.   The inter-State range in the proportion of bonus is from less than one per cent to over thirteen per cent.[10] It is well known, however, that inter-firm variations within an industry and in the entire industrial sector are much more.   In the years of high profits some companies have paid as much as six months' basic wages as bonus.   On the other hand, there are companies that have not paid bonus at all in several consecutive years.   In view of its importance, bonus has been a subject of industrial dispute on many occasions.[11]

Another factor which mechanically raises earnings is the dearness allowance which is linked up with the cost of living index number of the relevant city or region.   The variation in earnings is determined by the method of calculation of dearness allowance which is not uniform.   The dearness allowance may be a flat rate, or may vary with wage or salary groups. It may be a fixed amount for the given points change in the CPI, or be graded by income groups.   The variety is endless and has been a cause for despair to the trade

10. See *Indian Labour Journal*, January 1966, p. 15, and April 1966, pp. 337-338.

11. In order to regulate the payment of bonus and minimise it as a cause of friction between labour and management, the Payment of Bonus Act, 1965 has been legislated. The Act has laid down the minimum and maximum bonus at 4 per cent and 20 per cent respectively of the wage or salary that is defined to include basic wage and dearness allowance but exclusive of all other cash benefits. See in this connection, Kamala Mathur, "Bonus Legislation in India", *Indian Journal of Industrial Relations*, Vol. 1, No. 4, April 1966, pp. 457-475.

unionists and the researchers alike.[12] Unlike in the case
bonus, no attempt has been made to control dearne
allowance through legislation. However, like basic wag
and bonus, this, too, has been regulated by the industri
tribunals.

Behaviour of Real Wages

The principal concern of workers is not with the pa
packet and its composition, but with the quantum of goo
and services that it can buy. Therefore, unions are primari

12. A glimpse of the jungle that is made of the "principles" governing dearne
    allowance can be had from the following words of Palekar:

    The amount of dearness allowance is calculated from a rate whi
    is either linked or not linked to a cost-of-living index. It goes witho
    saying that in the latter case it is a misnomer to call it a dearn
    allowance. In between these two extremes there is a bewilderi
    variety of rates—rates which start off on different levels of the cost-
    living index; rates which change inversely with the basic wage rate
    those which taper as the cost of living index rises; rates which dif
    according to the degree of neutralisation awarded by the tribun
    different rates for different industries depending on the long-ter
    capacity of the industry or a firm to pay; flat or graded rates; rates bas
    on the size of the firm, lower rates being awarded for small firms; ra
    which vary according to systems in this respect already existing in t
    particular firm, or in similar firms in the locality; rates which dif
    according to the nature of the employer's business, i.e., whether bas
    on profit motive or not; rates which differ according to the to
    emoluments of the workers including such perquisites as free housir
    free fuel and lighting; a different, rising or falling, rate for differe
    slabs or range of variation of the cost-of-living index; rates whi
    differ according to the leading rate, such as the cotton textile rate,
    which they are linked; flat rates as percentage of income; fixed rat
    but dearness allowance varying according to the number of da
    worked during the month; rates fixed in such a way that the dearne
    allowance, irrespective of any other consideration, does not fall belo
    a certain minimum amount; rates which differ according to the gener
    level of wages of similar categories of workers in any particular regio
    even different rates for men and women workers;—one could go o
    with this list ad infinitum.

    Shreekant A. Palekar, Problems of Wage Policy for Economic Develo
    ment, With Special Reference to India, Bombay, Asia Publishing Hous
    1962, pp. 54-55. Also see "Dearness Allowance", Indian Labo
    Gazette, Vol. VII, No. 1, July 1957, pp. 1-10.

erested in the real wages of workers rather than in earn-
gs as such. The index numbers of real wages of factory
d mining workers are set out in Table 15. These
e derived by deflating the index numbers of earnings by
e All-India Consumer Price Index numbers with base year
ifted to 1951. In the same table are given data on index
mbers of physical production in the manufacturing
d mining sectors and the corresponding series on labour
oductivity. The data on selected industry groups for index
mbers of real wages, employment, labour productivity,
d degree of unionisation are given in Table 16. These data

TABLE 15

index numbers of production, productivity and real wages in (i) factories
and (ii) mining (1952 to 1954)

(Base year 1951=100)

Year	Factories			Mining		
	Index Numbers of			Index Numbers of		
	Produc-tion	Produc-tivity	Real Wages	Produc-tion	Produc-tivity	Real Wages
	2	3	4	5	6	7
52	103.0	99	109.2	105.6	104	107.8
53	105.8	104	106.6	104.6	97	104.6
54	113.2	109	112.0	107.1	103	112.1
55	125.6	171	123.7	111.6	104	120.2
56	137.2	116	115.4	114.9	100	143.6
57	141.7	117	114.3	126.0	106	151.3
58	145.7	118	107.5	133.3	113	154.4
59	157.7	126	105.6	141.0	125	158.9
60	175.3	135	110.2	157.7	133	160.5
61	185.0	137	115.5	169.3	138	165.0
62	201.0	142	116.3	185.4	149	165.5
63	216.2	144	113.8	202.2	159	171.4
64	233.5	148	102.0(P)	194.4	156	152.5

urces: (i) *Index of Production* and (ii) *Index of Real Wages*, see *Indian*
Labour Statistics, 1966, p. 198.
(iii) *Index of Productivity*: Based on Index of Production divided
by Index of E ployment.
(iv) *Index of Employment*: Based on Average Daily Employment
under the Factories Act. See (a) *Statistical Abstract of*
India, 1963 & 1964, p. 526, (b) *Indian Labour Statistics*, 1966,
pp. 36-37.

TAB

Index numbers of (a) *employment,* (b) *productivity,* (c) *real wages, and* (
(*Base year*

| Industry | 1956 | | | |
	Employ-ment	Pro-ducti-vity	Real Wages	Degr of Unic nisa tior
1	2	3	4	5
1 Food, Beverages & Tobacco ..	85.5	145.0	..	235
2 Textiles ..	101.3	126.0	116.2	124
3 Wood & Cork, Furniture & Fixtures ..	81.1	223.0	97.2	287
4 Paper & Paper Products ..	103.7	145.0	110.5	123
5 Leather & Leather Products ..	110.0	82.0	90.9	225
6 Rubber & Rubber Products ..	108.0	123.0	114.4	55
7 Chemicals & Chemical Products ..	103.4	133.0	118.1	133
8 Products of Petroleum & Coal ..	136.3	1114.6	146.9	
9 Non-metallic Mineral Products (Excluding Petroleum Products) ..	90.1	172.0	117.8	
10 Basic Metal Industries ..	100.9	116.0	113.2	79
11 Metal Products (Excluding Machinery & Transport Equipment) ..	112.9	163.0	117.4	186
12 Machinery (Excluding Electrical) ..	106.5	208.0	113.8	230
13 Electrical Machinery, Apparatus Appliances ..	106.0	216.0	107.7	562
14 Transport Equipment ..	110.1	197.0	124.6	780

Sources : (i) *Index of Employment*

Based on Average Daily Employment data collected under t Factories Act. See

(a) *Indian Labour Journal,* Vol. XI, July 1953 to June 19: pp. 260-261.

(b) *Indian Labour Gazette,* March 1958, pp. 906-941.

(c) *Indian Labour Statistics,* 1965, pp. 20-29.

(d) *Ibid.,* 1966, pp. 20-29.

(ii) *Index of Productivity*

Based on Index of Industrial Production (base shifted to 1951 See *Monthly Statistics of the Production of Selected Industries India,* for January and February, 1966, C.S.O., pp. 235-245.

(iii) *Index of Real Wages*

Based on Index of Money Earnings and All-India Consum Price Index. See *Indian Labour Statistics,* 1966, p. 298.

16

degree of unionisation in selected industrial groups for 1956, 1961 and 1964
1951=100)

1961				1964			
Employ-ment	Produc-tivity	Real Wages	Degree of Unioni-sation	Emp-loyment	Prod-uctivity	Real Wages	Degree of Unio-nisation (1963-(1964
6	7	8	9	10	11	12	13
125.7	138.0	..	179.9	133.8	144.0	..	206.2
107.8	128.0	116.8	158.6	118.6	139.0	116.2	158.3
108.1	251.0	69.0	269.9	245.9	149.0	121.3	142.0
155.6	176.0	112.7	202.3	200.0	179.0	103.2	165.6
111.0	95.0	121.9	382.9	144.4	88.0	137.2	432.9
162.5	128.0	104.4	148.1	204.2	129.0	90.0	240.4
162.2	144.0	131.1	147.4	195.6	157.0	115.1	125.6
163.6	1419.5	126.6	..	154.5	2113.2	103.2	..
173.9	1161.0	130.7	..	198.2	1169.0	103.7	..
174.5	125.0	105.2	114.6	241.2	129.0	75.6	77.6
217.7	129.0	122.9	306.2	304.8	136.0	102.2	239.8
200.9	296.0	107.8	316.5	260.7	349.0	93.3	263.1
271.9	154.0	106.8	318.1	412.5	157.0	87.1	322.3
172.9	164.0	128.3	3240.0	201.9	208.0	94.2	2580.0

(iv) *Index of Degree of Unionisation*
Based on (1) Average Daily Employment and (2) Membership of Workers' Unions. For (2), see (i) *Indian Labour Statistics*, 1959, pp. 86-91 (ii) *Indian Labour Statistics*, 1966, pp 105-116.

Notes: (i) *Index of Productivity* is derived by dividing the Index of Prodution by the Index of Employment.

(ii) *Index of Real Wages* is derived by deflating the Index of Money Earnings by the All-India Consumer Price Index. The formula is

$$\frac{\text{Money Wages}}{\text{Consumer Price}} \times 100$$

(iii) *Index of Degree of Unionisation* is constructed on the basis of the Workers' Union Membership divided by the Average Daily Employn:ent. The formula is

$$\frac{\text{Workers' Union Membership}}{\text{Average Daily Employment}} \times 100$$

relate to 1956, 1961, and 1964 and have a common base year in 1951. The yearly data are included in the Appendix.

The trends revealed by the series in Tables 15 and 16 on real wages should be interpreted with caution. While the data on money earnings can be considered broadly correct, the same may not necessarily hold true for real wages. Our confidence in earnings data on the manufacturing sector has been enhanced by the similarity in trends revealed by the index numbers prepared on the CIM and the ASI data on the one hand and the Payment of Wages Act data published by the Labour Bureau on the other. These are given in the Appendix. However, due to the well-known limitations of the All-India Consumer Price Index numbers which have been used for computing real wages, we are inclined to interpret the series on the latter as indicative of trends in broad magnitudes rather than precise figures.

Table 15 shows that the real wages of factory workers have been moving erratically. These seem to rise in 1954 and 1955, fall in the next four years, move up again in the next three years, and then decline once again. If the provisional figures for 1964 can be relied upon, it would appear that the real wages in this year had fallen to about the same level as in 1951. As compared to 1961, the decline in 1964 was of the order of 11.2 per cent. This severe reduction was evidently not due to curtailment of earnings which actually show a rise (see Table 13). The volume of industrial production also rose during this period (see Table 12). The consumer prices were, however, rising steadily during the course of the Second and the Third Plans, and prevented the real wages from moving up. Their decline since 1962 is largely due to prices which rose by 7.6 per cent during 1962-1964.

In contrast to industries, the real wages of mining workers have shown a general tendency to increase during the period 1951-1963. However, in 1964 the real wages declined sharply. While comparing the mining workers with their factory counterparts, it should be noted that, in relation to the pre-Second World War level (1939=100), the real wages of the former had systematically lagged behind those of the latter during 1939-1950. In 1950, the real wages of factory workers were already at 100, but those of the mining workers stood at 91. The latter, however, had generally caught up with the former by 1955.[13] The steady rise in real wages of mining workers since 1957 is partly due to the upward revision in the basic wages and the dearness allowance resulting from the awards of the industrial tribunals and the labour appellate tribunals.[14]

Table 15 shows that, over the period 1951-1964, real wages have generally lagged behind labour productivity. In the First Plan period, real wages kept pace with productivity in the factories sector but moved far ahead in mining. During the Second Plan period real wages stagnated in the factories while productivity continued to rise. In the mines, too, productivity outpaced real wages. The latter increased by only 14.8 per cent as compared to 38 per cent rise in the former. This tendency has not only persisted in the Third Plan period but, in fact, the two have started moving in opposite directions.

THE ROLE OF UNIONISM

Unionism and Real Wages

The data on productivity and real wages for 14 industries (given in Table 16) confirm that, by and large, real wages have systematically fallen behind productivity. Table 16 also shows data on the employment and the degree of unionisation. It is sometimes said that unionisation has positively contributed to raising real wages. The logic behind this relationship is that unions have successfully restricted entry into the labour market under their jurisdiction and used this power for introducing an escalator into the wage clauses of the collective bargaining contracts which automatically adjusts wages in accordance with a rise in labour productivity. In the long run, these practices may

3. S. A. Palekar, (op.cit.), Chapter III, pp. 64-109. Particularly see Table 20 on page 68. It appears that this catching-up was facilitated by a more than average decrease in foodgrain prices in Bihar during 1952-1955 which lowered the deflator used in calculating the real wages of mining workers.

4. See Indian Labour Year Book, 1955-56, pp. 87-96.

result in real wages rising alongside productivity with unionism playing a positive role in the process.[15] The investigations conducted so far, however, do not show unambiguous and conclusive evidence to this effect. It is more likely that unions have accentuated the inequality of incomes between the unionised and the non-unionised workers rather than generally raised the level of real wages. The Indian data show that the relationship between unionism and real wages is inverse which, in terms of the logic stated above, is clearly absurd. It may be pointed out that the postulated relationship is not likely to be validated if data over a longer period are analysed. This is evident from the fact that real wages in 1964 were only slightly higher than the 1939 level in the manufacturing sector, whereas the progress of union movement has been quite rapid since then. It is, therefore, necessary to conclude that in Indian conditions the effect of trade unionism on real wages has not been positive; it may even be nil.

Unionism and Money Earnings

Is it possible, however, that unionism has played a positive role in raising money earnings? It may be said that real wages are largely determined by the cost of living over which trade unions have no control. Indeed in an inflationary period the probability of real wages falling is higher than their rising. In India inflationary conditions have continued, with a break of three years during 1953-1955, ever since the outbreak of the Second World War. During these years, unions have fought a defensive battle against rising prices and might have contributed indirectly in stabilising real wages in several sectors if not everywhere. Moreover, the actual battle is always fought, among others, on the issue of raising money earnings, and not on stabilising or raising real wages. It has been, therefore, argued that unions are a factor in raising money earnings. This theory

15 H. Gregg Lewis, *Unionism and Relative Wages in the United States An Empirical Inquiry*, Chicago, The University of Chicago Press, 1963 Chapters II, III, and IV.

has been tested by A. Fonseca.[16] His results show that while the contribution of unionism to earnings is positive, it is not significant. Taking the same explaining variables, *viz.*, degree of unionisation, Consumer Price Index, and physical productivity, we retested the theory for the period 1951-1961. Let y denote money wages and x_1, x_2, and x_3 the explaining variables respectively. It is hypothesised that y is determined by x_1, x_2, and x_3 if the values of simple and multiple correlation coefficients are significantly different from zero. The technique used is the Pearson Product Moment Coefficient. The values of simple, partial, and multiple correlation coefficients are set out in Table 17.

TABLE 17

Results of simple and multiple correlations analysis

Correlations	Values
1. Simple Correlations	
r y x_1	+.75
r y x_2	+.88
r y x_3	—.02
r x_1 x_2	+.86
r x_1 x_3	—.01
r x_2 x_3	—.04
2. Partial Correlations	
r y $x_1.x_2$	—.04
r y $x_2.x_1$	+.69
3. Multiple Correlation	
r yx_1 x_2 x_3	+.84

16. Fonseca has formulated the theory that money wages are determined by the degree of unionisation, the cost of living index, and the productivity of industry and tested to Indian data over the period 1939-1956. Let X_1 stand for money wages and X_2, X_3, and X_4 for the three explaining variables, then the regression equation would be as follows:

   $X_1 = .234 X_2 + .874 X_3 + 2.166 X_4$.

   In order to eliminate multicollinearity the author used the linear formula developed by Tinbergen and re-estimated the equation as follows:

   $X_1 = .18 X_2 + .91 X_3 + 2.09 X_4$.

   See A. Fonseca, S.J., *Wage Determination and Organised Labour in India*, London, Oxford University Press, 1964, pp. 194-201.

The table shows that the simple correlation between earnings and degree of unionisation is quite high, *viz.* +.75. However, when the effect of Consumer Price Index (x_2) is partialled out, the value drops not only to an insignificant level but acquires a negative sign. This demonstrates unambiguously that the degree of unionisation has no direct effect upon earnings. On the other hand the value of r_{yx_2} is quite high at +.88. When x_1 is partialled out, the coefficient of correlation drops to +.69 which is also quite high. By comparison to these, the simple coefficient of correlation between earnings and productivity is not significantly different from zero. The value of multiple correlation coefficient is +.84. It is, however, clear that the principal determinant of earnings in the manufacturing sector is the Consumer Price Index. It operates partly through dearness allowance, and partly through bonus, overtime, and similar other factors.

Though our test has formally repudiated the theory that trade unions have anything to do with workers' earnings, it would, indeed, be rash to draw such a conclusion. It is even doubtful that statistical techniques can truly bring out the significance of a social institution like trade unions that operate through a complex of interacting variables simultaneously upon the status, the earnings, and the security of workers. It may seem at first sight that the earnings have risen in a particular industry because of the award of an industrial tribunal or a wage board. Ostensibly, the rise is related to a measurable yardstick which is acceptable to everyone. But, it is probable that the tribunal or the wage board would not have been constituted if a union with the threatening posture had not been there.

The principle of dearness allowance itself has been won by unions after many struggles, and the matter of suitably linking it with the CPI is even now causing disputes. The political pressure the unions have been exerting on the government for revising the consumer price indices and on the question of raising dearness allowance to government employees cannot suitably be picked up in the correlation analysis. It, nevertheless, has been significant in bringing material benefits to workers.

On the other hand, this argument can be carried too far to the point of denying any positive interest among employers in the well-being of workers. Enlightened employers may find it no less in their interest to keep workers satisfied by paying them more in some form or the other. The principle of *ex gratia* bonus is an instance in point. It preceded the emergence of a significant trade union movement in the country and has been traditionally related to profits, attendance, etc. Similarly, the government, too, is interested in the welfare of workers. It may have decided, in Indian conditions, to safeguard workers' standard of living on unassailable grounds of equity, social welfare, and political expediency. The threat of unions exercising their power to halt production and cause civil commotion during the Second World War probably had spurred the government to raise the question of dearness allowance in 1943 in the Standing Labour Committee and even propose that this might be statutorily regulated. It should be put on record that employers were not opposed to the payment of dearness allowance although they opposed its compulsory enforcement.

In a planned economy, the government needs the support of workers who in return must be assured of the bare subsistence without which the physical capacity to labour is bound to dwindle. Indeed this argument is so stark and real that there has been a community of interest among the workers, the employers, and the government in keeping the production lines functioning normally and providing the former with amenities that will make it possible. The unions have no doubt articulated this position on workers' behalf, often to great advantage, particularly in securing the conformity of recalcitrant employers. But they have done so in a social setting where the broad principles have found mutual acceptance and the conflict is limited to their practical implementation.

The Reverse Effect

Table 17 shows simple correlations between explaining variables. It is significant that x_1 and x_2 are highly correlated while x_1 and x_3, and x_2 and x_3 are wholly independent of each other. What is the significance of high correlation between the degree of unionisation and the Consumer Price Index? So far, this relationship has been completely ignored by scholars, though in Indian conditions, and probably in similar developing countries as well, it is of great significance. While the correlation analysis has refuted the hypothesis that earnings may be related to the degree of unionisation, it has yielded powerful evidence for its reverse, that is, the progress of unionisation is determined by the trend in consumer prices. The reverse effect flows via earnings and money illusion.

This is fully consistent with the working hypothesis stated in Chapter 1 that the basic strategy of unionism in India had been defensive and that it had been aided by inflation. The high value of correlation coefficient between x_1 and x_2 implies that workers take to unionising as their earnings rise but real wages stagnate. The former creates an illusion of prosperity that rising prices almost as speedily dash to the ground. With every round of increase in the CPI the discontent in workers grows and along with it the need for an organisation and a leadership that can fight with the employers. If the union exists, the discontent is transformed into a set of demands on employers and finds public expression in the form of meetings, agitations of various kinds, threats of strike, etc. When some of these demands are met, as is likely due to higher profits occasioned by rising prices, the union as an institution is validated and workers find the effort of organising and agitating around it worthwhile. In the next round of price increase, the same experience may be repeated and the union gets the credit for protecting workers' real wages. Success in one factory is likely to be emulated in the neighbouring firms and the process grows spatially as well as in depth. This is facilitated by the growth in employment which the expanding economy naturally generates, and the rise in expectations which is a normal accompaniment of economic development.

The union leader finds in rising productivity and stagnating real wages the moral basis for organising and inspiring workers. Sooner or later, the workers get the message and find it in their interest to organise. This process can sometimes produce phenomenal results. In the transport equipment industry, employment doubled over a period of 13 years while real wages fell by almost 6 per cent, but the degree of unionisation rose by 2,480 per cent. Such a meteoric rise in unionism may not take place in all industries. Those industries which had reached a high level of unionisation in the base year, such as basic metal industries, would grow only slowly. The transport equipment industry is probably an exception. But, a careful scrutiny of data shows that this relationship is generally present and appears to be stronger than any other plausible relationship.

CONCLUSIONS

To sum up the discussion in this chapter, it has been seen that the economy has been operating under boom conditions since 1956. Economic planning under the aegis of the government has been responsible for taking the country quite far on the growth path, initiating important structural changes in the manufacturing sector, raising output, employment, and prices, and causing real wages either to stagnate or even fall (see Table 16). The latter result is a common experience in developing countries and may have been generally in accordance with the expectation of planners themselves even though the extent of inflation that has actually occurred may have taken them by surprise. It may be pointed out that the successive five year plans have never held out an assurance of a general rise in real wages even though promised a fair deal and more rights to workers.

Considering the stage of development of trade unions in India, the relationship between their growth and real wages has been significant in two respects. First, these have expanded rapidly in those industries where the increase in employment has been substantial but real wages have fallen. Second, the increase in unionisation may have enabled workers to increase their earnings although the significance of this effect is not felt directly. The effect is indirect and has probably taken the form of capitalising in favourable situations and securing the implementation of socially approved principles through public articulation of workers' demands with or without the accompaniment of threat of action. Among favourable situations, the most important has been the sheltered state of market for most industries and the rise in aggregate demand caused by the sustained expansion in the public sector including the so-called non-developmental activities. In a way, trade unions in India have grown rapidly under rather artificial circumstances which have been created by the decisions of the government to (i) take leadership in developing the economy, (ii) adopt economic policies that have led to inflation, (iii) insulate domestic enterprise from foreign competition, and (iv) protect the real wages of workers in so far as it may be possible.

The existence of positive relationship between growth in employment (a passing factor by itself), and rising prices (as an active determinant) and unionism raises two questions. First, what is the line of causation between the CPI and the degree of unionisation, and second, what is the role of the government in controlling this process? Since the government has sought to control trade unionism in respect of both its activities and its distribution among the recognised centres, its trade union policy is reviewed first in Chapter 4. The response of trade unions to rising prices and other problems in the form of disputes and conflicts (as defined therein) is analysed in Chapter 5. It is also indicated that through conflicts trade unions have been adding to their membership. The line of causation in a simple scheme may be illustrated as shown in the Chart opposite.

In this scheme, the government policy operates at all levels. Its primary purpose is to raise A, as determined by the five year plans, and consequently B, mitigate the effects of C on D through fiscal measures of taxation and selective subsidies and controls of various kinds, stabilise E or permit it to rise gently, regulate F administratively, with the aid of the tripartite machinery, and politically, prevent or minimise G and promote H consistent with the requirements of a developing economy. In view of this comprehensive scope and influence, the government policy is discussed in the next chapter and is referred to in Chapters 5, 6, and 7. For the same reason, suggestions are made in Chapter 8 to revise it.

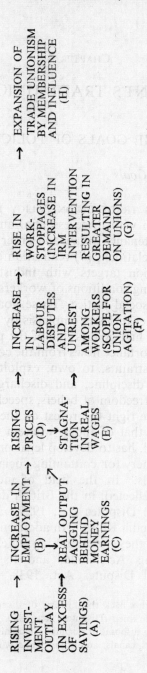

RISING INVESTMENT OUTLAY (IN EXCESS OF SAVINGS) (A) → INCREASE IN EMPLOYMENT (B) → REAL OUTPUT LAGGING BEHIND MONEY EARNINGS (C) → RISING PRICES (D) → STAGNATION IN REAL WAGES (E) → INCREASE IN LABOUR DISPUTES AND UNREST AMONG WORKERS (SCOPE FOR UNION AGITATION) (F) → RISE IN WORK-STOPPAGES (INCREASE IN IRM INTERVENTION RESULTING IN GREATER DEMAND ON UNIONS) (G) → EXPANSION OF TRADE UNIONISM BY MEMBERSHIP AND INFLUENCE (H)

CHAPTER 4

GOVERNMENT'S TRADE UNION POLICY

THE GOALS OF POLICY

Interdependence of Goals

THE GOVERNMENT'S TRADE UNION POLICY IS DERIVED FROM its primary concern with three essential and interdependent goals, *viz.*, (*i*) maintenance of law and order and its corollary, stability in social relations; (*ii*) realisation of feasible investment and production targets with industrial peace; and (*iii*) raising the living conditions of workers and securing for them natural and social justice. These goals are shared in common with greater or lesser emphasis by all contemporary democracies. The first goal is one of the primary functions of the state. Its importance flows from the constitutional right subject to legal restraints, to own, exploit, and dispose of property; to hire, discipline, and discharge labour on the one hand, and the freedom of beliefs, speech, and association accompanied by the right to protest on the other. A social economy, such as that of India, wherein these conflicting rights are permitted, has to develop legal procedures and administrative machinery for containing social conflicts within manageable bounds. In the field of industrial relations this concern was reflected, in the British days, in the enactment of the Trade Disputes Act, 1929,[1] and in rule 81-A of the Defence of India Rules. In addition, there were provincial enactments, the notable among which are the Bombay Industrial Relations Act, 1946, and its predecessor the Bombay Industrial Disputes Act, 1938, and the Central

---

1. It is possible to trace back the history of disputes legislation to the Employers and Workmen (Disputes) Act, 1860. This Act was passed for providing speedy disposal of disputes concerning wages of workmen employed in railways, canals, and other public works.

Provinces and Berar Industrial Disputes Settlement Act, 1947 (Madhya Pradesh). In the new India, under the Interim Government, one of the first enactments to be adopted by the Legislative Assembly was the Industrial Disputes Act, 1947.

In order of priorities the second goal naturally follows from the first. It is also a fact that since Independence, next to law and order, the government's major concern has been with production.[2] With the commencement of economic planning, this goal has been repeatedly emphasised by the government. The importance of this goal has led the government to develop instruments of policy which, depending upon the severity of symptoms, can either eliminate or mitigate the causes that mostly account for the breakdown of industrial peace. These include the creation of an adjudication machinery for compulsory referral of disputes, the *ad hoc* wage boards, the institution of tripartite conferences, and the committees and the Labour Panel of the Planning Commission.

The third goal implies a promise to workers that the society they are helping to build will be fair and just to them. It also recognises the patent fact that the society had not been hitherto fair to workers in respect of their collective share in output nor was just in the rights they were given to enjoy

---

[2]. This was eloquently brought home by Jawaharlal Nehru in a speech delivered at the Industries Conference, New Delhi, on December 18, 1947. After dwelling on the subject of conflicting ideologies and viewpoints which came in the way of production, he said:

Nevertheless, the major fact confronts us that all manner of perils face us in India today. And although some for the moment are at the forefront, the ultimate peril is the slow drying-up of the capacity of the nation to produce. That affects us politically, economically and in every other way, and gradually our strength goes down to resist these very perils that face us. Therefore, you have to stop this drying-up of our productive capacity.

I believe you have been thinking about this and you have also passed a number of resolutions on the subject. We must increase our production; we must increase our national wealth and the national dividend and only then can we really raise the standard of living of our people.

Government of India, Ministry of Information and Broadcasting, Publications Division, *Jawaharlal Nehru's Speeches*, Volume One, 1946-1949, New Delhi, 1949, p. 95.

either within the industry or sometimes even as citizens of the country. The imparting of these rights had been recommended by the I.L.O. conventions, and had already found a pride of place in the demands of the organised trade union movement in India. The rights to natural and social justice had also been powerfully projected in the Gandhian doctrine of non-violent resistance in the cause of truth. It should also be noted that although this goal had been purposefully projected by the government in the post-Independence India the underlying principles had gradually made their way into the statute built up by the erstwhile British government.[3]

Conditions on which their Realisation Depends

It can be readily seen that the realisation of these goal is crucially dependent upon the cooperation of organised labour with managements on the one hand and of both o these with the government on the other. For the govern ment it has been relatively easier to secure the cooperatio: of managements in expanding output and in setting up ne industries. There may also be mutuality of interest, fc instance, rising output will frequently yield more profits t the employers and higher tax revenue to the governmen However, the securing of unions' participation in these task is relatively difficult; indeed it bristles with complications an may even endanger the *entente* between the government an the employers.

First of all, the cooperation, if at all meaningful, has be at the institutional level. It may take the form of a de or understanding which binds the government and the unio:

---

3. The first comprehensive legislation for regulating labour in factories v passed in 1881. In the subsequent decades there were several advan on the original Act. All of these were consolidated in the Factories A 1934, which was further amended eight times up to 1947. The Facto Act, 1948, which was passed by consolidating all the previous amendme: is currently in force and has already undergone several amendme: For a brief history of factory legislation in India, see K. N. Vaid, *S: and Labour in India*, op. cit., Chapter 3 : "History and Growth of B: Labour Legislation", pp. 33-50.

to a certain course of action.   By its nature this is a political relationship which, to be effective, must meet two conditions, *viz.*, (*i*) the parties concerned, say, unions, are truly representative of their constituents, and (*ii*) the leadership is in a position to discipline the conduct of their respective organisations and through them the behaviour of the rank and file. In India these conditions have not been satisfactorily fulfilled by either the government or unions.   In the case of the former the labour ministry has not been able to either represent or condition the behaviour of others, particularly the economic ministries.   On the side of labour the unions have been traditionally weak. This is in part due to the uncertainty about the loyalty of workers to unions and partly due to the political rivalry among the leaders.   This weakness has been aggravated by the anxiety of the government to secure the commitment of organised labour to its policy—a factor which has often resulted in the involvement of the former in the policies of the latter.   In India the institutional relationship between the government and the unions has remained unstable, to a large extent, due to the partial absence of the two conditions stated above.

Second, there is a basic conflict of interests between the government and the employers on the one side and the organised trade union movement on the other.   The first two are generally interested in maintaining the *status quo* and the latter in disrupting it.   The trade unions in India, as in many other democratic countries, are waging relentless battles for securing concessions and rights from employers and the government and must strive, for their existence and progress, to alter the balance of power in their favour.   However, this conflict of interests is susceptible to compromise, particularly in a democracy where trade unions can form ideological alliances and exert pressure upon the government directly as well as indirectly through the party in power. Fortunately in India the scope of compromise has been large partly because the leadership of the Indian National Congress was already committed to meeting some of the demands of organised labour well before Independence and partly due to its ideological movement towards the left.   An additional factor has been the political stake of the Congress in the survival and progress of the INTUC.[4]

Third, the government has a better chance of securing the commitment of labour to its policies if it can persuade the latter to accept its goals.   There may still be differences on tactics but with common goals it is easier to reach compromises on practical problems. The setting up of common goals is to be viewed as a first but vital step which by itself does not assure agreement on tactics but without which even a dialogue cannot start. In this, too, it has been partly successful. The partial identification has been aided by (*i*) the adoption of the "socialist pattern of society" as the ultimate goal of planning, (*ii*) the diversion of resources to the public sector, particularly the heavy industries, (*iii*) the related policies of increasing employment and avoiding retrenchment wherever possible, (*iv*) the extension of civil liberties to all shades of political opinion, and finally (*v*) the foreign policy of non-alignment. These policies have widened the area of agreement between the unions and the government and thereby have facilitated the implementation of the five year plans in vital sectors. To some extent this has been at the cost of cooperation between the government and the employers. Some among the latter have felt estranged and sometimes engaged in hostile criticism of the government's economic and labour policies.[5]

---

4. The close link between the ruling party and the trade union movemen is not unique to India. It is common to many underdeveloped countrie See Bruce H. Millen, *The Political Role of Labour in Developing Countrie* Washington, D.C., The Brookings Institution, 1963, pp. 80-111.

5. The importance of political element in this process cannot be understate To cite an instance, in 1948, after the adoption of the Industrial Tru Resolution in December 1957, the government was complaining of polit cal strikes. It appealed to the all-India organisations of labour to impl ment the resolution faithfully. In response, the General Council of th AITUC passed a resolution in February 1948 which declared, *inter ali* that: "So long as the competitive system of private industry for prof remains, one can endeavour only to minimise strikes and this can t achieved to some extent only if firm and effective measures are taken t restrict profits, dividends and rents, to reduce, regulate and stabili prices and to organise suitable distribution by rationing of all essenti commodities." The resolution further states: "One of the necessary co ditions to be fulfilled is the speedy nationalisation of the basic industrie

The entire purpose of the government's policy has been to secure the acceptance by union leaders of the principle of reciprocity between rights and obligations. Its concern for the welfare of workers and their protection as the weaker party has lent moral weight to this posture. It would, however, be a mistake to read into it no more than an extension of Gandhian philosophy to the realm of industrial relations. The government's more material concerns in respect of maintaining law and order and economic development have already been noted. To these may be added its vested interests as the biggest employer in the country. These diverse strains have sometimes introduced elements of uncertainty and ambivalence in the industrial relations policy.[6]

REVIEW OF INDUSTRIAL RELATIONS POLICY

The Formulation of Policy

As pointed out earlier the period 1946-1948 witnessed acute industrial strife. The number of disputes rose from 820 in 1945 to 1,629 in 1946, and to 1,811 in 1947, but fell to 1,259

---

banks, etc., which would give a feeling to the workers that the production is for the public good and not primarily for private profits." *Summary of Proceedings of the Standing Labour Committee (Tenth Session)* held in New Delhi on the 15th, 16th and 17th April, 1948, p. 133. A decade later the same AITUC signed the Code of Discipline in Industry and was calling upon the workers to strengthen the public sector.

6. See in this connection Van D. Kennedy, "The Sources and Evolution of Indian Labour Relations Policy", *Indian Journal of Industrial Relations*, Vol. 1, No. 1, July 1965, pp. 15-40. Kennedy explains the evolution of the government's policy on industrial relations in terms of (*i*) the British heritage,(*ii*) paternal concern for workers, (*iii*) Gandhian belief in harmony, (*iv*) belief in norms, (*v*) the concern for production, and (*vi*) the role of labour ministers.

By using these explaining variables Kennedy has dramatised the uniqueness of India. It is, however, possible to analyse the making of Indian policy in terms of the social and economic goals which are commonly shared among most underdeveloped countries. Indeed the question may be asked: Given the overriding necessity of developing the country under the aegis of the state, the importance of internal political stability and the commitment to constitutional democracy what could be the in 1948. In the same way the number of mandays lost increased from 4.0 million in 1945 to 12.7 million in 1946, and to 16.5 million in 1947, but declined to 7.8 million in 1948.[7] This colossal waste of industrial potential showed up in the declining industrial production. The Interim Index of Industrial Production (1937=100) fell from 120.0 in 1945 to 109.0 in 1946, and to 102.4 in 1947, and rose to 114.0 in 1948. It is remarkable that similar trends can be seen in the index number of profits and in the average total daily employment in factories.[8] There are some problems of comparability of data in these series on account of partition and the merger of native states in the Indian Union. But the general downward trend in these series up to 1947 and their revival in 1948 are unmistakable. The portents of economic crisis, no less than the political disturbances that presaged Independence, caused deep anxiety to the government. This was reflected in the labour minister's address to the eighth session of the Indian Labour Conference in April 1947. He referred to the "wave of industrial unrest" that had been sweeping the country and warned the labour leaders that while the government would back workers in their reasonable demands, it also expected that every effort would be made to maintain industrial peace. He added :

If the worker has a right to expect assistance from the community and the state representing the community, and now-a-days, no abiding improvement will be possible unless the demands of the workers are backed by public opinion and the authority of the state, where-

---

rational labour policy? Kennedy does not ask this question and therefore tends to overemphasise the moralistic and personal factors in the evolution of policy.

7. Manager of Publications, *Statistical Abstract* for 1946-47, Delhi, 1949, Table No. 197, p. 458, and Labour Bureau, *Indian Labour Statistics*, 1961, Simla, 1961, Table No. 10.1, p. 170.

8. See Manager of Publications, *Statistical Abstract, India*, 1950, Delhi, 1952, Tables No. 181-A and 180, pp. 658-659 respectively. Also see *Indian Labour Year Book*, 1950-51, Delhi, Manager of Publications, 1953, Table 1, pp. 2-3.

ever necessary, the community equally has a right to expect that its normal activity should not be disrupted except under the gravest of provocations. I am mentioning this because our recent experience in several cases has shown that *no government can function if it allows the workers to be made a pawn of political parties interested not in bringing about an improvement in working conditions consistent with the general economic conditions in the country, but to secure a position of advantage for their own parties.*[9] (emphasis added)

What could the government do under these circumstances? It followed a three-pronged policy. First, it enacted the Industrial Disputes Act, 1947, and promptly enforced it to curb work-stoppages. Some of the provisions of this Act had been vehemently opposed by trade union leaders. Second, simultaneously with the consideration of the Industrial Disputes Bill the government announced a five year plan of labour legislation to meet some of the long-standing demands of workers. Most of the proposed bills were routed through the Indian Labour Conference or the Standing Labour Committee. Third, the government also decided to take steps for steering the trade union movement along healthy and responsible channels. For this purpose the Indian Trade Unions (Amendment) Act, 1947, was passed.[10] However, due to strong opposition from within the government the Act was not enforced.

9. Government of India, Ministry of Labour, *Summary of the Proceedings of the Indian Labour Conference*, Eighth Session, New Delhi, 21st and 22nd April, 1947, p. 2. Also see the reports of the Provincial Governments annexed to Appendix II. Several of these mention political factor in strikes. One report mentions the subversive activities of communists under a separate heading. The report does not hesitate in saying that "some unions sponsored by communists have accordingly been declared unlawful," p. 89.

10. This Act was passed to meet a genuinely felt need. The government believed that trade disputes should, as far as possible, be settled through mutual negotiations. This was possible only if employers agreed to recognise a union and dealt with it on an equal basis. Indeed the subject of trade union recognition was one of the most important causes of work-stoppages. When these disputes were referred to compulsory adjudication

These measures reflected not only the concern of the government to meet a temporary crisis but also the convictions of national leaders as to what would be the proper arrangement for the country in the long run. Whether the latter was indicative of the paternalistic beliefs of leaders or the political doctrine that sought to give the state the twin roles of mediator and arbiter for maintaining balance among the contending classes is not of much relevance for our purpose. It is, however, important to know whether the policies were conceived with due deliberation and represented as broad a consensus of political opinions as was possible under the circumstances. To this question the answer is clearly an affirmative one.

On labour matters the sub-committee of the National Planning Committee had submitted its final report in 1940. It had recommended state regulation of living and working conditions of employees and considered it of "paramount importance that certain essential human standards be maintained." It had made a series of recommendations on hours of work, child labour, health and safety, wages, housing, and holidays with pay, which, among others, found their way into the Factories Act, 1948. On trade unions the sub-committee proposed that "legislation should be passed to recognise trade unionism as an essential and integral part of the economic system." On trade disputes the recommendation was that "machinery for the settlement of disputes should be provided by government in the form of a conciliation board and an industrial court." It further added that "under planned economy legislation should be passed for adjudication of industrial disputes."[11]

the adjudicators "generally hesitated to give a clear finding or lead in th matter, holding that it was unwise to accept the demand unless the poin was accepted on an all-India scale." See Annexure XV to Appendix I (Brief Report of United Provinces) in *Summary of Proceedings of th Indian Labour Conference*, (op. cit.), p. 94. Also see in this connectio Van D. Kennedy, (op. cit.), pp. 19-20.

11. *Report*, National Planning Committee, (op. cit.), pp. 155-157. Ther were reservations on the last recommendation by two members of th sub-committee. The basis of reservation of the labour leader N. M. Josh was that he would not express any opinion on so vital a matter until h knew more about the nature of the state to come.

Quite aside from the recommendations of the National Planning Committee, the experience of the Congress administrations under the provincial autonomy had led them to assigning a positive role to the government in the field of labour relations. In 1938 the Congress ministry of Bombay had declared:

With regard to trade disputes, government are determined to pursue an active policy with a view to maintaining industrial peace in the Presidency, endeavouring all the time to see that the workers obtain a fair deal. It is the intention of government to provide legislation aiming at the prevention of strikes and lockouts as far as possible. The basis of this legislation would be the requirement that no reduction in wages or other change in conditions of employment to the disadvantage of the workers should take effect till they have had sufficient time and opportunity for having the facts and merits of the proposed change examined and all avenues of peaceful settlement of the dispute explored either through the channel of voluntary negotiation, conciliation, or arbitration or by the machinery of the law. A corresponding obligation would rest on the workers in respect of demands on their behalf.[12]

The declaration goes on to say that since no legislative programme could be a substitute for trade unions the government will encourage their growth and promote collective bargaining.

It is possible to support the line of thinking revealed by the National Planning Committee report and the above quoted declaration by several other excerpts. All of these unambiguously demonstrate that the national leadership in India never assumed that industrial relations should at all be allowed to be moulded by the free interaction between labour and management. Instead the government would protect workers, encourage trade unions so that this might be

12. This declaration was reproduced by the National Planning Committee report on Labour, (op. cit.), p. 31.

achieved better, promote bilateral settlements of disputes, to the extent possible, but more than anything else maintain industrial peace. It could not be that the leaders were not aware of the contradiction between the most important objective of avoidance of work-stoppages and the secondary goal of encouraging trade unions. By stating the priorities in this manner the Congress leadership was no doubt differentiating the national interest in maximising output from the sectional interests of workers. The passing of the Industrial Disputes Act and the Indian Trade Unions (Amendment) Act in 1947 shows that the government was keen on proceeding with the above policy doctrine which may now be termed as "promotion of trade unions subject to the maintenance of industrial peace".

It may be briefly noted that this doctrine received full support from the officials who had accumulated considerable experience with the working of rule 81-A of the Defence of India Rules. To them, too, industrial peace was a matter of the highest importance, but it was clear that this was not possible without legislating for union recognition and securing it against victimisation. Towards the same end collective bargaining also merited encouragement but only to the extent that it did not jeopardise industrial peace.[13]

Within the framework of this doctrine there is room for modification of strategy, for experimentation with new ideas and even calculated risks but none for shifts in priorities. The development of industrial relations policy since 1947-48,

---

13. During the Second World War the tripartite forums were consulted on the revision of the Trade Disputes Act, 1929, with a view to doing away with rule 81-A on the return of normalcy. By 1944 the government had already made up its mind on setting up a permanent industrial court, the manner of referring disputes to compulsory arbitration, the extension of the definition of public utility to all trades that were considered important to the life of the community, the prohibition of strikes or lockouts in the course of statutory conciliation or arbitration proceedings and the insertion of a strike notice clause in the revised legislation. At about the same time the government had circulated a Trade Unions Bill which formed the basis of the 1947 enactment. See Government of India, Department of Labour, *Sixth Labour Conference*, (held at New Delhi on the 27th and 28th October, 1944), *Summary of Proceedings*, New Delhi, Government of India Press, 1945, pp. 21, and 28-36.

when the foundations were laid, up to 1965 shows that while the points of emphasis have changed, the basic policy has not. The more striking change has, however, been in the idiom of policy, in the modes of communicating with labour and managements, and in the political and administrative procedures for dealing with industrial relations.

Shift in Policy

The first significant shift in emphasis occurred with the gradual return of the economy to normalcy and the completion of the basic tasks of free India, *i.e.*, the restoration of law and order and the unification of native states, and not with the change in the stewardship of labour ministry as is often believed. In 1949 the Labour Relations Bill and the Trade Unions Bill were introduced in the Constituent Assembly. Both of these were comprehensive legislation and were meant to replace the existing Acts in their fields with a view to introducing uniformity in the provisions throughout the country.

The Trade Unions Bill excluded from its scope the armed forces and the police, and placed restrictions on the unions of government servants. It had certain features of the 1947 amendment Act on compulsory recognition and in addition imposed certain responsibilities on the registered and recognised unions. Moreover, the number of outsiders on the executive committee was restricted to one-fourth or four, whichever was less. The scope of the Labour Relations Bill was extended to all categories of employees other than civil servants, defence forces, domestic servants, and establishments employing less than ten persons. It laid considerable emphasis on collective bargaining and provided for bipartite negotiations as a preliminary step to the settlement of a dispute.[14] Since the issue of retrenchment of surplus labour was becoming urgent in view of its explosive potential, the Bill had provided for its regulation through an independent tribunal and payment of gratuity to those retrenched.

14. Manager of Publications, *The Indian Labour Year Book*, 1949-50, Delhi, 1951, pp. 116-117 and 113. Also see Van D. Kennedy, (op. cit.), pp. 20-21.

It may be further noted that although the two Bills taken together had sought to strengthen trade unions and encourage collective bargaining, the governmental discretion on compulsory referral of disputes to adjudication had been retained. These were no doubt bold proposals and showed an inclination to experiment with new ideas and take certain risks. However, partly due to the opposition from trade union leaders but largely from the employing ministries the Bills were allowed to lapse.

The principle of sponsoring collective bargaining through legislation was not confined to the two Bills mentioned above. By an amendment to the Industrial Disputes Act, 1947, in 1950 the appropriate governments were authorised to order the setting up of works committees in all undertakings employing 100 or more workers. The purpose was "to foster the spirit of joint consultation between the employers and the employees" and "to promote harmonious relations" between the two. But, simultaneously, by the same amendment the discretionary powers of the government to refer disputes to boards of conciliation, courts of inquiry and industrial tribunals were also greatly enhanced.[15] The Act as amended automatically binds the parties concerned to the award of an industrial tribunal unless the same is rejected or modified by the appropriate government. It may be noted that these developments took place about the same time the two ill-fated Bills had been placed on the agenda of the Constituent Assembly. This raises the question whether the government had accepted without reservation the principle of promoting collective bargaining. It is evident in retrospect that while there was willingness to experiment on a selective basis, provided the unions accepted their share of responsibility for giving collective bargaining a fair trial and the restraints that go with it, no major risks could be taken.

Aside from the reasons which led the Bills to their inevitable doom, there were two other powerful factors operating against them. First, the government had started thinking in terms of economic planning and the work on the First

15. *The Indian Labour Year Book*, 1949-50, pp. 120-123.

Five Year Plan had begun. It might not have appeared opportune to commence the First Plan under conditions of uncertain industrial relations. Second, the INTUC was not at all convinced that compulsory adjudication had proved harmful to trade unions. On the contrary, the union movement as a whole had gained in strength, the workers in many industries had received protection, and subversive political activity in their ranks had been checked.[16] These constellation of forces proved too powerful even to permit a limited experimentation with the principles embodied in the two Bills.

The Giri Interlude

The period 1952-1954 may be considered as an interlude of acute ambivalence in the history of government policy on industrial relations. The principal source of this ambivalence was the forceful drive of V. V. Giri, the then labour minister, to alter the priorities in labour policy. He believed in collective bargaining as good in itself and in a strong, independent trade union movement that could serve responsibly the workers as well as the country. He also believed, and said so publicly, that compulsory adjudication had done much harm to industrial relations and retarded the growth of trade unions and therefore the time had come to charter a new course. In order to secure the acceptance of this policy by the Cabinet it would no doubt be necessary to enlist the support of the principal trade unions and employers' organisations and the State Governments. Accordingly he made a fervent appeal to the delegates at the 12th session of the Indian Labour Conference (1952) to agree to the following important changes.[17]

    (i) Accept the principle of internal settlement in preference to compulsory arbitration. Free the two

16. See the speech of Harihar Nath Shastri at the 12th session of the Indian Labour Conference, 1952, in *Proceedings of the Indian Labour Conference, Twelfth Session*, held in Nanital on the 8th to 11th October, 1952, pp. 26-29.

17. See V. V. Giri's speech reproduced in the *Proceedings of the Indian Labour Conference, Twelfth Session*, (op. cit), pp. 5-24.

parties from the shackles of adjudication in as wide a field as possible. A beginning may be made with non-public utilities.

(*ii*) Revise the Industrial Disputes Act, 1947, to make it simpler and affirm the above principle and to introduce uniformity throughout the country.

(*iii*) In non-public utility concerns strikes and lockouts should be prohibited during the period of binding awards (agreements) and also perhaps during the initial period of notice of change but not on other occasions.

(*iv*) Agree to the immediate abolition of the Labour Appellate Tribunal. Several other authorities, such as conciliation boards, commissions of inquiry, and labour courts, should also be abolished.

(*v*) Legislate for the certification of "bargaining agents" and also "recognised" unions. When two or more unions are contending for the certificate the representative status should be determined by election through secret ballot of all workers employed in the concern. If no union qualifies for the certificate the most representative among them should be "recognised" for purposes of bargaining.

The delegates while endorsing the general sentiment in favour of collective bargaining were divided on the steps that could be immediately taken. Giri could not obtain the endorsement of the Conference on the abolition of several authorities he had earlier proposed. The opposition to the proposed abandonment of compulsory adjudication was sufficiently strong and widespread to slow him down and even stall the proposal for the time being. There were operating at the same time powerful factors which favoured continuity and would have foredoomed any radical shifts in policy.

The First Five Year Plan which, let it be remembered, emerged after extensive deliberations in the Planning Commission, the higher echelons of the Congress party, consultations with the State Governments and debate in the Parliament, had assigned the task of maintaining industrial peace to the government, and for weighty reasons. The planners stated that

> Harmonious relations between capital and labour are essential for the realisation of the targets of the Plan in the industrial sector...
>
> ... Economic progress is also bound up with industrial peace. Industrial relations are, therefore, not a matter between employers and employees alone, but a vital concern of the community which may be expressed in measures for the protection of its larger interests.

This is one reason for state intervention. The second is the protection of the weaker party. The Plan states :

> The employer usually possesses superior strength which may become a source of injustice and oppression unless he is imbued with a high sense of fairness and uses his advantage with scrupulous regard to the rights and interests of others.... Experience of many years has demonstrated that in the majority of labour struggles, owing to the ignorance and the mistakes of the workers and their organisational and bargaining weakness they have failed to gain their ends irrespective of the merits of the disputes. The community has, therefore, to intervene for redressing the balance in favour of the weaker party to assure just treatment for all concerned.[18]

Giri was willing to take the risk of work-stoppages in order to promote collective bargaining, but not the planners. This is what they said:

> Whatever may be the apparent outcome of a labour conflict, the resulting loss far outweighs any advantage secured by a party and in most cases all concerned stand to lose.
>
> In normal times and in ordinary cases whether the right

8. *First Five Year Plan*, (op. cit.), pp. 572-573.

to strike or lockout should be circumscribed is an open question. An economy organised for planned production and distribution, aiming at the realisation of social justice and the welfare of the masses can function effectively only in an atmosphere of industrial peace. India is moving in this direction. It is also at present passing through a period of economic and political emergency. Taking the period of the next few years, the regulation of industrial relations in the country has to be based on these two considerations and it is incumbent on the state to arm itself with legal powers to refer disputes for settlement by arbitration or adjudication on failure of efforts to reach an agreement by other means. However, the endeavour of the state has all along to be to encourage mutual settlement, collective bargaining and voluntary arbitration to the utmost extent and thereby to reduce to the minimum occasions for its intervention in industrial disputes and the exercise of special powers. The restrictive aspects of any existing or future labour legislation must be judged in the light of these considerations.[19]

This was the stated policy of the government at the time Giri was pleading for a basic change in it. In retrospect there can be no doubt that his personal intervention though forceful and impassionate was foredoomed to frustration. He could not possibly move the solid rocks on which labour policy had been founded. While he was in office there was some ambivalence in policy pronouncements and it appeared that the government was speaking with two voices and spelling out its goals in contradictory terms. With his resignation these anomalies also went out of sight.[20]

19. *Ibid.*, pp. 572-573.
20. Indeed Giri accepted the defeat of his policies well before his resignation. In January 1954 he admitted: "Detailed consultations during and after that Conference (12th Session) have, however, convinced me that the conditions in the country are not favourable for a change in the basic policy that now governs the administration of labour laws." He referred to falling profits and the weak bargaining power of workers and then said "I cannot, therefore, blame workers and their organisations if they feel that we have chosen the wrong time to make them self-reliant. This is also another important reason why we should avoid any radical experi-

Restoration of Priorities

The successor to Giri was like him a distinguished labour leader. But unlike him, Khandubhai Desai could find no place for the "law of jungle" which resulted in work-stoppages in a state-directed economy. Industrial production was rising while the cost of living had fallen. As a result, the standard of living of workers had shown perceptible increase. But the economic situation was far from satisfactory. The unemployment problem was getting worse. Particularly for the trade unions the threat of retrenchment was beginning to assume ominous proportions. This was beginning to show up in the data on disputes and mandays lost in them. The number of disputes had fallen from 1,071 in 1951 to 772 in 1953, but thereafter it gradually rose to 840 in 1954, to 1,116 in 1955, and to 1,203 in 1956. The corresponding series on mandays shows a decline from 3.8 million in 1951 to 3.4 million in 1953, but a steady climb beginning with 3.4 million in 1954 to 5.7 million in 1955, and to 7.0 million in 1956.[21] The response of the government to this trend was the strengthening and streamlining of the adjudication machinery, the setting up of tripartite committees of employers and labour leaders to sort out their problems, and the acceptance of the principle of wage determination

---

ments for the present. The First Five Year Plan is only halfway through, and it is of the utmost importance that we should all pull our weight together in the full implementation of it. The Plan is for the benefit of the country as a whole and it would not be proper for sectional interests to indulge in activities or methods which might retard the progress of the Plan even though these might otherwise be unexceptionable. I have, therefore, come to the conclusion, no doubt, as you will have realised, much to my disappointment, that compulsory adjudication must continue to remain an important feature of labour-management relations for some time more, although it should be the bounden duty of all of us interested in the eventual building up of a strong trade union movement to give the largest measure of support to the policy of mutual negotiation and settlement of disputes." This speech was welcomed by several union leaders. Government of India, Ministry of Labour, *Summary of Proceedings of Indian Labour Conference, Thirteenth Session*, Mysore, January 1964, pp. 11-12.

Indian Labour Statistics, 1966, Tables 12.1, 12.7, 3.1, and 10.1 on pages 191, 198, 41 and 165 respectively.

through wage boards. In respect of the first change, the government abolished the Labour Appellate Tribunal in 1956 and constituted a three-tier labour judiciary in its place. It consisted of labour courts, industrial tribunals, and national tribunals. On the second, the Joint Consultative Board of Industry and Labour, which had been in existence for several years, was reconstituted in 1954 to advise the government on important matters, such as norms and standards for remuneration to labour and amendment to labour legislation. On the third, a wage board for working journalists was set up in 1956.[22] Later, in 1957 the government had also appointed central wage boards for the cotton textiles, sugar, and cement industries.

Meanwhile, the Second Five Year Plan had dittoed the policy laid down in the First Plan with an added emphasis on labour's participation in management as the first step towards the development and reorganisation of the economy on the socialist pattern. The planners had also decided to strengthen the public sector and take deliberate risk of moderate inflation. The government realised that the implementation of the Second Plan would strain the economy in many ways. Consequently new techniques were needed to mitigate the stress and secure the cooperation of labour and management. It was, therefore, not at all accidental that after the second general election the labour portfolio was handed over to the Minister of Planning, Gulzari Lal Nanda. Besides his experience in planning, Nanda had long been associated with the labour movement at Ahmedabad, and was the labour minister in Bombay before joining the Central Government.

New Idioms for Old Policy

True to the expectations, Nanda opened the 15th Indian Labour Conference by referring to the critical phase through

22. *Indian Labour Year Book*, 1955-56, pp. 126-127, p. 169, and p. 146. Also see *Indian Labour Year Book*, 1955-56, pp. 336-342 and pp. 170-171. The award of this wage board was, however, declared *ultra vires* by the Supreme Court. The government, therefore, appointed another committee for fixing wage rates for working journalists. See *Indian Labour Year Book*, 1957, p. 338.

which the Second Plan was passing. He also said:

> The Plan sums up the hopes and aspirations of the people of the country. To all connected with industry, it offers an expanding horizon and a widening field of opportunity. The question that we have to ask ourselves in this context is what each one of us is prepared to do for the Plan. The question becomes pertinent now because the Plan has reached a stage in its career when to ensure its success we have to use all the energy we can muster together to push it along its path.

He referred to the problems of rationalisation, low productivity, workers' housing and indiscipline. On wage policy, Nanda said that though he was not proposing a wage freeze, particularly because of rising prices, he hoped that workers would "accept voluntary restraint on wage increases in the national interest."[23]

Nanda argued that the government was planning for more output and employment and rising productivity which alone could provide the material basis for higher wages and better housing. Since these were also the goals of trade unions they should cooperate with the government in implementing the Plan. Moreover, there was the promise of a socialist pattern of society towards which the government had decided on taking the first steps, *viz.* workers' participation in management, and a programme of workers' education. The initial response to this appeal was one of deep scepticism. The discussion that followed showed "deep cleavage of opinion" and "serious disagreement" between the parties; but despite them, two important conclusions were reached. The employers agreed to certain principles on the question of rationalisation which conceded to the unions the following important rights:

(*i*) Notice to workers of the "technological change" planned by the employers with full details.

(*ii*) Every reasonable step will be taken to absorb the sur-

. *Summary of Proceedings of the Indian Labour Conference*, 15th Session, New Delhi, 11th & 12th July, 1957, pp. 1-6.

plus personnel. No one will be retrenched as long as similar jobs are available in the same plant or under the same employer. Moreover, such workers will be trained by the employers for alternative jobs.

(*iii*) The union shall submit its proposals to the employers for discussion within a week. If there is an agreement between the two sides the employers may implement the plan in accordance with it.

(*iv*) Retrenchment will be in accordance with the principle of juniority from which departure may be made only in exceptional cases and for reasons which are duly recorded.

(*v*) If there are differences between the two parties, the dispute shall be referred for arbitration.

The unions in return agreed that the employers had the right to rationalise the industry and retrench the surplus workers in accordance with the law and this agreement.[24] The unions also signed a code of discipline which bound the two parties to "no-strike or lockout without notice", "no recourse to 'go slow' tactics", no violence and intimidation, and no deliberate damage to property. They also agreed to the blanket clause that "any action which disturbs cordial industrial relations should be avoided".[25] On its part, the government agreed to speed up workers' housing programme and the principle of minimum wages.

The labour minister was "greatly pleased and very much gratified" that it was possible "to have a process of give and take and some concessions are made by both sides in order to reach certain agreed conclusions". Similar sentiments were expressed by employers and union leaders.[26] Considering the diversity in the trade union movement and the

24. *Ibid.*, pp. 48-50.
25. *Ibid.*, p. 26.
26. *Ibid.*, pp. 28-29. In expressing these feelings the communist leader S. A. Dange was only a step ahead of others. His speech indicated the deep change that had come in the attitude of the AITUC. He is reported to have "expressed a hope that the decisions of the Conference would be implemented in the same spirit in which they were taken and that there would be mutual give and take of obligations and rights on either side.

growing restlessness among workers this was no doubt a signal achievement for the labour minister. But what made it possible? In part this was due to his persuasiveness and ingenuity, but to a larger part this was due to the change in the political postures of the different trade union centres.

First of all the trade union leadership in India was genuinely impressed by the performance of the First Plan and the dimensions of the Second. The INTUC gave its wholehearted cooperation in the implementation of the Second Plan.[27] The AITUC, too, extended support to the "progressive features" of the Second Plan. These features were identified as (i) expansion of the state sector, (ii) strengthening of heavy industries most of which were to be under state ownership, (iii) increased economic cooperation between India and the communist countries, particularly the Soviet Union, (iv) accent on land reforms, and (v) acceptance by Parliament of the goal of socialist pattern of society.[28] The communist leadership of the AITUC realised the danger to these goals in the non-fulfilment of the Second Plan. In the words of S. A. Dange:

We must remember that if the Plan fails, the results will not affect only the ruling party. It will spell immense economic difficulties for the whole country. No doubt the political responsibility of the failure will be of the ruling Congress Party. But then the misery will be for everyone to suffer. It may even give a political advantage for the genuine parties of the left. But the advantage will be

---

He added that a harmonious relationship on this basis would lead to better development of the economy and to the raising of standards of workers' living, not excluding normal profits on the other side and a peaceful existence for the Central and State Governments. He appealed to all concerned to extend their cooperation in this common task." (emphasis added), *Ibid.*, p. 29.

27. In fairness it may be added that the INTUC also made several demands on the government for improving wages and working conditions and enforcing the awards of tribunals, etc. See INTUC, *Labour Policy in the Five Year Plan*, Memorandum by INTUC. Also see INTUC, *Ninth Annual Session*, Madurai, 1st and 2nd January, 1958, "Resolutions", pp. 2-3.

28. S. A. Dange, *General Report at Ernakulam*, Silver Jubilee Sessions, All-India Trade Union Congress, December 25 to 29, 1957, pp. 10-11.

far greater, if we can save the best and the basic features of the Plan and defeat the monopoly capitalists in their game against the people.[29]

As far as the HMS is concerned, it gave official support to the Second Plan, but its voice had been weakened by the split in the Praja Socialist Party and the consequent feud among its leaders. The dominant line had been laid down by Asoka Mehta who not only supported the Plan but proposed the doctrine that trade unions should strive to subordinate the demand of immediate wage gains and similar considerations to the development of the country.[30] The UTUC, too, despite reservations on the economic policies of the government decided on a constructive attitude towards the Second Plan. In 1958 the general secretary of the UTUC declared:

In spite of the inherent limitations of the Second Plan, the working class of India cannot, therefore, set its face against the increased accent on industrialisation in it. The working class of India would rather like to take a constructive view about the Plan provided all others concerned, *viz.*, the government, the capitalists, employers, managements of the private and public sectors of our economy, all look upon the Plan as a true national effort and not one for which only the working class and the common masses of the people will be called upon to tighten up their belts and bear the burden of sacrifice.[31]

Second, for a sizeable section of trade union leadership it was a package deal which was binding upon them only to the extent that other parties to the agreements also lived up to their respective roles. As Dange had made it clear, all the three parties were bound to their respective responsibilities

29. *Ibid.*, p. 15.
30. A. Mehta, "The Mediating Role of the Trade Union in Underdeveloped Countries", *Economic Development and Cultural Change*, October 1957, p. 16. Also see Harold Crouch, *Trade Unions and Politics in India*, Bombay, Manaktalas, 1966, Chapter VIII entitled "The Hind Mazdoor Sabha", pp. 202-227.
31. United Trade Union Congress, *Report* presented by Jatin Chakravorty, Secretary, at the 3rd All-India Session, April 2 to 6, 1958, Quilon, Kerala, p. 13.

on the conclusions of the Fifteenth Tripartite pertaining to wage policy, rationalisation, housing, and code of discipline.[32] Probably each side had reservations on the real value of these conclusions but had agreed to them under the prevailing circumstances. The effect of these reservations began to show up in the mounting wave of work-stoppages in the following year.

The labour minister realised that this trend could be checked mainly by strengthening the area of agreement between the government and the trade union leaders of different political shades and use this opportunity for binding the latter more closely to the basic goals of the Plan. The Code of Discipline was the principal instrument for achieving this purpose. Nanda sought and secured the ratification of the Code from employers and trade unions at different levels. But it had also become clear that the implementation of the Code was conditional on the solution of the problem of union recognition and the mitigation of trade union rivalry. To these problems at least a partial solution could be found in the Code of Conduct. In 1958 Nanda said:

Inter-union rivalry is the bane of the labour movement in the country and is the major factor in the disturbed conditions of industrial relations in many places. Trade union conflicts have been undermining the strength and solidarity of the working class. The ideal condition would be to have a unified trade union structure throughout industry. This cannot come about till the working of trade unions is divorced from party politics or the bulk of the labour finds itsef in a single party or the working class form a party of its own....I am sure at least that a working class party, by itself, is neither a practicable nor a desirable proposition in the conditions of India for a long time. *If multiplicity of unions cannot be avoided, is there not a way to arrange the mutual relations of the competing unions in the same field so that the workers are saved from harm, the industry is not injured and the national interest*

2. *Sixteenth Tripartite*, Introduction by S. A. Dange, AITUC publication, August 1958, pp. 5-15.

does not suffer. With this end in view, the Standing Labour Committee at its meeting last year recommended that different organisations should meet together to discuss and settle matters affecting inter-union relations. I have been asked repeatedly to make a personal effort to bring this about. I wrote to all the central organisations of workers offering to use my good offices for bringing them together so that a Code of Conduct may be evolved, setting out the "do's" and "don'ts" which trade unions should observe for the sake of the good of the working class and the progress of the country.[33] (emphasis added)

The proposal of Nanda was adopted, and so were others dealing with works committees, model grievance procedure, and joint management councils. The Conference reiterated its belief in the principle of bipartite settlement of disputes and simultaneously affirmed the paradox by resolving that the time was not yet ripe for suspending adjudication even for a temporary period. The Sixteenth Tripartite achieved the highest watermark in taking vital decisions on industrial relations since its commencement 16 years ago. It completed the work started in 1957; from now on the labour ministry would be concerned with implementing the decisions in so far as it could and making refinements in the policy.

The principal achievement of Nanda was not in giving the labour policy a new direction but in seeking to enhance its effectiveness by reformulating it in new idioms. The *modus operandi* was to secure a political consensus at the top and transmitting the same down the line in the organisational structures of different interest groups. The beauty of this method lay in the reconciliation of opposite interests in howsoever paradoxical statements with the explicit purpose, that was clearly understood by all the parties, of giving the Second Plan a fighting chance of succeeding. There already existed in the country a consensus of sentiments to this effect;

33. *Summary of Proceedings of the Indian Labour Conference*, 16th session Nainital, 19th-20th May, 1958, pp. 12-13. Also see Appendix I entitled "Report of the Committee on Industrial Relations and Other Items" pp. 31-43 and Appendix III entitled "Inter-union Code of Conduct", p. 53.

this could not have been contrived by the government. But it is to the credit of Nanda and his advisers that this sentiment was transmuted into a formal structure of mutually reinforcing codes and norms. The novelty of this method lay in two respects. First, the labour minister, by using the political process, secured the commitment of labour to the basic principle of mutuality of rights and social obligations—a goal that had been steadfastly kept in view by his predecessors but which, nevertheless, had been evading them continuously and could neither be legislated nor enforced otherwise. Second, like all political agreements, the codes could endure only to the extent that the underlying consensus on the basis of which these had been structured also survived. There could possibly be no presumption that the consensus would be everlasting.

No wonder, the codes, though temporarily reinforced by the resolution on industrial truce, have been eroded by time.[34] Their success, measured against the criterion of work-stoppages, was not impressive in any year, although they were probably instrumental in slowing down the trend of disputes in the beginning and thereby avoided a catastrophe to the Second Five Year Plan. In 1957 the country lost a total of 6.4 million mandays. In 1958 the loss increased to 7.8 million—a figure that had not been exceeded since 1950. In 1959, even though the number of disputes rose marginally, the mandays lost fell down to 5.6 million. In the next three years the figures were 6.5 million, 4.9 million, and 6.1 million respectively. There was a drop in the mandays lost to 3.3 million in 1963, but a sharp reversal in 1964 when the figure jumped to 7.7 million. It is, thus, clear that by itself or in comparison to the period of the First Plan this is an unsatisfactory record.

It appears that there were three important reasons why the codes have not fulfilled the principal purpose for which they had been designed. First, as Dange had warned in 1958, the codes were part of a package deal. The labour ministry could not ensure the compliance of the government to its

34. The choice of this criterion has been based on the emphasis noted in the official utterances on the yardstick of disputes resulting in work-stoppages while appraising the Code of Discipline.

stated or implicit responsibilities far less of the employers or the unions. It can even be asserted that the political agreement on the codes far exceeded the powers of the parties concerned to commit their respective constituents. Accordingly, the codes were gradually reduced to pious wishes with high moral fervour but low practical content. Second, the inter-union Code of Conduct, which was an essential complement to the Code of Discipline rocked on the hard realities of trade union rivalry. When the rival union leaderships are struggling, at the ground level, for their life and existence they are unlikely to pay much regard to a code to which their top leaders had been signatories with deep reservations. Union security is the foundation of good conduct, but neither the government nor the union leaders could ensure it. Third, the principal responsibility of implementing the labour policy is of the State Governments. For reasons right or wrong, complaints against them by the trade unions of practically every political shade or opinion, not excepting the INTUC, have multiplied. In retrospect it appears that the principal drive behind the codes was that of the labour ministry at the Centre; it has found little genuine practical support from the States which themselves in some cases have been deeply involved in trade union politics.[35]

The one material gain was the assumption of moral responsibility by the Union labour ministry to process grievances of either labour or management on violations of codes and to redress them as speedily as possible. This has also resulted

35. These complaints have covered a wide field. The INTUC stated in 1960, in its Memorandum on Labour Policy in the Third Five Year Plan, that the State Governments had not either promoted voluntary arbitration, or set up joint consultative machinery, at the State or the unit level or rigorously enforced the tribunal awards, etc. The AITUC had also charged the government of complicity in "delay and sabotage by employers of agreements, laws, awards, conventions" and "helping disruption of working class unity by means of patronage in recognition of trade unions and by other means". There are many other charges besides these. See S. A. Dange, *Report at Coimbatore*, 26th session, January 6-12, 1961, AITUC publication, pp. 61-63. The employers, too, have complained against the working of the implementation machinery in the States. In fact in 1960 only six States had deployed whole-time officers to man the implementation machinery.

in prompt enforcement of tribunal awards in the private sector and some reduction in dilatoriness in the public sector on implementing labour laws. Moreover, some progress has also been made in introducing grievance procedures in establishments where these had not existed and in promoting out-of-court settlements.[36]

For several years the government has been trying to form joint management councils in larger establishments with a reasonably peaceful record of industrial relations. An official report has found them doing useful work in several companies. It is, however, also reported that in many cases neither the management nor the unions have shown much enthusiasm in retaining them and quite a few have become inactive. This scheme has been received with widespread scepticism and it is not at all certain that, in its present form, it will be carried over into the Fourth Five Year Plan.[37]

INFLUENCE ON TRADE UNIONISM

On the question of the influence of government policy on trade unionism there is much diversity of opinion among serious students of the subject as well as among trade union leaders. This is surprising, considering that both the policy and the development of trade unions are susceptible to an objective analysis. True, the data are inadequate; in certain vital respects these may even be unreliable. But these should account for no more than marginal differences in opinions, and having been recognised as such can be suitably discounted in serious discussions. However, it seems that the reasons are more basic; these relate to the concepts in question and the selection of appropriate facts.

While discussing whether trade union movement in India

36. The Code of Discipline, the Inter-Union Code of Conduct, the Industrial Truce Resolutions, the Model Grievance Procedure and the procedures under them have been well publicised by the government. For their texts and other details, see Government of India, Ministry of Labour and Employment, Implementation and Evaluation Division, *Implementation and Evaluation Machinery, Its Functions and Procedures*, second edition, October 1963.

37. Ministry of Labour and Employment, *Reports on the Working of Joint Management Councils*. Most of these reports relate to 1961 and 1962.

has grown stronger or weaker one can have any of the following three concepts in mind:

(i) The qualitative aspects of trade unionism, i.e., whether the union movement has gradually become increasingly self-reliant and independent of the government machinery set up for conciliation and adjudication of disputes. Some commentators might widen the concept to include independence from political parties as one of the indicators of improvement in quality. It might, however, be sufficient to confine the concept to its narrower meaning.

(ii) The quantitative aspects of trade unionism, i.e. whether the movement has grown numerically and by reported membership.

(iii) The growth of trade unionism may be judged by what it has done for the working class. In this case the indicators used will be the rights won either through legislation or in tripartite forums or in the normal process of conciliation and adjudication of disputes.

It may be noticed that though each of the concepts seems to be perfectly neutral, in practice they are not, and are in fact value-loaded. Some scholars like to compare trade unionism in India with that in the developed countries, such as the U.S.A. and the U.K., and come out with the inevitable conclusions that it has not progressed much and may even have become weaker. On the other hand, the defenders of the government policy and some others who may have profited from it would prefer the second concept. As has already been demonstrated in the preceding chapter the evidence in support of the contention that the movement has grown in India is indeed overwhelming. Then there are some trade union leaders who like to cite the third kind of indicators to prove that unions despite all odds and difficulties have done well for workers.

It may, however, be stated that all the three propositions are basically correct; the disagreement can only be on emphasis rather than on substance. To re-state, it is factually correct that:

(*i*) The trade union movement has grown in size and reported membership. It has also gained in status at the hands of both the government and the employers. The Planning Commission and Parliament have considered it important enough to assign it the vital responsibility of improving the lot of workers and, of course, cooperating in the implementation of five year plans.

(*ii*) The trade union movement has won for workers important rights. It is no longer possible to lay off or retrench workers without compensation. The principle of seniority has found wide acceptance. The principle of equity in industrial wage determination has been repeatedly upheld by the wage boards. The right to hearing in accordance with the "due process" is now enshrined in case law. The principle of social justice has been advocated by the party in power, affirmed in successive five year plans, and has won adherents at all levels of the judiciary. These are solid achievements which might not have been possible but for the relentless pressure of trade union leaders on the government and the employers. The fact that these have been secured through democratic and judicial processes cannot render them less significant.

(*iii*) The trade unions in the country, barring outstanding exceptions which can be counted on the finger tips, have been inextricably tied down to the judicial process. It is lacking in resilience and vitality that come from a profound mutual commitment of leaders and workers to their trade unions. In the social order workers are illiterate and poor but, more, they have not yet learnt to use their organised power through the collective will forged in a union in a disciplined and orderly manner. There can be no doubt that this has produced grave weaknesses in the union movement which probably cut across not only ideological barriers but pervade every layer of organisation.

Like (*i*) and (*ii*) the third effect can also be traced to the policies of the government. It is not implied that the government is the sole or even the most powerful factor influencing the quality of trade union movement. Probably illiteracy among workers and their rural background should be accorded the highest rating among the causes of the qualitative weakness of the trade union movement in India. The government has, however, played a notable role in this direction. It has been most unwilling to take chances with industrial peace and let the unions grow into strong as well as responsible institutions. In this the government has received general support from a sizeable section of union leadership. One cannot really blame the government for it because it has never been the goal of policy-makers to make unions strong. Rather, the policy has been directed at the workers who as a key factor of production are of strategic importance. The purpose of the policy has been to improve the conditions of workers rather than to strengthen their unions. It is obvious that the primary purpose cannot be fulfilled without the political support of trade union leaders. So it is inescapable that the hands of union leaders are strengthened in the process.

On balance the general influence of government policy has been (*i*) to accord workers higher status; (*ii*) to strengthen the hands of union leaders by involving them at the level of policy-making as well as in the implementation of policies and by other means; and (*iii*) to weaken the organisational basis of trade unions. The policies to this effect have been rationally conceived and ably carried out. These flow directly from the commitment of the government to use the state as the principal instrument of economic progress and social reconstruction. Since the main purpose behind the elaborate legal and the extra-legal frameworks has been to eliminate work-stoppages as far as possible, it should be seen how far this has been served in practice. Moreover, the government, to further its essential goals, has sought the help of union leaders which in most instances has been formally given. Ordinarily this consensus should be reflected in the reduced incidence of work-stoppages, increased production and a heightened sense of partnership between unions and managements. However, as has been shown in Chapter 3, the economic climate has not been conducive to industrial peace.

Moreover, it is not just the government that demands reciprocity between rights and obligations; the union leaders, too, have demanded that, for the rights they concede (maintain industrial peace regardless of the issues involved) the government and employers should live up to their parts of the bargain. In essential respects these demands have centred round higher earnings (protection or raising of real wages), job security (protection from the employer's right to retrench surplus workers) and union security. The next chapter shows that despite consensus on principles conflicts have grown in practice.

CHAPTER 5

TRADE UNIONS AND INDUSTRIAL DISPUTES

DEFINITIONS, DATA, AND GENERAL CONSIDERATIONS

IT HAS BEEN SHOWN IN CHAPTER 4 THAT AN ABIDING CONSIDERA-tion of the government's labour policy has been the main-tenance of industrial peace. It has also been indicated that, despite this concern, industrial disputes leading to work-stoppages were not only a recurrent feature but, in several years, gained in strength and appeared to nullify the whole purpose of the elaborate industrial relations machinery created for their prevention. Earlier in Chapter 3 it has been noted that economic conditions in the country, parti-cularly since 1956, had provided the material basis for dis-content throughout large sections of the working class. It was also seen that the progress of unionism in India has been aided by inflation and growing employment. This has raised the possibility that the intervening variable that con-nects the growing discontent resulting from scarcity of es-sential consumer goods and rising prices with unionism is the bahaviour of disputes and conflicts. In this chapter the latter concepts are defined, their statistics analysed and, within the limitations of data, the linkage between conflicts and unionism is quantitatively determined. In this context the interaction of government policy and trade unionism is further explored.

Legal Definitions and their Effect upon Data

The term "industrial dispute" is defined by the Industrial Disputes Act, 1947 as "any dispute or difference between employers and employers, or between employers and work-men, or between workmen and workmen, which is connected with the employment or non-employment or the terms of employment or with the conditions of labour, of any person."[1] This definition is very wide and covers all possible contingencies that may result in work-stoppages. It is almost identical to the definition of "dispute" in the British Trade Disputes Act, 1906. In a strict judicial sense it would not exclude strikes in support of workers in another industry, or, for that matter, in some other country. "Any person" may conceivably include workers employed in a given factory as well as anywhere else. However, if the dispute does not relate to either the employment or the terms of employment of "any person" anywhere in the world it is not covered by the law. From this it follows that while sympathetic strikes are covered by the Indian law the political strikes are not.[2]

Despite the wide scope of the term "dispute" in theory, in practice it is quite limited. According to the Industrial Disputes (Central) Rules, 1957, a dispute is deemed by the government to exist only when an application is made by one of the parties stating, among other details, the specific matters in dispute and the number of workmen likely to be affected by it.[3] Evidently this rule limits the practical scope of the Industrial Disputes Act to those disputes which can be clearly identified as existing between an employer and his employees, and by implication excludes political and sympathetic strikes. This limitation has caused serious consequences for data collection. The government not only does not recognise the existence of disputes that may not be specific to an undertaking but also does not publish data pertaining to them. In describing the limitations of data on industrial disputes leading to work-stoppages, the Labour Bureau states that "the statistics, *inter alia*, do not cover political strikes or sympathetic demonstrations and the like as they are not connected with any specific demand of

1. See Industrial Disputes Act, 1947, section 2(k).
2. For a similar interpretation of British legal provisions, see Olga L. Aikin, "Legal Perspectives" in B. C. Roberts (ed.), *Industrial Relations, Contemporary Problems and Perspectives*, London, Methnen & Co. Ltd., 1962, pp. 195-226.
3. See Industrial Disputes (Central) Rules, 1957, Part I, rules 3, 4, 5, and 6.

employees lying within the competence of the employers concerned to redress and closures not connected with industrial disputes sponsored by the employers for reasons like shortage of raw material, breakdown in machinery or supply of power, or financial reasons."[4]

It is apparent from the reasons stated by the Labour Bureau that the government has decided in some measure to judge the issues even before collecting information on them. This decision, though now partially corrected, has handicapped the formation of informed judgement on the full range of causes underlying industrial work-stoppages. Moreover, the rule made by the Central Government is not consistent with the wording in the Act, and should be revised. There are two more reasons which may motivate the government to collect and publish complete information on strikes and lockouts. First, work-stoppages which are due to macro-causes, whether political or economic, are important symptoms of deeper discontent and may deserve investigation. Second, the conditions that each dispute must (i) relate to specific demands of employees, and furthermore that (ii) it should be within the competence of the employer concerned to redress the same, are generally untenable.

It is well known that strikes occur not only because of specific demands but quite often due to the accumulation of numerous unredressed grievances over a period of time. The great strikes that occurred in the country after the First World War, and maybe after the Second World War, too, could not always be attributed to a single cause. Such strikes probably occur even now and, if so, should be brought to the notice of the public, the Parliament, and the research workers. It is probable that some of these merit thorough investigation which may throw much light on the actual state of industrial relations in the country. The government itself might decide to take suitable steps to mitigate serious situations, possibly caused by some deep-seated malaise, once all the relevant facts are known and have been objectively analysed. Moreover, how can the administration decide whether disputes resulting in work-stoppages are such

4. *Indian Labour Statistics*, 1962, "Scope and Limitation", p. xviii.

that the same are capable of redressal within the competence of the employers concerned? Cases are not unknown when undertakings have been permanently shut down as a result of disputes which could not be mutually settled. These may be exceptional instances in India, but for the same reason they deserve to be brought to public knowledge.

The Scope and Limitations of Data

Data on work-stoppages are available over the entire period covered in this book. However, the basis of industrial classification has undergone several changes rendering the data non-comparable. This problem is particularly serious for the period before 1955. It may also be noted that the data are collected on a voluntary basis, and so they may not be complete for every sector. The information pertaining to work-stoppages in the manufacturing and mining sectors is, however, quite reliable. In addition to strikes and lockouts, the government publishes limited information on disputes handled by the industrial relations machinery in the States and at the Centre. This is available at one place only from 1959 onwards. The data for the previous years may be available in the annual reports submitted by the labour ministries of States to their respective legislatures, but these are not readily accessible. It may, therefore, be worthwhile for the Labour Bureau to collect and publish this information over as long a period as may be possible.

For descriptive purposes industrial disputes in India may be grouped into four classes: (i) disputes that lead to work-stoppages and are published; (ii) disputes that lead to strikes or lockouts but are not published because they are not defined as disputes by the Labour Bureau. Since 1962 the Labour Bureau has been publishing data on political and sympathetic strikes, by months and States only in which these occur, but not by industry groups and other associated variables; (iii) disputes that are referred to the industrial relations machinery; and (iv) disputes that are settled without reference to the industrial relations machinery. Among these four classes nothing is known on (iv). Therefore, their existence has to be ignored. In class (iii) are included disputes which

may or may not have led to work-stoppages. To an unknown extent these overlap with (*i*). Assuming, however, that
all cases of work-stoppages, sooner or later, get referred to the
industrial relations machinery, it may be safe to consider
class (*iii*) as inclusive of (*i*). Accordingly, the data on (*iii*)
will be treated as of gross totals and the proportion of (*i*) to
(*iii*) can be interpreted as indicative of the "breakdown rate",
i.e., as a measure of the breakdown of the industrial relations
machinery.

The concept of "breakdown rate" can be differently interpreted. The whole purpose of creating the industrial relations machinery through the Industrial Disputes Act has
been the prevention and settlement of disputes between labour and management that may lead to work-stoppages.
In accordance with the stated purpose a reference to the
industrial relations machinery may be made either by the
parties directly in dispute, singly or jointly, or by the government itself. Once a dispute is referred to conciliation or
adjudication and is pending disposal, strikes and lockouts
are illegal. It is, thus, possible that legal strikes and lockouts
may not occur at all if the appropriate government is sufficiently vigilant to intervene in all disputes that may have
occurred or have been apprehended. Such an interpretation
would mean that any breakdown of the industrial relations
machinery is solely due to failure of the government in some
particular respect.

It is possible, however, that labour administrations in
India do not generally view their role as strictly as stated in
the Act. Moreover, there may be other normal limitations,
viz. inadequate staff, failure to apprehend a dispute due to
preoccupations with more important matters, lack of timely
information on disputes that may be brewing or may have
broken out, unreasonableness of the parties to disputes, etc.
The failure of the industrial relations machinery to prevent
a strike or lockout may also conceivably be due wholly or
partly to the unwillingness of labour and employers to seek
conciliation. Possibly some strikes are caused by fierce power
struggles between rival unions that are keen on a trial of
strength. A few strikes may have been instigated by management for the sole purpose of embarrassing union leadership

or for justifying a lockout it wants to declare anyhow.

In view of these and other probable considerations it is not reasonable to interpret the "breakdown rate" as indicative of the failure of one party or the other to play a fair game. It is better to view its trends as symptoms of social discontent of which the causes lie deeper and are probably common to most societies passing through similar stages of development. Even so, the fact remains that, to the extent conflicts occur, the declared purpose of the Industrial Disputes Act and similar legislation in States is not fulfilled. In saying this it is not our purpose to view every work-stoppage as an indictment of the disputes legislation but only to point out that, no matter how well conceived, work-shutdowns cannot always be prevented. Indeed there is no method known to democratic societies that can prevent all disputes. However, if the government puts the responsibility for preventing work-stoppages on the industrial relations machinery, as, in our judgement, is the case in India, then the failures should be analysed in order to determine whether the goals themselves are properly set.

Our Definitions of Conflicts, Disputes, and Grievances

In the literature on the subject, including government publications, the term "industrial dispute" is used to denote work-stoppages as well as those differences between labour and management that are settled through the industrial relations machinery. This can be a source of confusion. We will, therefore, use the term "industrial conflicts" for denoting the former and "industrial disputes" for the latter. The distinction between the two terms is based on the common observation that not all disputes may lead to work-stoppages, the latter being symptomatic of an open conflict. However, in both cases third party intervention is usually involved. The third party may be the industrial relations machinery, the police, or a prominent personality. Besides these, there may be yet another kind of dispute which is settled directly between the union and the management usually without the intervention of a third party. These may be termed "industrial grievances". The settlement of industrial grievances is one of the primary functions of trade unions and managements. If this function is carried out satisfactorily the number of industrial disputes can be greatly reduced. On the other hand, if the bipartite machinery at the plant level is not working well, petty industrial grievances may grow into disputes and jam the functioning of the industrial relations machinery. Similarly, if the industrial relations machinery cannot resolve all disputes to the satisfaction of both parties, some of them may reappear before it and the others may take the form of conflicts.

Due to the complete absence of data it will not be possible to analyse industrial grievances and the process of their settlement. This is a major gap in the statistics on labour matters published in India. It is suggested that the Labour Bureau should start collecting data on grievances that were formally taken up between labour and managements at the plant level and settled mutually. This would include grievances taken up in the works committees, in the joint management councils and other bodies involving unions or a group of workers on the one hand and managements on the other. Published data on grievances will enable the government and the public to assess the overall magnitude of the problem and its relationship with disputes and conflicts. The government can determine with greater precision the trend in industrial relations at all levels and assess the performance of its policy accordingly.

TRENDS IN INDUSTRIAL DISPUTES AND CONFLICTS

Trend in the Breakdown Rate

Data on industrial disputes referred to the industrial relations machinery are available for the country as a whole since 1959. These, along with the number of conflicts and the ratio of the latter to the former, are given in Table 18. This ratio has been referred to above as the "breakdown rate". The table shows the percentage of disputes which have developed into conflicts, indicating thereby the extent of failure of the industrial relations machinery in fulfilling its stated legal obligation. As already explained, the breakdown rate is not to be interpreted as a failure of the government alone, but the measure of the nonfulfilment of a purpose to which it is committed.

TABLE 18

Disputes, conflicts, and the breakdown rate

Year	Number of Disputes referred to Industrial Relations Machinery	Number of Conflicts	Breakdown Rate (3/2) (in percentage)
1	2	3	4
1959	22,259	1,531	6.87
1960	33,896	1,583	4.69
1961	34,113	1,357	3.97
1962	27,991	1,491	5.32
1963	29,977	1,471	4.90
1964	33,538	2,151	6.45
1965	30,656	1,689	5.51

Source : Annual Reports of the Ministry of Labour & Employment.

The table shows that the breakdown rate has ranged between approximately 4 and 7 per cent. It may be said that considering the overall magnitude of disputes handled by the industrial relations machinery the breakdown rate is not abnormally high. It is notable that the lowest figure for the breakdown rate was in 1961 which was a normal year. This may or may not be the year of peak efficiency for the industrial relations machinery. However, if 1961 can be taken as a representative normal year, the breakdown rate of 3-4 per cent may be expected as the lowest possible floor. It may be considered as a norm that the industrial relations machinery might seek to reach. On the other hand, if the breakdown rate shows a rising trend it can be indicative of two possible tendencies. First, the industrial relations machinery is no longer able to resolve disputes and may be

developing symptoms of organisational fatigue. Second
the two parties concerned, whether unilaterally or together
are showing diminishing inclination to have the dispute
settled peacefully. This may, of course, be in part due to th
intractable nature of the issues in dispute. If the latte
cause is at all true it would call for immediate investigatio
and a possible change in policy. The figure for 1964 i
indeed a pointer to such a possibility.

The breakdown rate is determined by the "conflicts" com
ponent of industrial disputes. Industrial conflicts occur du
to a variety of causes. Most of these are related to condi
tions and terms of employment and may be susceptible t
redressal either through bipartite negotiations, or the conci
liation of a third party, or adjudication. But some conflicts
even though originating in factory premises and on specifi
issues, may be due to larger causes which lie hidden in mor
general labour unrest. Superficially it may appear that work
ers are struggling for higher material benefits or job securit
or shorter working hours, etc., but these may be merely mani
festations of the underlying social upheaval that generall
accompanies the transformation of a society from th
primitive or feudal stage to the modern.

Western scholars have observed that the widespread labou
unrest in the post-Second World War period, in the under
developed world, is frequently due to deeper causes, such a
over-population, sub-human living conditions in urban slums
malnutrition, deficiencies in education and recreational faci
lities, personal indebtedness, corruption in public life, etc.
In most colonial countries labour unrest was an inseparabl
part of the nationalist movement before the attainment o
political independence. These attitudes of defiance o
authority have not died down with the change in the politica

5. William H. Knowles, *Industrial Conflict and Unions*, University c
California, Institute of Industrial Relations, Reprint No. 159, 1961; an
Walter Gallenson (ed.), *Labour in Developing Economies*, Berkele
University of California Press, 1962. Contributors to this volume hav
generally concerned themselves with the political and ideological aspec
of labour problems in the emerging countries. Also see Sidney C. Sufrii
Unions in Emerging Societies, Frustration and Politics, Syracuse, N. Y
Syracuse University Press, 1964,

et-up. It is, therefore, possible that the so-called industrial onflicts are part of more general labour unrest in the ountry.

In India it is possible that some of the strikes and lock-outs, in certain years, have been due to food scarcity, resentment against government policies, hostility towards managements drawn from linguistic groups or castes that are different rom those of most of the employees, etc. These may take he form of wild-cat strikes, or follow a formally constructed charter of employees' demands, or may be occasioned by some ostensibly justifiable causes. In practice, it would be difficult o separate them from "bread and butter" unionism leading o strikes or even lockouts. It is, therefore, possible to read oo much into the analysis of work-stoppages by causes as s regularly done by the Labour Bureau. However, in the absence of data on other pertinent variables, it is not possible o sort out the factor of "labour unrest" from the trend in conflicts. One might suppose that the Labour Bureau's decision to eliminate sympathetic and political strikes from the data has, in a way, solved the problem by factoring out labour unrest. We are not sure, however, that such a favourable interpretation is permissible on a premise of uncertain validity and will therefore proceed on the assumption that general labour unrest may be present in some measure in the data on conflicts.

Measures of Industrial Conflicts and Trends

The data on industrial conflicts and related matters are presented in Table 19. The period covered is 1950-1965. It may be noted, however, that due to the reorganisation of States, the data up to 1956 are not strictly comparable to those of the later period. Prior to 1956 the data related mostly to Part A States, Delhi and Ajmer, and some Part B States; but since the reorganisation of States, these cover the whole of India excepting Jammu and Kashmir.

In 1950 there were 1,201 conflicts involving 0.89 million workers resulting in a loss of 4.28 million mandays. In 1956 there were 1,203 conflicts affecting 0.72 million workers and

TABLE 19

Trends in industrial conflicts, 1950-1965

Year	No. of Industrial Conflicts	No. of Workers Involved (in '000)	No. of Mandays Lost (in '000)	Index Nos. of Mandays Lost (Base = 1951 = 100)
1	2	3	4	5
1950 ..	1,201	892	4,284	107.7
1951 ..	1,166	746	3,977	100.0
1952 ..	1,178	1,118	3,904	98.2
1953 ..	1,225	737	4,146	104.2
1954 ..	1,128	659	4,381	110.2
1955 ..	1,285	646	6,309	158.6
1956 ..	1,203	729	6,992	175.8
1957 ..	1,630	889	6,429	161.7
1958 ..	1,524	929	7,798	196.1
1959 ..	1,531	694	5,633	141.6
1960 ..	1,583	986	6,537	164.4
1961 ..	1,357	512	4,919	123.7
1962	1,491	705	6,121	153.9
1963 ..	1,471	563	3,269	82.2
1964 ..	2,151	1,003	7,725	194.2
1965 ..	1,689	779	6,174	155.2

Sources : For columns (2), (3), and (4).

 (*i*) For Years 1950-1962 : K. N. vaid, *Industrial Disputes in India*, Industrial Relations Statistical Series V, Shri Ram Centre Press, New Delhi, pp. 8, 14, and 19.

 (*ii*) For Years 1963-1965 : *Indian Labour Statistics*, 1966, Table No. 10.1.

Notes : Figures relating to col. (3) and col. (4) have been rounded off to thousands and hence may differ slightly from the actual numbers.

causing a loss of 6.99 million mandays.[6] This comparison makes it obvious that neither the number of disputes nor the number of workers involved provides a satisfactory index of industrial conflicts. The former are indicative of the incidence of strikes and lockouts while the latter are suggestive of the impact they have made on workers. The effect upon the economy can be measured most satisfactorily by the figure on mandays lost. This is an aggregate of many conflicts and cannot by itself indicate the harm done to individual sectors of the economy. Nor can it measure the relationship of industrial conflicts to the mandays available for productive work. For this purpose the Labour Bureau uses the concept of severity rate which is the ratio of industrial disputes (conflicts) to one hundred thousand mandays scheduled to work. It has also constructed an index number of industrial unrest. This is defined as the percentage of the ratio of mandays lost to mandays scheduled to work for the given year with 1951 as the base year. These series have been published up to 1961 only.

It appears that the data on mandays scheduled to work are available, on the basis of the Census of Manufacturing Industries up to 1958 and the Annual Survey of Industries for 1959-1962 only. Since the ASI reports are generally three to four years behind the year to which these relate, the series on severity rate and the index number of industrial unrest can never be kept uptodate. Moreover, these are based on the manufacturing sector as covered by the ASI only. Due to these limitations it is not particularly useful to rely upon the Labour Bureau concepts. A table on these series is, nevertheless, given in Appendix. We have largely relied upon the data on mandays lost as indicators of industrial conflicts. Accordingly, index numbers of these series with 1951 as the base year have been prepared. On comparing with the series on severity rate it is found that the two have generally moved alike.

The indices of mandays lost show that the years 1950, 1956, 1958, and 1964 are marked by abnormally high industrial

. K. N. Vaid, *Industrial Disputes in India,* Industrial Relations Statistical Series V, New Delhi, Shri Ram Centre Press, 1965, Tables 1 and 3.

unrest. The table also shows that 1955 is the dividing line that separates the previous period, characterised by a declining trend in mandays lost, from the latter period in which these have been relatively high. This coincides with the behaviour of prices, which generally fell during 1952-1955 and have been rising since 1956. It was noted in Chapter 4, that, for the period 1951-1961, the degree in unionisation correlated with the CPI and was interpreted to mean that rising prices had spurred the union movement. The data on mandays lost generally support this finding.

When prices rise the discontent among workers grows and rallies them round one or more unions. Declining or stagnant real wages in the face of rising productivity provide the union leadership with a justifiable basis for militant agitation leading to strikes and lockouts. In this situation of either incipient or growing militancy inter-union rivalry, where it exists, can often act as fuel to the fire. The more militant leadership may be able to attract workers under its banner and lead them to strikes, either with the motive of enforcing the union demand, or to undermine the influence of the rival union, or both. As a result it is probable that the moderate unions will suffer a relative decline in influence in relation to more aggressive rivals. This was brought out in Chapter 2, Table 5. Between 1955 and 1960 the percentage of INTUC membership in the total of the four centres declined from 56.61 to 53.78. On the basis of limited evidence in our possession it is possible to conclude that the same factor (rising prices) that has strengthened unionism in the country has also contributed to work-stoppages and, further, that inter-union rivalry has generally been a complicating and aggravating factor.

Workers' Participation in Conflicts

What has been the extent of workers' participation in industrial conflicts? How are union members involved in strikes and lockouts? To these questions general answers can be given on the basis of Table 20. The table gives data on the number of workers involved per conflict, the membership involvement ratio, the degree of unionisation, and the

TABLE 20

Trends in (i) *Workers involved per dispute,* (ii) *Membership involvement ratio,* (iii) *Degree of unionisation, and* (iv) *Average duration of conflicts,* 1950-1964

Year			Workers Involved Per Conflict	Membership Involvement Ratio (in percentage)	Degree of Unionisation	Average Duration of Conflicts (days)
1			2	3	4	5
1950	..	..	743	50.8	..	4.8
1951	..	..	640	37.5	33.9	5.3
1952	..	..	949	53.4	34.8	3.5
1953	..	..	602	35.0	35.4	5.6
1954	..	..	584	30.4	35.7	6.6
1955	..	..	503	28.5	36.2	9.7
1956	..	..	606	30.7	35.4	9.5
1957	..	..	545	29.6	43.9	7.2
1958	..	..	610	25.6	51.2	8.4
1959	..	..	453	17.7	55.4	8.1
1960	..	..	623	24.7	55.2	6.6
1961	..	..	377	12.9	53.3	9.6
1962	..	..	473	19.2	48.5	8.7
1963	..	..	383	14.4	49.7	5.8
1964	..	..	466	..	..	7.7

Sources :

1. *Factory Employment*
   (i) For Years 1951-1955: *Statistical Abstract of India,* 1962, p. 511.
   (ii) For Years 1956-1963: *Indian Labour Statistics,* 1966, p. 36.
2. *Employment in Plantations and Railways and Posts & Telegraphs*
   (i) For Years 1951-1961: *Indian Labour Statistics,* 1964, pp. 32-33.
   (ii) For Years 1961-1963: *Indian Labour Statistics,* 1966, p. 39.
3. *Employment in Mines*
   (i) For Years 1951-1956: *Indian Labour Statistics,* 1959, p. 28.
   (ii) For Years 1957-1961: *Indian Labour Statistics,* 1964, p. 30.
   (iii) For Years 1962-1963: *Indian Labour Statistics,* 1966, p. 36.

average duration of conflicts. The first concept is self-evident, the second is the ratio of workers involved in industrial conflicts to the reported union membership expressed as a percentage, the degree of unionisation relates to factories, mines, plantations, and transport and communications, and the last is the ratio of average mandays lost per conflict to the average number of workers involved per conflict.

Table 20 shows that the number of workers per conflict generally declined up to 1955, rose in the next three years, and tended to fall again. On the whole the trend seems to be in the downward direction. The membership involvement ratio shows a clearer trend towards decline. It may be seen that in the same period the degree of unionisation shows a rise. Columns (3) and (4) together suggest that as the trade union movement gains in strength the participation of members in conflicts tends to rise. In other words, the proportion of union members in the workers involved in conflicts has been going up.[7] Under Indian conditions a falling ratio may mean either increased participation of membership or higher membership enrolment following work-stoppages. The former interpretation is suggestive of growing union solidarity and the latter of the process of union penetration into the ranks of workers, *i.e.*, of a measure of union dyna-

---

7. The concept of membership involvement ratio was originally developed by A. M. Ross and P. T. Hartman in their book *Changing Patterns of Industrial Conflict*, New York, John Wiley & Sons, Inc., 1960, Ch. 2. They interpret the ratio "as roughly equivalent to the percentage of union members who go on strike although it overstates the latter percentage insofar as some workers may strike more than once in a year and some non-unionists may participate in strikes. More precisely, the membership involvement ratio is the sum of all workers involved in all strikes during the year, divided by the average number of union members during that year. Workers are counted once for each strike in which they participate." p. 11.

The interpretation of this ratio by Ross and Hartman is erroneous on two grounds. First, the ratio measures the participation of union members in the ranks of strikers, not in strikes. If the purpose is to find out the extent of unions' participation in strikes, it could be done through the ratio of union members involved in strikes to the number of strikes in each year. Second, if the ratio falls, as it does for many countries, it does not necessarily mean that there is a "gradual decline in the proportion of union members going on strike", (*Ibid.*, p. 18). It would actually imply that the denominator (average unions' membership) has exhibited a higher growth rate than the numerator (workers involved in strikes). Conversely, in a situation where the strike activity is going down it would mean that union membership is falling at a slower rate than workers involved in strikes. Ross and Hartman have wrongly interpreted a falling trend in the ratio as indicative of declining membership involvement. In fact it is exactly the opposite.

ism. The latter interpretation appears to be more in keeping with the state of the trade union movement in India. The general decline in the number of workers involved per conflict is the probable result of two causes. First, there as been a rapid growth in the number of relatively smaller r medium size firms. Strikes or lockouts occurring in these firms are likely to involve a smaller number of workers n an average. Firms which are larger than the size that permits intimate personal relationships between employers nd workers are probably more conflict-prone than the lder and bigger undertakings, which may have developed more stable and peaceful relations with unions. Second, here has been considerable increase in the number of small ze unions. The process of unionisation is generally accompanied by a higher incidence of conflicts. We should ot expect one-to-one correspondence between the growth f firms in different employment class and the trends in disutes grouped accordingly. However, the data on selected ears presented in Table 21 generally support the conclusion hat the decline in the average size of firms and unions has bearing on the number of workers involved per conflict. table in Appendix gives yearly figures.

Duration of Conflicts

The data on average duration of conflicts show a decline p to 1953, a gradual rise that lasted till 1956, a steady fall ntil 1961, and unsystematic behaviour since then. To some xtent the duration of conflicts is controlled by the government. Since the declaration of the Emergency in 1962 the government has been able to order the reopening of factories nder the Defence of India Rules. Even prior to it, the government had discretion to refer a dispute to adjudication nd thereupon to declare the strike or the lockout concerned llegal. Since 1958 the Code of Discipline has also been nvoked to terminate open conflicts. It is possible that governmental efforts have been responsible for reducing the verage duration of conflicts since 1958. Without the intervention of the authorities industrial conflicts, on an average, might have been more prolonged, causing heavier losses in mandays.

Trends in average size of employment per factory, average size of union

Sl. No.	Industry	1952		
		Average Daily Employment per factory[a]	Average Union Membership per factory	No. of Workers Involved per Dispute[b]
	1	2	3	4
1	Manufacturing	85	32	966
2	Food, Beverages & Tobacco ..	41	14	251
3	Textiles	303	137	1518
	(a) Cotton	445	221	1931
	(b) Others (Jute, Silk, & Woollen)	478	202	532
4	Clothing, Footwear and Made-up Textile Goods	46	79	N.A.
5	Wood and Cork, Furniture and Fixtures	31	4	N.A.
6	Paper and Paper Products	207	70 ⎫	
7	Printing, Publishing and Allied Industries	38	14 ⎬ ⎭	305
8	Leather and Leather Products (except Footwear)	28	17	169
9	Rubber and Rubber Products ..	170	48	N.A.
10	Chemicals and Chemical Products ..	71	37	340
11	Non-metallic Mineral Products including Products of Petroleum and Coal	89	30	250
12	Basic Metal Industries	144	87	868
13	Manufacture of Metal Products ..	35	7	N.A.
14	Manufacture of Machinery (except electrical)	48	8	N.A.
15	Manufacture of Electrical Machinery, Apparatus and Appliances ..	129	17	408
16	Transport Equipment	186	7	N.A.
17	Miscellaneous Industries	33	15	N.A.
18	Electricity, Gas, Water and Sanitary Services	58	108	144

Notes and Sources:

(a) Data refer only to Part "A" and "C" States. See *Statistical Abstract of India*, 1952-53, pp. 525-543.

(b) & (c) Workers involved per dispute is only an estimated average as the industry groups have been adjusted to suit the set-up of the table. See *Indian Labour Statistics*, 1963.

(d) Average daily employment data obtained from *Indian Labour Journal*, March 1958, pp. 906-941.

21

membership per factory, and number of workers involved per dispute

	1956d			1963e	
Average Daily Employment per factory	*Average Union Membership per factory f*	*No. of Workers Involved per Dispute c*	*Average Daily Employment per factory*	*Average Union Membership per factory*	*No. of Workers Involved per Dispute*
5	6	7	8	9	10
86	31	638	77	31	389
50	19	545	38	16	307
332	129	1,108	224	108	684
566	156	1,213	388	110	731
272	187	744	161	41	909
62	38	N.A.	105	39	73
25	5	N.A.	23	3	50
174	58 ⎫		153	65	188
	⎬ 104				
35	20 ⎭		36	78	73
42	22	54	57	52	42
166	21	N.A.	104	51	330
82	38	191	102	44	148
90	39	236	91	40	388
140	84	259	145	83	153
41	12	N.A.	15	20	251
56	13	N.A.	59	16	149
111	26	677	129	39	209
177	7	N.A.	163	21	714
98	36	N.A.	68	19	264
48	117	150	69	165	825

(e) Average daily employment data obtained from *Indian Labour Statistics*, 1966.

f) *Data on Union Membership*:
   (i) For 1952-53, see, *Trade Unions in India*, Industrial Relations Statistical Series IV, New Delhi, Shri Ram Centre Press.
   (ii) For 1956-57, see, *Trade Unions 1956-57*, Labour Bureau, Ministry of Labour & Employment, Government of India.
   (iii) For 1963-64, see *Indian Labour Statistics*, 1966.

ANALYSIS OF CONFLICTS BY CAUSES AND RESULTS

Causes of Conflicts

As stated earlier, labour conflicts may be caused by wages, employment conditions and related as well as other reasons. Among the latter the questions of trade union recognition (mostly in bargaining territories contested by multiple unions), representative leadership in the recognised union (generally known as the problem of factionalism), and suspicion of the good faith of employers in conducting bipartite negotiations, are probably the most important. It is even possible that conflicts on seemingly "bread and butter" issues are in fact caused, partly if not wholly, by unsolved problems such as those stated above. On the basis of data published by the Labour Bureau it is not possible to indicate the relative importance of "other causes". Hence it will be assumed, for the sake of simplicity, that the "causes" listed by the labour Bureau are true and the questions listed above, among others, are all subsumed in the residual category. In Table 22 are set out data on the proportions of causes listed as "wages and allowancess", "bonus", "personnel and retrenchment", "leave and hours of work", and "others". This distribution is given on the number of conflicts only, for 1950-1964, and on mandays lost for 1956-1964.

Table 22 reveals that the causes of conflicts relating to the earnings of workers (see column 7) have grown relatively in importance. In the six-year period, 1950-1955, these together accounted for 36 per cent of the conflicts shown in the table; in the next six years, 1956-1961, the percentage rose to 40, but fell to 38 during 1962-1964. In terms of mandays lost these were even more important. During 1956-1961 the percentage of average total mandays lost was 41.5 but went up to 50 for the period 1961-1964. On the other hand, the proportion of conflicts relating to job security (column 4) has shown a tendency to decline gradually. In respect of the total number of cases the percentage was 31 for the average of 1950-1955, 30 for 1956-1961, and 25.5 for 1962-1964.

In relation to mandays lost these cases accounted for 26 per cent in 1956-1961 and 17 per cent in 1962-1964.

It may be noted that the increase and decrease in the relative weights of the causes related to earnings and job security respectively are in respect of a rising total of conflicts involving a growing number of mandays lost generally. The decline in the latter is due mainly to the legal protection afforded to workers against arbitrary retrenchment and the general stabilisation of their employment status. This has been due in part to the gradual implementation of the Industrial Employment (Standing Orders) Act, 1946, the settlement of a large number of disputes involving retrenchment and dismissal through adjudication, and in part to the efficacy of the conciliation machinery in resolving personnel disputes. It appears that issues involving dismissal, lay-off, and retrenchment of workers have been increasingly settled through the industrial relations machinery. The conciliation-cum-adjudication machinery has proved its adequacy in preventing disputes on these matters from growing into conflicts. In the absence of statistics on the nature of disputes handled by the industrial relations machinery, it cannot be said whether the trend is towards an increase or a decrease. It is, however, our impression that a sizeable portion of the industrial relations machinery time is taken up in personnel disputes. With the amendment of the Industrial Disputes Act in 1964, which enabled issues related to dismissals to be raised by individual workmen as industrial disputes before the industrial relations machinery, it is likely that fewer conflicts on these matters will occur.

Just as the government has tried to reduce industrial conflicts occurring due to personnel causes by making them justiciable on the basis of the principle of natural justice as embodied in standing orders duly certified by the appropriate authority, and the Industrial Disputes Act, it has also sought to minimise conflicts due to wages, allowances, and bonus. For several years now the government has relied upon industrial and national tribunals for settling wage and bonus questions. But increasingly the government is having recourse to wage boards for resolving these issues. These are tripartite bodies, consisting mostly of representatitves of

TABLE

Causes of industrial

(in

Years		C	A	U
		Wages and Allowances	Bonus	Personnel and Retrench-ment
	1	2	3	4
1950		27	9	24
1951		28	7	28
1952		29	10	33
1953	(No. of Conflicts only)	26	10	34
1954		28	7	35
1955		23	17	32
1956	No. of Conflicts	27	8	35
	Mandays Lost	22	10	19
1957	No. of Disputes	30	14	31
	Mandays Lost	30	17	26
1958	No. of Disputes	30	11	33
	Mandays Lost	40	13	29
1959	No. of Disputes	27	10	29
	Mandays Lost	19	9	29
1960	No. of Disputes	37	10	25
	Mandays Lost	40	7	21
1961	No. of Disputes	30	7	29
	Mandays Lost	22	20	29
1962	No. of Disputes	30	12	25
	Mandays Lost	26	35	13
1963	No. of Disputes	28	10	26
	Mandays Lost	33	11	14
1964	No. of Disputes	35	8	27
	Mandays Lost	36	9	23

22

conflicts, 1950-1964

percentages)

S	E	S		
Leave and Hours of Work	All Others	2+3	Total 2+3+4+5+6	Total Number of Cases
5	6	7	8	9
8	32	36	100	814
8	29	35	100	1,071
9	19	39	100	963
5	25	36	100	772
10	20	35	100	840
5	23	40	100	1,166
5	25	35	100	1,263
1	48	32	100	
5	21	44	100	1,556
2	25	47	100	
3	22	41	100	1,514
1	16	53	100	
4	30	37	100	1,492
1	42	28	100	
2	25	47	100	1,506
0	32	47	100	
3	30	37	100	1,314
8	20	42	100	
1	32	42	100	1,491
2	23	61	100	
5	32	38	100	1,471
2	40	44	100	
2	28	33	100	2,151
0	32	45	100	

Sources : *Indian Labour Statistics* for the years 1964 and 1966.

K.N. Vaid, *Industrial Disputes in India*, (op. cit.), Table 5.

Indian Labour Journal, October 1964, p. 862, and December 1965, p. 1083.

employers and unions with an independent chairman nominated by the government. When their recommendations are unanimous the industry concerned is expected voluntarily to implement them. The government has occasionally threatened to legislate for compulsory enforcement of wage boards' recommendations but so far has refrained from doing so. The government has retained the discretion to modify any recommendations, but does not usually exercise it.

There is no legal requirement that strikes and lockouts shall not take place during the pendency of the proceedings of a wage board although the government generally expects of both parties to maintain industrial peace. Furthermore, it is expected of employers that they should faithfully implement the wage board awards, and of the unions that they should be patient and generally facilitate this process. The government, for its part, is committed to using persuasion and, if necessary, pressure upon recalcitrant employers to reorder their wage structures in accordance with the wage board award.[8] So far the experience has been that the wage boards' recommendations are implemented though with considerable time lag.[9] It is probable that the general effect of

8. In this book the terms "award" and "recommendations" have been used interchangeably in relation to wage boards. Strictly speaking wage boards can make recommendations only since there is no legal sanction behind them. However, for all practical purposes these are treated as awards which, if made unanimously, are considered binding upon employers.

9. There are in fact three kinds of time lags involved:
One is between the date of constitution of a wage board and the date of its recommendations. The second is the time involved in the government taking a decision on accepting the recommendations and notifying them to the public. The third is the time taken by the employers concerned in implementing the recommendations of the wage board. These three lags may add up to several years. In the case of the cotton textile industry the first wage board was appointed in March 1957; it submitted its report on 1st December, 1959; the recommendations were accepted by the government within one month; but it took more than four years to fully implement them. The first wage board for the sugar industry took almost three years to submit its report, and it took about four years to put it into practice in all factories. It was a shade better in the cement industry. But there are wage boards which were appointed in 1960 and 1961 and have yet to

settling wage questions through wage boards has been to dampen down industrial conflicts arising due to them. The data show that the number of strikes and lockouts and the mandays lost due to wage questions dropped significantly after the appointment of wage boards. These, however, began to pick up later. The latter might be on account of impatience among workers about the delays in the implementation of wage boards' recommendations.

The lags mentioned above are not an unmixed evil. By slowing down adjustments of wages to rising prices and physical productivity, the pace of inflation is retarded and the employers save on costs for some years and in addition have the advantage of uninterrupted production. The unions, too, are saved from the prospect of fighting for workers' rights through trials of strength which may cause, at least some of them, grave embarrassment, even possible extinction. However, the delay in implementing awards, and unanimous awards in particular, probably carries the implication of a promise given but not carried out. If repeated too often, there is a danger that the promise will not be believed and the moral basis of the authority of wage boards will be eroded. Such a development cannot but undermine both the labour policy and the prestige of the government.

The problem of delay in implementing decisions taken by appropriate bodies is not limited to the recommendations of wage boards. It is present in other spheres, too, and has been causing industrial conflicts. In 1963 there occurred 69 conflicts on the issue of non-implementation of labour enactments, awards, and mutual agreements. These together resulted in 0.18 million mandays lost. In 1964 the figures were 47 conflicts and 0.25 million mandays lost.[10]

---

submit their final reports. It may be mentioned that wage boards often prescribe dates by which the recommendations are expected to be implemented. The lags are inclusive of the period of implementation as laid down by the wage boards.

See Ministry of Labour & Employment, *Report*, 1962-63 (Vol. I), and 1964-65 (Vol. I). Also see the Appendix for a list of industries for which wage boards have been set up, the dates on which these were constituted and the dates on which they submitted their reports, if any.

10. *Indian Labour Journal*, October 1964, p. 863 and December 1965. pp. 1083-1084.

Among the factors affecting workers' earnings in India bonus is one of the most important. As Table 21 shows conflicts due to bonus caused 10 per cent of the total man-days lost in 1956. This figure went up to 20 in 1961, and to 35 in 1962. Meanwhile the Supreme Court in a judgement on a bonus case expressed the view that it might be desirable to have the mode of determining bonus reviewed comprehensively by a high powered commission. In the light of this influential opinion, the government appointed a tripartite Bonus Commission in December 1961 with wide terms of reference. These included the defining of the concept of bonus, the methods of its determination, the fixation of minima and maxima, and any other matter jointly agreed upon between employers and workers.[11] The Commission submitted its report in 1964 which was accepted by the government with a few modifications. This was followed by prolonged consultations with labour and employers which proved infructuous. The government therefore proceeded on its own to declare an ordinance in May 1965 and pass an enactment later in the same year.[12] Some of the provisions of the Bonus Act, however, have been declared *ultra vires* by the Supreme Court and the matter is once again pending settlement.

The issue of bonus is an important illustration of how the government handles controversial subjects affecting labour and management relations. The government has probably succeeded in removing bonus as an important cause of conflict, but only by making it a serious nagging dispute to be handled as well as possible by the conciliation and adjudication machinery. Legislation may not eliminate friction but may be effective in reducing work-stoppages in some measure. The alternative cost in time consumed by the managements and unions together with the resources of society in men and money consumed by the industrial relations machinery, the High Courts, and the Supreme Court, would no doubt be substantial. But in the reckoning of the government all this is probably worth the saving in

11. See *The Indian Labour Year Book*, 1961, pp. 114-115 and *The Indian Labour Year Book*, 1964, pp. 125-126.

12. See Kamala Mathur, (*op. cit.*).

production which the method entails.

It has been often said that unions in India are the weaker side in a conflict situation. This is a belief which rests on the fact of the obvious organisational strength of employers in contrast to the disunity, indiscipline, and disarray of a large number of unions. There is, however, a more basic source of weakness in unions. Workers earn their living through the sale of labour time. But when they are on strike their earnings are sharply curtailed and are often reduced to nil. Employers, understanding this only too well, may decide to beat a union by letting the workers starve. The most effective method of doing so is locking out the factory. Most conflicts are started by unions but those that drag out are generally the ones in which strikes are followed by lockouts.

In 1964 there were 170 lockouts, of which 101 were preceded by strikes. These together cost the country 1.5 million mandays or 19.3 per cent of the total of all conflicts. The other 69 lockouts resulted in 0.5 million mandays lost. There are no statistics as to why these latter lockouts were declared. It may be that the provocations in these cases were in the nature of slow-downs, indiscipline, sabotage, or others.[13] Whatever the causes, it is significant that about 8 per cent of conflicts involving lockouts were responsible for 26 per cent of the total mandays lost in 1964.[14]

There is no doubt that these were really trials of strength. No statistics are available on how workers or their unions fared in such cases. The Labour Bureau publishes data on the results of strikes and lockouts in the aggregate. These are built on the basis of information received on individual conflicts. It might be instructive to know the distribution of successful, partially successful, and unsuccessful conflicts which entailed either strikes or lockouts and those which

13. *Indian Labour Journal*, December 1965, pp. 1071-1072.
14. It may be noted that 1964 was a year of Emergency although it would appear that the effect of the latter on industrial conflicts had nearly worn off. The comparable data for 1959 and 1960 show that the effect of lockouts on mandays lost was even more severe. In 1959 the number of lockouts accounted for 7.2 per cent of all conflicts, but for 35.7 per cent of mandays lost. In 1960 the figures were 5.6 per cent and 27.6 per cent respectively. See, *Indian Labour Journal*, November 1961, pp. 1034-1035.

had both. It might also be useful to know the consequences of the intervention of the industrial relations machinery in the three types of conflicts. Such data are already published in the aggregate. All that the Labour Bureau has to do is to give further breakdowns.

Analysis of Results

The data on percentage distribution of conflicts by results are set out in Table 23. Success and failure are related to workers' important demands. If a conflict has ended successfully it means that workers' demands have been met; if only some of the demands have been conceded, it is said that there is partial success, and so on.

TABLE 23

Percentage distribution of conflicts by results, 1951-1964

Year	Successful	Partially Successful	2 + 3	Failure	Indefinite	Total No. of Conflicts
1	2	3	4	5	6	7
1950	18.7	11.9	30.6	49.4	20.4	814
1951	17.2	16.7	33.9	49.5	16.6	870
1952	23.1	13.7	36.8	44.5	18.7	862
1953	17.8	14.0	31.8	41.6	26.6	687
1954	16.9	12.0	28.9	37.8	33.3	692
1955	20.4	8.3	28.7	28.2	43.1	1,034
1956	25.8	12.0	37.8	40.5	21.7	1,148
1957	30.8	15.0	45.8	33.4	20.8	1,557
1958	32.3	15.9	48.2	28.1	23.7	1,457
1959	23.7	14.0	37.7	32.3	30.0	1,388
1960	33.0	11.3	44.3	30.4	25.3	1,377
1961	28.8	19.5	48.3	29.5	22.2	1,139
1962	30.2	18.3	48.5	30.7	20.8	1,488
1963	23.4	17.9	41.3	41.0	17.7	1,422
1964	27.7	14.8	42.5	37.2	20.3	2,092

Sources: *Indian Labour Journal*, October 1964, and December 1965.
Indian Labour Year Book, of respective years.
K. N. Vaid, *Industrial Disputes in India*, (op. cit.), Table 6.

Table 23 shows that in a large number of cases the results are uncertain. From the point of view of unions this should be interpreted as a partial, if not a complete, failure. Thus interpreted, columns 5 and 6 can be lumped together as failure in part or whole and conversely the sum of columns 2 and 3 as given in column 4. The trend in column 4 generally indicates that the performance of unions in industrial conflicts is gradually improving. Since most of these are, in the immediate sense, started by unions, it is possible to read in the trend an indication that they are slowly gaining in strength.

Why is it that in a country where unions are known to be generally weak their score of gains in conflicts is so high? In answering this question we must ask how most industrial conflicts have been terminated. The results of the conflicts are closely tied up with the methods of their termination. In 1964, as many as 38 per cent of the 2,092 conflicts reported by the Labour Bureau were settled through government intervention—mostly through mediation and conciliation. In 24.6 per cent cases a settlement was mutually reached. However, in 30.3 per cent cases the employees decided to resume work voluntarily. In the remaining cases the results are not known. Of the cases in which the government intervened, 58 per cent full or partial success was reported. In cases of mutual settlement the comparable figure was 63.7 per cent, whereas in conflicts which were unilaterally wound up by workers the rate of complete or partial success was 4.6 per cent only.[15]

The data for the previous years show that the industrial relations machinery intervened in approximately 43 per cent cases in 1963, 42 per cent in 1962, and about the same number in 1960. Conflicts which were mutually terminated were 20 per cent, 24 per cent, and 22 per cent in these respective years. Those which were unilaterally ended were 39 per cent in 1963, 27 per cent in 1962, and 28 per cent in 1960. The success rate (including partial success) in 1963 was 58 per cent for governmental intervention, 63 per cent for mutual settlements, and 3.7 per cent for unilateral withdrawal of conflicts. The respective figures for 1962 and

15. *Indian Labour Journal*, December 1965, p. 1086.

1960 were 62 per cent and 56 per cent for governmental intervention, 67 per cent and 62 per cent for mutual settlements, and 7.8 per cent and 3.7 per cent only for the third type.[16]

The above analysis shows that the government plays a significant role not only in terminating disputes but also, in the course of so doing, in influencing the terms of settlement. Having regard to the way the industrial relations machinery is positioned in India it is inevitable that its influence is felt not on the basis of careful assessment of the relative strengths of labour and management so much as on the merits of the issues in dispute.   This goes without saying in cases that are settled through adjudication.   But to a large extent the approach of the conciliators is also quasi-judicial.   The success rate of unions in such conflicts should only partly be attributed to their strength; it is largely conditional on the presence of the industrial relations machinery and the policy of the government to use its legal and moral authority for terminating work-stoppages as speedily and judiciously as may be possible.

The strength of unions is no doubt as evident in the second kind of conflict termination as their weakness is in the third kind.   It is significant, indeed, that in a greater number of work-stoppages the employees had to return to work unconditionally.   These are instances of unconditional surrender that testify to the general weakness of the trade union movement that is commonly observed in the country. At the same time it is important to note that in a large number of cases, which are indeed increasing over the years, the unions have forced the management to open negotiations.   This trend may be interpreted as indicative of a growing core of strong and self-reliant trade unionism.

ANALYSIS OF CONFLICTS BY AFFILIATION

How are work-stoppages related to union affiliation?   It is normally to be expected that a union, regardless of its poli-

16. See *Indian Labour Journal*, October 1964, p. 866, November 1963, p. 1184, and November 1961, p. 1050 for the data pertaining to 1963, 1962, and 1960 respectively.

tical affiliation, will act in the interest of the workers and the organisation. It is possible, however, that in respect of either interest, unions may act differently in similar situations due to their ideology as well as the fact of inter-union rivalry. Some unions, affiliated to a political centre with militant ideology, may try to embarrass and outwit rivals through higher than average recourse to work-stoppages. On the other hand, it is also possible, indeed probable, that despite revolutionary beliefs a union centre that is generally weak may proceed cautiously and exhibit marked conservatism in forcing shutdowns. Data on these matters are not available in all respects and for the entire period. The published statistics on industrial conflicts by affiliation are presented in Table 24. The information pertains to the number of work-stoppages and the mandays lost in them.

Table 24 shows that the AITUC is the most conflict-prone centre in India. This would accord with the fact that its leaders are drawn mostly from the ranks of the former Communist Party of India, now split into left and right groupings. However, despite its Marxist ideology, its strike-proneness is going down. In 1959, the AITUC unions accounted for 53.8 per cent of mandays lost in the total of conflicts associated with all political centres, but in 1964 the figure came down to 27.8 per cent. It may be recalled from Table 5 in Chapter 2 that in 1962-63 the share of the AITUC in the total membership of the four centres was approximately 23 per cent. The trend in the AITUC-associated conflicts appears, therefore, to be moving closer to its relative weight in the trade union movement.

In the case of the INTUC the trend seems to be in the opposite direction. Its share in mandays lost in work-stoppages went up from 24.6 per cent in 1959 to 45.2 per cent in 1963; it fell, however, to 38.6 per cent in 1964. It is rather remarkable that the growth in militancy in the INTUC has followed a period of decrease in its share of the total membership of the four centres. Is it possible that the INTUC leadership has realised the danger to its organisational strength stemming from a total formal commitment to passive methods of dispute settlement? Or is the symptom of militancy indicative of the fact that the INTUC unions,

TABLE 24

Work-stoppages classified by the affiliation of unions, 1959-64

Year		Unions					Total
		AITUC	INTUC	HMS	UTUC	Multiple Unions	
1		2	3	4	5	6	7
1959	A	368	214	146	69	..	794
		(46.2)	(26.9)	(18.3)	(8.6)		(100.0)
	B	2.09	0.95	0.60	0.23	..	3.87
		(53.8)	(24.6)	(15.5)	(6.1)		(100.0)
1960	A	281	176	138	79	..	674
		(41.7)	(26.1)	(20.5)	(11.7)		(100.0)
	B	1.37	0.75	0.69	0.51	..	3.32
		(41.2)	(22.7)	(20.8)	(15.3)		(100.0)
1961	A	253	201	124	40	57	675
		(37.5)	(29.8)	(18.4)	(5.9)	(8.4)	(100.0)
	B	1.40	0.61	0.16	0.65	0.89	3.73
		(44.7)	(19.6)	(5.2)	(2.1)	(28.4)	(100.0)
1962	A	306	233	104	51	96	790
		(38.7)	(29.5)	(13.2)	(6.5)	(12.2)	(100.0)
	B	1.09	0.58	0.22	0.78	2.09	4.06
		(26.8)	(14.4)	(5.6)	(1.9)	(53.3)	(100.0)
1963	A	242	250	102	23	80	697
		(34.7)	(35.9)	(14.6)	(3.3)	(11.5)	(100.0)
	B	0.43	0.70	0.21	0.02	0.19	1.55
		(27.6)	(45.2)	(13.6)	(1.2)	(12.4)	(100.0)
1964	A	374	317	173	34	115	1013
		(36.9)	(31.3)	(17.1)	(3.4)	11.3)	(100.0)
	B	1.17	1.62	0.60	0.11	0.69	4.20
		(27.8)	(38.6)	(14.4)	(2.7)	(16.5)	(100.0)

A—No. of work-stoppages

B—Mandays lost (in million)

Note:　　The figures may not add up to the totals in respect of either the ab
solute numbers or the percentage as these have been rounded off.

Source:　*Indian Labour Journal*, October 1960, p. 1086; November 1961
p. 1050; February 1963, p. 159; February 1963, p. 1187; Octobe
1964, p. 868; December 1965, p. 1088.

in many undertakings, have reached a level of development
where formal no-strike commitments do not serve any pur-

pose and are increasingly taking decisions on calling strikes, on grounds of necessity and expediency? On the basis of information in our possession it is not possible to give explicit answers to these questions. It is, however, probable that the answer to the latter question is in the affirmative.

In the case of the HMS and the UTUC there are no clear-cut indications of either an increase or a decrease in conflict-proneness. The UTUC is too small a centre to make such difference in the total strike situation. It shows a decline in conflicts for several years, but there is a sudden reversal in 1964. The same holds true for the HMS.

The conflicts associated with multiple unions can be treated as the most significant affirmation of the theory generally held in India, that inter-union rivalry is a cause of strikes. It is also possible, however, that the shutdowns in multiple union undertakings are to some extent indicative of concerted action that would have been taken in any case but because of it may be more effective.

The Combined Weight of Political Centres

If the data in Tables 18 and 24 are collated it will be seen that the proportion of conflicts associated with the political centres has not exhibited much variability. It was 52.0 per cent in 1959, 42.5 per cent in 1960, 49.0 per cent in 1961, 52.3 per cent in 1962, 47.3 per cent in 1963, and 47.0 per cent in 1964. The average for the period 1959-1964 is 48.3 per cent. However, the combined weight of political centres in industrial relations is not truly revealed by the above figures. This is better indicated if the number of political and sympathetic strikes and the mandays lost in them are added to the respective figures on industrial conflicts. The data on political strikes have been published by the Labour Bureau for 1962, 1963, and 1964 only. These along with other relevant details are given in Table 25.

If the data on conflicts and mandays lost associated with the four centres viz., INTUC, AITUC, HMS, and UTUC, and the multiple union situations are adjusted for political strikes, their combined weight increases enormously. The average number of conflicts for 1962, 1963, and 1964 in which

TABLE 25

The weight of political centres in industrial conflicts

		1962	1963	1964
	1	2	3	4
1	Number of political & sympathetic strikes	66	111	287
2	Mandays lost in political & sympathetic strikes (in millions)	0.12	1.08	1.01
3	Number of industrial conflicts associated with political centres including multiple union undertakings	790	697	1013
4	Mandays lost in (3)	4.06	1.55	4.20
5	(1 + 3)	856	808	1300
6	(2 + 4)	4.18	2.63	5.21
7	5 as percentage of all conflicts in Table 19	57.4	54.9	60.4
8	6 as percentage of mandays lost in all conflicts as in Table 19	68.3	80.4	67.4

these centres were involved rises considerably. The average for three years of the total conflicts (row 7 in Table 25) and of the mandays lost (row 8 in Table 25) are 57.5 per cent and 72.0 per cent respectively. This is much more than the share of the combined total of the four centres in the reported union membership.

It is highly significant that the percentage of mandays lost in all conflicts, including political strikes with which the four centres are associated, is the highest for 1963. The significance of this lies in the fact that in November 1962 all of them had adopted, together with employers, a resolution on industrial truce. They had pledged that "under no circumstances shall there be any interruption in or slowing down of production of goods and services." Furthermore, the resolution stated, "In respect of their economic interests, both workers and employers will exercise voluntary restraint and accept the utmost sacrifice, in an equitable manner, in the interest of the nation and its defence efforts."

It is true that the mandays lost declined sharply in 1963, but among those which occurred the political centres were involved in more than 80 per cent. The AITUC, of course, had expressed its reservations both in a letter to Gulzari Lal Nanda, the then Minister of Labour and Employment, and in a formal resolution.[17] It nevertheless succeeded in bringing down its share in conflicts and mandays lost. However, the INTUC, though complaining against the one-sided implementation of the Industrial Truce Resolution, had given it wholehearted support.[18] Despite this its involvement in work-stoppages increased absolutely as well as relatively to others. In fact, the INTUC is the only organisation that participated in a larger number of conflicts causing higher mandays losses in 1963 as compared to 1962. This is inexplicable except as an indication that the compulsion of a union's commitment to workers is stronger than to a resolution such as the Industrial Truce Resolution or to national pledges as the Code of Discipline.

CONCLUSIONS

From the foregoing analysis of industrial conflicts, four principal conclusions emerge. First, and probably the most important, is that the government policy of trying to prevent work-stoppages has generally operated under economic conditions which would normally tend to increase and aggravate them. When prices rise, real wages fall, and the share of wages in factory output declines; it is natural for labour to express its discontent in various ways including work-shutdowns. These adverse trends had been gaining in strength since 1956 and showed rapid deterioration in the latter phase of the Third Plan. In a developing economy

7. See AITUC, *Twenty First Tripartite*, Papers Relating to 21st Session of the Indian Labour Conference (New Delhi, July 1963), Analysis of Working of Industrial Truce Resolution, August 1963, pp. 1-23.
8. General Secretary's Report to the 14th Session of Indian National Trade Union Congress, May 1963, pp. iii-iv, pp. 8-11, and Appendices, pp. xi-xiii. Also see INTUC, 15th *Report*, December 1964, pp. 15-17.

as that of India two additional forces operate autonomously to raise the number of conflicts: (*i*) The rapid increase in the number of factories with managements and labour relatively new to their tasks and consequently leading to greater likelihood of breakdowns in mutual dealings and of work-shutdowns. (*ii*) The rapid expansion in the number of trade unions may also be a factor in increased conflict rates particularly in the newly emerging industries.[19] This is partly because unions are more strike-prone in the early stages when they are fighting for existence. In part, strikes of short duration may be the only practical way of securing the intervention of the industrial relations machinery so as to obtain natural justice and a fair settlement of issues in conflict. It may also happen that new unions are formed after the need for them has been collectively felt, for instance, in the aftermath of a wild-cat strike.

Second, the government, despite enormous legal powers that can virtually outlaw work-stoppages, has found it necessary to reinforce the industrial relations machinery with political action involving tripartite negotiations and moral persuasion. The Code of Discipline and the Industrial Truce Resolution are instances of this policy. The settlement of wage disputes through wage boards is another. Where the wage board machinery has been found to be inadequate, as on the question of bonus, the government has had recourse to legislation. The effects are that (*i*) the work of the industrial relations machinery is growing; (*ii*) unsettled issues continue to disturb industrial relations despite adjudication at the highest level; and (*iii*) the cumulative lag between the occurrence of a dispute and its final settlement has probably increased. The effect of government policy on unionism has been to promote moderation among trade union leaders

---

19. It is implied in these propositions that the trend in industrial conflict is directly associated with the growth in the populations of worker managements, and unions. This is probably a delayed response of workers and unions to the growth in industry and the accompanying stresses It is further implied that in the course of evolution the intensity of conflic grows up to a point and, then, as managements and unions mature gradually diminishes. The data appear to indicate that India is still passing through the first stage.

and make them more dependent upon official machinery for the settlement of outstanding disputes rather than relying on their own resources and dealing with managements directly. In a general way the labour policy has aimed at counteracting the conflict-generating effect of the economic policy not through discouraging the expansion of the trade union movement but by attempting to deflect it into constitutional channels and persuading union leaders to commit themselves to the national purpose. This dual purpose policy—of encouraging the growth of unionism directly by granting unions legal rights and political facilities and indirectly by the judicial and quasi-judicial methods of disputes settlement, which permit relatively weaker unions to survive, and at the same time of curbing the conflict-proneness of unions—has simultaneously increased the dependence of unions on outside leaders and the government, the former partly because they are wanted for dealing with the latter.

Third, the four political centres, viz., INTUC, AITUC, HMS, and UTUC, together have been strongly associated with industrial conflicts, particularly with mandays lost in them. This association is not implicitly taken to mean that they severally or jointly are to blame for conflicts. But the political centres derive their weight not only from the reported union membership represented by them but, much more, by their active association with mandays lost in strikes and lockouts. Furthermore, it appears that the leaders of the political centres are caught between two loyalties. On the one hand they have given pledges to the government to eliminate strikes as far as possible, and on the other they are under pressure from below to fight for workers' demands through all possible methods, not excluding strikes. The net result of these opposite pulls is such that trade union leadership in India has to speak in conflicting voices, with a pronounced tendency to blame the employers for their failure to live up to the signed pledges. It appears that the government understands the dilemma of union leaders but has been so far unable to develop policies that will show a way out. This can only mean, as is becoming increasingly evident, that despite assertions to the contrary, policy instruments, such as the Code of Discipline and the Industrial Truce

Resolution will fall into disuse.

Fourth, the issues in disputes and conflicts are increasingly of a kind that invite macro-solutions. The most important causes of conflicts relate to wages, allowances, and bonus. These cannot be settled, in a large number of cases, at the level of a single firm. This problem is not unique to India. In the U.K. and many European countries labour unions and employers negotiate agreements at the national level with the government playing a role, sometimes active and on other occasions passive, depending upon the importance of the industry in question. These agreements are not necessarily followed at the plant level; sometimes they are deliberately violated, creating serious problems for the government and the industry alike. The problem of "wage drift" is the most widely known and discussed among these. In many countries which have experienced full or near-full employment over the main stretch of the post-Second World War period, the governments are becoming increasingly involved in the process of settlement of outstanding issues between labour and managements. This has been of necessity not of choice. The nature of agreements no less than the method of reaching them, can cause serious repercussions on the economy. A government deeply concerned with slowing down inflation, bridging the balance of payments gap, maintaining defence preparedness, and keeping the aid promises made to foreign countries, cannot afford to stand idly by watching bipartite settlements likely to harm the economy taking shape. In the United States the government, under the Taft-Hartley Act, can force the disputants to return to work and resume negotiations. Thereupon it can work quietly towards a satisfactory mutual settlement. The U.S. Government has in many instances made public appeals for the conclusion of non-inflationary collective agreements and in some cases has even followed them up with political pressure. In the U.K. the government is committed to an incomes policy which now functions through legislated powers to enforce wage restraint upon unions. In Norway and Sweden the governments for many years have been actively associated with settlement of national disputes between organised labour and employers.

In India, too, the government is committed to regulating industrial relations in the interests of developing the economy. It would like workers to be "made aware of the relentless economic principle that for the working class as a whole no appreciable rise in real wages along with the statisfactory growth in employment opportunities is possible without a corresponding increase in productivity per worker. This should, therefore, become the principal concern of the trade union organisations in the country even more than that of the employers. The workers have at the same time to realise that while to evoke the best in them they must have suitable conditions and facilities provided for them, their remuneration, whether as wages or bonus, cannot be very far out of alignment with the prevailing standard in the country even if the profitability of a particular establishment or industry may make that possible. Labour has to function as an organic part of the entire community."[20]

The above passage makes it clear that, from the viewpoint of the government, the basic demands of labour can be fulfilled in the long run only through the development of the economy through a series of five year plans. In a democracy such as India their success is dependent, among other factors, upon labour's willing acceptance of the sacrifices inherent in the process of development. Consequently, the government has tried to involve trade union leaders in every stage of formulating the Plans as well as their execution. The union leaders probably understand clearly what the government expects from them. But even though accepting the validity of a pinciple in theory they may not be in a position to implement it in full. However, they also know that most of the problems are essentially of a national character. For this reason, from the commencement of the planning era, but more particularly since the publication of the draft outline of the Second Five Year Plan in 1955, some of the trade union leaders, particularly of the INTUC, have been trying to influence the size and the shape of the successive

20. Speech of the Union Minister of Labour and Employment and Planning, Gulzari Lal Nanda, at the 19th Session of the Indian Labour Conference, 1961. *Report*, 1961-62 (Volume 1), Ministry of Labour and Employment, pp. 79-80.

five year plans. Probably this interest has not been as much as the government might have desired.[21] However, considering that in some issues the trade union leaders have taken greater interest than in others, it is necessary to locate the extent of their participation in the formulation of plans and involvement in the implementation of schemes affecting workers. Moreover, planning the economy is a political process which not only affects the sectional interests within the country but the rest of the world as well. It should, therefore, be expected that some of the trade union centres will try to influence the direction of government's economic policy. These and related matters are analysed in the next chapter. In it are discussed the policies on which the trade union centres, singly or collectively, and the government have moved towards each other and those on which they have moved apart.

21. In a speech delivered at the Ninth Annual Conference of the Indian Society of Labour Economics in December 1965, Asoka Mehta, Deputy Chairman of the Planning Commission, called upon trade unions to widen their participation in the formulation of the Fourth Plan. He asked them specifically to "help in fixing targets for specific industries, railways, transport and other sectors, in the Plan." He listed a wide variety of programmes in which unions could collaborate with the government in implementing the plan. The author is not aware of any significant response to this plea from the trade union leaders. See Asoka Mehta, *Dynamics of the Labour Movement*, Varanasi, December 29, 1965, pp. 15-16.

CHAPTER 6

TRADE UNIONS AND THE FIVE YEAR PLANS

UNIONS AND NATIONAL OBJECTIVES

The Need for Consensus on Goals

THE RELATIONSHIP BETWEEN THE TRADE UNIONS AND THE
five year plans can be discussed at three levels. First, the
government is interested in securing as wide support as
possible for the broad national goals laid down in the five
year plans. The wider the agreement on the goals, the
greater will be the clarity with which it can define its task
and chart out paths of action. For instance, if the society
is by and large in agreement with the goal of "socialism",
it is relatively easier to determine the approximate methods
of achieving it. This may be attempted, as has been the
case in the Second and the Third Plans, through enlargement
of the public sector, controls over corporate managements,
particularly the managing agency system, expansion of
educational and other facilities to backward communities,
land reforms, egalitarian fiscal policy, etc. There can be
no doubt that without a national consensus in support of
socialism all such policies would be more difficult to justify
and some of them might not be even considered. Therefore,
in planning for the economy and the society, it is a matter
of the utmost importance that active interest groups, such
as the recognised political centres of trade unions, should be
in sympathy with the broad national objectives. In India,
the government has steadfastly striven to win the support
of the trade union leadership in these respects and with
considerable success. Second, given the agreement on
general goals there may still be serious differences of opinion
on (*i*) their interpretation in practical terms, and (*ii*) the modes
of implementing socio-economic policies. If so, how are
these differences resolved? If some of the issues are too

deep to be settled by agreement what has the government done to diminish the cleavage and prevent it from adversely affecting the working of the plans. Third, how have the union leaders resolved the in-built conflict between their commitments to self-denying principles, as in the Code of Discipline and the Industrial Truce Resolution, and to the workers, who may be practically asking for their abrogation? One way out of this dilemma is to go on upholding the principles in theory while violating them in practice and putting the blame for such behaviour on other parties. There may be other escapes, too.

One of the striking facts of the post-Independence period in India is that there has been general agreement on the purpose of government policy in economic and social spheres. This may be due to four interrelated reasons. First, there has been no significant difference of opinion on the nature of the basic economic problems. These are clearly to raise production as speedily as may be possible and to eradicate poverty. Second, despite the preponderance of agriculture in the economy, there has been a consensus among the leading members of the elite that industry ought to be given a higher priority. The Bombay Plan and the People's Plan were aimed at industrialising the country. There was a strong sentiment among the Indian members of the civil service in the erstwhile British India that "tariffs should be raised and India industrialised as quickly as possible."[1] Third, there has never been serious disagreement on the pivotal role assigned to the government in planning the economy. In fact, the former British government had tacitly accepted this role by setting up a planning department in 1944. From the side of the trade union movement, the pressure for greater involvement of the state in the economic affairs of the country has never abated. Fourth, there is broad support for the proposition that, without economic emancipation of the

---

1. Maurice Zinkin, "Some Aspects of Change in Indian Society, 1938-60, A Reminiscence" in N. V. Sovani and V. M. Dandekar (ed.), *Changing India*, Essays in Honour of Professor D. R. Gadgil, Bombay, Asia Publishing House, 1961, p. 334. Also see W. H. Morris-Jones, *The Government and Politics of India*, London, Hutchinson University Library, 1964, pp. 109-110.

people, democracy will not be able to strike roots in the country and for its corollary that this will not be possible without the government pursuing "progressive" policies which will not only augment production but also ensure its equitable distribution. These sentiments have found expression in the Directive Principles of the Constitution and later in the incorporation of the goal of a "socialist pattern of society" in the Second Five Year Plan and its sequel.

Goal of Socialism and Trade Unions

The goal of a "socialist pattern of society" was adopted by the Indian National Congress at its Avadi session in January 1955. There are no indications that the Congress leadership was under any pressure from below to adopt such a resolution.[2] The INTUC leadership, too, while avowing socialism since 1955 was until then committed to the goal of *Sarvodaya*. However, the INTUC influence on the government was on the side of progressive policies wherever these affected workers in respect of continuity of production, employment and other matters. Therefore, the INTUC did not hesitate to welcome the new orientation in the government's thinking and declared in a resolution: "It implies in the present circumstances within the framework of the present mixed economy, with private sector functioning under more and more controls and regulations, a greater and speedier elimination of the vested interests and their subordination in the larger interests of the nation. Thus the state in a sense assumes the sacred trust of producing and supplying the essential and basic needs of the country."[3]

One of the principal roles of the INTUC leadership, since 1955, has been to remind the government of its promises and the distance yet to cover on the road to socialism. In a memorandum submitted to the government on the eve of the Third Plan, the INTUC complained that despite the acceptance of the objective of socialism "there was little substantial change in the labour policies and programme under the Second Five Year Plan. In fact, the Second Five

2. W. H. Morris-Jones, (op. cit.), p. 178.
3. Indian National Trade Union Congress, Seventh Annual Session, Nagpur, January 1955, *A Brief Review*, Appendices, pp. 2-3.

Year Plan had nothing second about it so far as labour policies were concerned and it appeared to be a continuation of the First Plan itself."[4]   Four years later, the INTUC repeated the charge that the government had been neglecting the interests of labour and further that there had been no "significant progress in the march of labour to its objectives". In its 15th Report the INTUC went on to say: "In fact, labour could not feel that there was any third stage in planning because of the Third Plan. It appears to be almost an endless series of successive years of deprivation and sufferings with history repeating itself too often and too painfully."[5]

It is evident that sharing of common objectives does not necessarily lead to a common programme of action. The ultimate ends may be the same but the means and methods of realising them are not only different but to an interest group like labour may appear to be such as to defeat the very purpose. The INTUC leadership is clearly disillusioned with planning even though for political reasons it may continue to harp on common goals.

Another group that was deeply affected by the Avadi resolution was the HMS and its socialist leaders. The resolution divided the leadership and this has since gradually widened into a permanent rift. The HMS has been split and what has remained of the organisation is now a house divided against itself into several recognised ideological and personal factions. It has lacked the resources to study the five year plans and crystallise its thinking in terms of concrete proposals and demands. Apparently, the organisation has suffered from excessive turnover in affiliated unions, so much so that at its 11th Convention in 1963 an important delegate from Bombay remarked: "Every year we are told that new unions come into the HMS and some old unions go out. Is the HMS some kind of a Kumbha Mela? We must see not only that new unions are brought in but also that old unions are retained and helped to grow."[6] Under

4. INTUC, *Labour Policy in the Third Five Year Plan,* 1960, pp. 4-5.
5. INTUC, *15th Report,* Appendices, pp. 12-13.
6. See F. M. Pinto's speech in Hind Mazdoor Sabha, *Report of the Eleventh Annual Convention,* Dalmianagar, 11-15 April, 1963, p. 8.

these circumstances it would be too much to expect of the HMS leadership clearly to determine the planks in the government policy which merit support and others that must be opposed. Having been led by leaders in the opposition the HMS has had no difficulty in criticising the government for repeatedly failing to fulfil its pledges. By and large the HMS has been concerned with "bread and butter" issues rather than national goals and priorities in the successive five year plans.[7]

Among the political centres in India the AITUC alone has gradually evolved a policy of selective support of the five year plans without making specific commitments on the strategy it might follow on either labour problems or issues concerning the direction of economic policy. It has had the organisational resources to study the problems, formulate attitudes, and propagate them effectively. In these the AITUC is no doubt aided by its close association with the Communist Party of India. Indeed it has reflected the standpoint of the latter on all important matters to an extent that it is generally believed that the two are one and the same. Like those of the Communist Party, the attitudes of the AITUC towards the labour and economic policies of the government can be grouped into two phases. The period 1947-1954 was characterised by much ideological opposition to the Congress government. However, gradually the Communist Party position softened and, by 1955, India under Nehru was counted among the forces of peace which merited some support. This is reflected in the shift of the AITUC attitude from hostility towards the First Five Year Plan to support for the progressive features of the Second Plan.[8] The official policy of the AITUC has not undergone any significant change since 1957.

7. See Hind Mazdoor Sabha, *Reports* of the Seventh, Eighth, Ninth, Tenth and Eleventh Annual Conventions held in December 1958, February 1960, December 1960, May 1962, and April 1963 respectively. Also see Harold Crouch, (op. cit.), Chapter VIII, pp. 202-227, and Hari Kishore Singh, *A History of the Praja Socialist Party* (1934-59), Lucknow, Narendra Prakashan, 1959, pp. 207-228.

8. See Harold Crouch, (op. cit.), Ch. VII, pp. 154-201. Also see *Twenty-fourth Session of the All India Trade Union Congress, Report and Resolutions*,   May 27-29, 1954, pp. 24-35, pp. 43-51.

At the Silver Jubilee Session of the AITUC, in 1957, the problem of economic development was formulated as one of struggling for the creation of an independent, self-reliant economy free from the control of foreign monopoly capital. In the report of the General Secretary a question was specifically asked in the context of India's fight for economic independence: What can the trade unions do? The answer given was that the AITUC unions should join neither in showering encomiums on the plan nor in denouncing it "as merely a conspiracy of the bourgeoisie to defraud the people", but rather "to educate the masses on the need to fulfil the plan and to defend it against the three main disruptors, namely, the foreign monopoly capitalists, the Indian monopolists, and their agents in the State."[9]

It is significant that the AITUC never gave formal approval to the "socialist" objectives of the Second and the Third Plans. Instead it supported their principal plank, viz., expansion of the public sector with extensive aid from the USSR and her allies. This policy might have involved the AITUC leadership in supporting complementary policies on increased taxation and possible collaboration with Western countries. The AITUC, however, safeguarded against such a contingency by declaring:

1. We defend the state sector. We ask for strengthening and extending it. We oppose its being handed over to private management or Anglo-American partnership.
2. We watch, expose and struggle against Anglo-American conspiracies to sabotage our independent economic development and inveigle us further into their net.
3. We emphasise the need to intensify plans for heavy industry, engineering, oil exploration and drugs, their build-up mainly through socialist aid in the state sector. Highest priority for heavy industry and oil.[10]

These attitudes were carried over to the Third Plan which

9. S. A. Dange, *General Report at Ernakulam*, December 25 to 29, 1957, AITUC, pp. 19-20.
10. There are several other demands which cover a wide range of policies See S. A. Dange, *Crisis and Workers*, (op. cit.), p. 47.

received powerful backing from the AITUC. In fact the support was widened paradoxically to include the defence of parliamentary institutions. Dange was categorical on this subject when he said: "The trade unions have a role to play in protecting, using and further developing the parliamentary democracy so that it is not either overthrown by military and personal dictators or used by the monopoly profiteers for their narrow class interests."[11]

How did the AITUC escape the dilemma of supporting the public sector and opposing higher taxation, wage freeze, etc.? : by demanding the nationalisation of banks, insurance companies and foreign monopoly capital. However, the support was at no time extended to the labour policy of the government.

The contrast between the attitudes of the INTUC and the AITUC is self-evident. The INTUC supported the goals and spelled out policies that it thought naturally flowed from them. Some of these policies were incorporated in the successive five year plans. To the INTUC these implied promises to the working classes which, however, was never the intent. It therefore complained of disillusionment, and developed the same ambivalence towards the plans which is found in the political centres located on the opposite extremity to itself. The AITUC on the other hand recognised the dualism of its policy from the day of its formulation and tried to make the greatest political capital out of it. On the questions of the overall dimensions of the Second and the Third Plans and the respective allocations to the public sector, the AITUC leadership was on the side of the government. It exerted pressure to move the government further left which, under the circumstances, appeared not only easier to achieve but perhaps was even sought by some in the Congress party. The INTUC could develop no such strategy. The policies it suggested, in respect of de-emphasising investment in the heavy industries sector, reducing the quantum of deficit financing, and allotting more funds to employment-generating industries etc., could not be acceptable to the

11. S. A. Dange, *Report at Coimbatore*, 26th Session, January 6-12, 1961, AITUC, p. 8, and also pp. 15-25.

government because it had already made up its mind on these matters. It is thus no wonder that, as disclosed in Chapter 5, the INTUC shows an increasing association with trends in industrial conflicts, despite commitments to the Code of Discipline and the Industrial Truce Resolution, while the AITUC does the opposite.[12]

ISSUES RELATING TO WAGES AND EMPLOYMENT

Conflict of Interests

Nowhere in the realm of problems pertaining to economic development is a greater conflict of interests between trade unions and the government as on the question of wages and employment. These two are inversely related. It is an axiom of the neo-classical economic theory that employment can rise only if the real wage rate falls and *vice versa*. This argument does not hold true in advanced countries where the economy is operating at significantly less than the full employment level. However, in underdeveloped economies, where full capacity output is reached with substantial unemployment, this theory remains valid. In such economies, as for instance in India, the level of employment cannot be raised significantly without simultaneously increasing the stock of capital and other complementary inputs. Keeping these in view one of the primary goals of economic planning is to raise the marginal propensity to save for financing rising levels of investment. Characteristically the rate of savings lags behind investment and the gap is financed partly through the net inflow of foreign capital and in part by inflation-induced forced savings. The problem is how to bridge the gap between planned investment and expected savings at rising levels of output without causing

12. In this discussion no space has been devoted to the UTUC for two reasons. First, the literature pertaining to it is extremely meagre. Second, from what is known the position it has taken on important national issues is not significantly different from that of the AITUC. See in this connection, United Trade Union Congress, *Report* at the 3rd All-India Session, April 2-6, 1958, and *Report* at the 5th All-India Session, August 28 to 30, 1964.

severe cuts in the living standards of the masses. In such a situation a general rise in real wages cannot even be contemplated, much less achieved. The best that can be hoped for is that real wages will not fall absolutely and that an increase in investment over time can be sustained by the diversion of an increasing proportion of rising real output into savings.

It can be readily seen that this problem will become more acute the larger the investment plan and the bigger the savings gap. In India it was faced for the first time with the adoption of the Second Five Year Plan. However, within two years the gathering economic crisis forced the government to pare the Plan and look around for foreign aid which was fortunately forthcoming in full measure. When the Second Plan was completed it was disclosed that about 30 per cent of investment in the public sector had been met through deficit financing and about the same through foreign aid in loans, grants, and trade credits. Employment had risen, but so had unemployment. As has already been shown, real wages in this period generally stagnated. The record of the Third Plan has been much worse in every respect.

Trade Union Demands and Government's Response

Let us now examine what the trade unions have asked the government to do for them in respect of wages and employment and with what degree of success. Before going into it, let it be said that the government had defined its position as early as 1952 in the First Plan and, despite a great deal of talk on mutual cooperation, socialism and several improvisations in policy tools, it has remained generally firm. Throughout this period the combined endeavour of the organised trade union movement has been to dislodge the government from its established position, but without much success. It has secured other concessions and rights but not on the vital though untenable demands for rising real wages combined with job security for the employed and the simultaneous creation of new employment opportunities.

As stated in the First Five Year Plan the wage policy of

the government aimed at two objectives : (*i*) restoration of the pre-war real wage, and (*ii*) removal of inequities and anomalies in the existing wage structure. The Plan also held out the distant goal of a living wage to be achieved as the productivity of workers rose.[13] To balance these policies the Plan proposed that similar restrictions be placed on remunerations to managements and on dividends.

The first goal was inadvertently reached by the end of the First Plan through the unexpected decline in the Consumer Price Index. With respect to the second goal, the government took no concrete measures until 1957 when the policy, announced earlier, of constituting wage boards was implemented in the cotton textile industry. It is noteworthy that during the First Plan period trade unions were not concerned so much with the wage question as with the problem of retrenchment. No doubt now and then the question of living wage was brought up by the trade union leaders in the tripartite conferences and on other occasions, but in the context of rising real wages this was not a matter of immediate concern. Instead, the threat of retrenchment was looming large. The principle of rationalisation, involving inevitable reductions in the employed labour force in the affected industries, had received general support in the First Plan. The government had proposed to mitigate the stress by measures that would in practice eliminate part of the implicit threat of victimisation and arbitrary discharge of workers. Moreover, the employers were expected to bear the cost of retraining the retrenched workers and also to provide alternative employments, if possible.[14]

These measures not only did not satisfy unions but met with stiff opposition from them. The union protest, coming as it did at a time of worsening employment, particularly in the cotton textile industry, had the effect of softening the government's position. The latter amended the Industrial Disputes Act in 1953 to make legal provision for retrenchment and layoff compensations.[15] The effect of this amendment was to render rationalisation a more expensive process

13. *The First Five Year Plan*, (op. cit.), pp. 583-585.
14. *Ibid.*, pp. 590-591.
15. See *Indian Labour Year Book*, 1953-54, pp. 122-123.

than had been visualised in the First Plan. In the Second Plan the government took yet another step to pacify the unions. It conceded the principle of rationalisation to employers but laid down the condition that as far as possible it should be carried out in consultation with unions.[16]   In taking this stand the government was merely expressing its concern at the grave risk of work-stoppages that unregulated rationalisation schemes would have certainly entailed.   In 1955, there had occurred a major industry-wide strike in Kanpur accompanied by considerable violence. The government could not afford the recurrence of such conflicts in other industrial centres.

The problem of rationalisation is an endemic one and still remains partly unsolved.   This problem is bound to arise as one industry after another is forced by the realities of market competition to shift from the older technology to more modern ones. From the point of view of planners it is tied up with growth in productivity which is considered a matter of over-riding necessity without which neither higher wages, nor increase in exports, nor stability in prices are possible. Accordingly, the Third Plan advised workers and their leaders to work not against but for rationalisation. It said :

Industry is being called upon to meet, as rapidly as possible, the claims on behalf of the workers for a living wage, better living and working conditions, the needed volume of employment opportunities and a fuller measure of social security. It must yield a reasonable return on capital and provide for capital formation on an adequate scale. Neither the exercise of their organised strength in industrial conflicts, nor laws and the intervention of the state can help the workers much in realising their aspirations. Their gains can arise only out of the strength and dynamism of the economy, the only enduring basis of which is a rising level of productivity....

For the workers no real advance in their standard of living is possible without a steady increase in productivity,

16. *Second Five Year Plan*, pp. 581-583.

because any increase in wages generally, beyond certain narrow limits, would otherwise be nullified by a rise in prices. Workers have, therefore, to insist on and not resist the progress of rationalisation in their own interest and in the larger interest of the country.[17]

It is not known how far this approach has been accepted by trade unions. However, due to either the reasonableness of the policy enumerated in the Third Plan or, more probably, the effectiveness of the industrial relations machinery in settling disputes on employment matters, the issue of rationalisation has receded into the background. There are also indications that important trade union leaders have accepted the inevitability of technological progress and the futility of labour's resistance to it.[18]

As the threat to job security has diminished in importance, the problems of wages and related matters have come to the

17. *Third Five Year Plan*, pp. 261-262.
18. See the Presidential Address of S.C.C. Anthoni Pillay in HMS, *Report of the Seventh Annual Convention*, December 1958, pp. 30-31. It is worth noting that in the 10th and 11th Annual Conventions held in May 1962 and April 1963 respectively, this subject was not referred to at all in either the General Secretary's reports or the Presidential Addresses.

The defensive posture was also adopted by the AITUC. In 1958, Dange put forward the ingenuous proposal that the AITUC would not object to automatic looms provided these were installed in the public sector. He was, however, "totally against allowing the existing mills to introduce automatic looms in their existing units." S. A. Dange, *Crisis and Workers*, (op. cit.), p. 153. At the 26th session of the AITUC held in 1961 there was, of course, no mention of this subject.

Unlike the HMS and the AITUC, the INTUC has expressed deep reservations on the employment aspects of the five year plans. It has not been so much opposed to rationalisation as to the whole approach to planning which, in disregard of the structure of factor endowments of the country, gives higher priority to investment in heavy industries. The INTUC leadership advised the government in 1959 to revise the Second Plan so as to decentralise production and lay greater emphasis on larger employment and raising the standard of living of the people. Similar advise was given in 1964 to revive "village industries which do not need heavy capital investment and can at the same time absorb more manpower." See Indian National Trade Union Congress, Fifteenth Session, *Report*, December 30, 1964, p. 15, and *Report* to Tenth Annual Session, February 1959, p. 129.

fore. The First Plan had proposed that wages be fixed through wage boards. This policy found general acceptance among the trade union leaders who probably found in this mechanism an escape from settling wage disputes through the tedious process of industrial tribunals. However, the realisation soon dawned upon them that wage boards could not be instituted just by asking for them and indeed required a great deal of agitation to carry conviction with the government on the justness of their demand. Furthermore, the delay involved in getting practical results from wage boards, first, by securing agreed recommendations and, second, their implementation, has caused much frustration and disillusionment. Trade unions of practically every shade and opinion have expressed these feelings on numerous occasions. In some quarters disenchantment with the wage policy of the government has given way to resentment, and may already be a factor in the growing incidence of industrial conflicts. The response of the government has so far taken the form of greater flexibility in setting up wage boards on the one hand and in securing better compliance with their recommendations on the other.

Since 1963 the trade unions have been demanding the revision of the index numbers of cost of living and the basis of fixation of dearness allowance. This agitation was started by the AITUC, but was quickly picked up by other unions. In fact, this was one way of reviving the demand for a need-based minimum wage which, though accepted at the 15th Indian Labour Conference in 1957, was virtually disowned by the government later on. The resolution never had a chance of being implemented. It was probably viewed by the government as an ultimate goal, and as a bait which could be dangled interminably before unions. But the militant union leadership thought differently and instead used the resolution as a weapon to unite the workers and embarrass the government. As Dange says, "The resolution became a memorable fact of history, a fact inconvenient to the employers but a weapon in the hands of the working class. No one ever suspected that that innocent resolution on minimum wages would ever resound in the TU movements as an immediate goal to be fought for, would provide such ammunition to the fighting workers, such defeat, embarrassment and lo of face to the government and become a source of confli and division inside the ruling circles. The Delhi Triparti will live down in history for this resolution. The fight f the minimum was raised to a higher level and the resolutic provided a banner and a unanimously agreed moral, econ mic, constitutional banner at that, to the whole TU mov ment."[19]

Even though the resolution had some utility to unions a weapon, its efficacy was bound to diminish with time. Th unions needed another rallying cry to revive the demand f higher wages. This was provided by the discovery th most index numbers of consumer prices were obsolete in or respect or another. Moreover, it gave the unions an oppo tunity of raising the question of the principle that shou govern the fixation of dearness allowance. The need f uniformity, or at any rate some order, in this matter has bee felt by managements and the government as well. S partly as a response to trade union agitation and partly settle a dispute with its own employees, the government the Centre and in the States earnestly took up the revision the CPI. The State governments appointed committees examine the existing series and suggest revisions. The La our Bureau, too, started publishing a revised series of CF for various centres and for all-India with 1960 as the ba year. As a result of these measures the demand for the rev sion of the CPI had lost much of its force by 1965. The pro blem of dearness allowance still remains and will probabl continue to be a morally just ground for union agitatio until reasonable stability is restored to the price level an some order to the chaos that characterises the method of fixing dearness allowance in the country.[20]

---

19. S. A. Dange, *Report at Coimbatore*, (op. cit)., p. 40.
20. In this respect some progress has already been made by the wage boar which have made final recommendations, as well as by the pay commi sions. These have generally recommended the linking of dearness a lowance with the CPI. There are, however, differences in details affectir different income groups and the extent of relief provided.

ISSUES RELATING TO SOCIAL SECURITY

Harmony of Interests

Unlike wage policy, the interests of the unions and the government have generally been in greater harmony on social security. The union leadership has for long been demanding social security measures. The first important legislation in this field in India was the Workmen's Compensation Act, 1923, which came into effect on July 1, 1924. The scope of benefit as well as the industries covered have been gradually widened.[21] However, the most significant legislation in this area has been enacted in post-Independence India. Important among the laws are the Employees' Provident Funds Act, 1952, the Maternity Benefit Act, 1961, and the Employees' State Insurance Act, 1948. Besides these, there are special laws conferring benefits upon mining and plantation workers among others.[22]

The demand for health insurance for workers has been raised in India ever since the ILO adopted the Sickness Insurance (Industry) Convention in 1927. However, the government has opposed its ratification on financial and administrative grounds. The demand for the introduction of some kind of health insurance received a great fillip by the publication of B. P. Adarkar's Report on Health Insurance for Industrial Workers in 1944.[23] This report was

---

21. For an excellent review of the working of this Act and the problems connected therewith, see Sunil Rai Choudhuri, *Social Security in India and Britain*, Calcutta, The World Press (P) Ltd., 1962, Chapters IV, V, and VI.

22. An adequate description of the three Acts referred to is given in P. C. Srivastava, *Social Security in India*, Allahabad, Lokbharti Publications, 1964, Chapters III-XIV. However, there seems to be an extraordinary dearth of scholarly publications on the working of the legislation relating to mining and plantation workers.

23. Because of the valuable work done by Adarkar he has been rightly acclaimed as the Beveridge of India and, according to one author, merits his name being "written in letters of gold in the history of social insurance in India": Sunil Rai Choudhuri, *Sickness Insurance in India and Great Britain*, Calcutta, The World Press (P) Ltd., 1966, p. 62. Also see Chapter 4, pp. 63-89.

welcomed from all quarters and formed the basis for the Employees' State Insurance Act, 1948.   The rationale for this legislation was provided by the concern of the state to secure the citizens of the country, particularly industrial workers, against the disabilities of disease and injury. Moreover, "the mandays lost on account of sickness and disability constitute a heavy drain not only on the slender resources of the industrial workers but also on the industrial output of the country.   Lack of social security impedes increased production, leads to larger labour turnover and prevents the building up of a stable and efficient labour force."[24]

In view of this approach and the lead the government had taken in legislating social security measures, the trade unions could ask for no more than (i) the extension of the scope of the Employees' State Insurance Act to areas not yet covered and also to families of the workers covered by it, and (ii) its more efficient administration for ensuring prompt relief to the needy.   By and large, the trade union movement has viewed the Employees' State Insurance Act as "a distinct gain won by the working class after years of struggle."[25]

In contrast to health insurance, whose main purpose has been to assure workers against known hazards and indirectly to raise production, the provident fund scheme has served a different purpose.   To the workers, covered by the various provident fund schemes, the legislation has provided some kind of a compulsory old age and retirement benefit.   Moreover, the government obtained additional resources for financing the investment envisaged in the five year plans. Since the government has stipulated that the net accruals to the provident funds, whether in public or private sector, must be invested in government securities, there is an automatic addition to domestic savings available to the public

24. *The First Five Year Plan*, (op. cit.).
25. While applauding this victory of workers, the AITUC, nevertheless, said that "the greatest drawback in the whole scheme is the top heavy bureaucratic administration."   It went on to declare that "the struggle for democratisation of the administration of social security schemes is thus a vital part of the struggle for social security".   See *Twenty-fourth Session of the All-India Trade Union Congress, Report & Resolutions*, (op. cit.), pp. 66-67.

exchequer for disbursement in accordance with the budgetary provisions. The pressing need for funds has given as much interest to the government in expanding the coverage of provident funds as to the unions. For similar reasons the former has been quite receptive to the demands made by unions, off and on, for raising employers' and employees' rates of contribution to the provident funds. This is seen in the progressive extension of the Employees' Provident Fund Act, 1952 from 1,400 establishments with 1.2 million subscribers in 1952-53 to approximately 27,500 establishments with over 4.0 million subscribers in 1964-65.[26] The total contributions have also gone up from 70.5 million rupees in 1952-53 to over 5.47 billion rupees in 1964-65

On the question of provident fund benefits, the unions have made four important demands, *viz.*, (*i*) the forfeiture provisions of the scheme should either be repealed or substantially modified because they involve punishing workers for involuntary severence of employment; (*ii*) the contributions of employers and employees should be raised from $6\frac{1}{4}$ per cent to $8\frac{1}{3}$ per cent; (*iii*) the provident fund scheme should be converted into an old age and/or survivorship pension scheme; (*iv*) the scheme should be extended to the large number of workers that are still outside the purview of the Act.

Among these demands the government has found it possible partially to accept the second and the fourth. The first and the third demands have been the most difficult ones to concede although there is a possibility that in the years to come the provident funds may grow to such a size as to render the financing of the third kind of benefits a feasible proposition. However, the government has already decided on an unemployment insurance scheme of limited scope that can be financed out of the enhanced contributions to provident funds.[27]

---

26. Central Provident Fund Commissioner, *Employees' Provident Fund Organisation, Statistical Abstract*, New Delhi, 1965, p. 7 and p. 14.

27. The government appointed a Study Group in 1957 to report on the feasibility of introducing a comprehensive scheme of social security for workers. In its report submitted in 1958 the Study Group made several recommendations for improving the existing schemes but expressed the opinion that "under existing conditions, any large extension of social

Grievances on Housing Policy

The demand for more and improved housing for workers has been one of the recurring themes in the proceedings and resolutions of trade union organisations. The government for its part has been willing, from the commencement of the First Plan, to divert as much funds for this purpose as has seemed feasible. Inevitably the union demands have tended to exceed what the government and the employers together have been willing to provide. It is, however, important that the former has assumed a part of the responsibility for meeting the long expressed workers' grievances in this respect. This in itself has been a significant union victory.

Most of the unions' grievances on housing policy are in respect of its implementation. In 1955, the INTUC categorically declared that "the Industrial Housing Scheme has not proved a success. The schemes drawn up are bureaucratic and wooden in character."[28]

This criticism went home. In the Second Five Year Plan the government budgeted 500 million rupees for building workers' houses in the industrial sector alone. Separate provisions were made for mining and plantation workers. But more important was the fact that the government conceded the point that the working of the subsidised industrial housing scheme had not been satisfactory and that "loans and subsidies permissible under the scheme have not evoked sufficient response from employers and from cooperative societies of workers."[29]

There were several reasons for the poor response of wor-

---

security measures will not be possible either in terms of coverage or actual benefit". Government of India, Ministry of Labour & Employment, *Report of the Study Group on Social Security*, New Delhi, 1958, p. 12. Also see pp. 8-39.

28. *INTUC Seventh Annual Session*, (op. cit.), The AITUC reviewing the housing situation in 1954, roundly condemned the employers and the government for what in its view was a "miserable" failure "to implement its own solemn promise to the workers". It also denounced the government for charging "exorbitant rents" and the "bureaucratic implementations of the various housing projects", etc. See *Twenty-fourth Session of the All-India Trade Union Congress*, (op. cit.), pp. 115-118.

29. *Second Five Year Plan*, pp. 586-587.

kers : (*i*) inconvenient location of houses, (*ii*) administrative delays in obtaining funds, (*iii*) scarcity of building material, (*iv*) soaring land prices, and (*v*) lack of coordination among the Centre, the States, and the employers.[30]

During the Second Plan period the main targets of union criticism were employers and the State governments. To meet this criticism, the Central Government agreed to raise the quantum of loan to employers from $37\frac{1}{2}$ per cent to 50 per cent of the total cost of construction. The Indian Labour Conference in 1959 also urged the States to expedite development of suitable lands for workers' housing. Moreover the Central Government agreed to give loans to States for this purpose.[31] Despite these measures, the progress of subsidised housing remained slow and as a result the achievements in the Second Plan fell substantially below the target. It appears that the high rents on newly constructed houses have been beyond the reach of many workers "with the result that in some areas the tenements which have been constructed have not been occupied by industrial workers".[32] There are also practical problems, such as providing workers with inexpensive transportation to enable them to move back and forth without loss of much time, terms of repayment of loans, and allotment of tenements, etc., that have not been wholly overcome.

Not all of these can be solved by agitation although unions have tried to use this method for speeding up the process of finding solutions that are advantageous to workers. In this effort the union leadership has been able to score points not only in getting the accepted principles modified but also in winning the important right to participate in the decision-making process. It appears that in this regard the union interests have coincided in large measure with the goals of the Central Government. The latter has been as keen as the former to develop suitable housing facilities for low-income groups. This would probably hold true for any democratically elected government, but to the Government

30. *Summary of Proceedings of the Indian Labour Conference*, 1957, pp. 19-21.
31. *Seventeenth Tripartite*, AITUC publication, 1959, pp. 26-27.
32. *Third Five Year Plan*, p. 683.   Also see pp. 681-686.

of India, it has had the additional attraction of appearing to be living up to the distant, though no doubt achievable, goal of socialism. On matters of housing, the government has apparently seen a constructive role in union criticism inasmuch as it has helped in securing the acceptance of housing policy by the employers and the States. Moreover, union pressure also helps the government in speeding up the resolution of the numerous practical problems that inevitably arise in a nation-wide programme of this nature.[33]

THEORETICAL UNDERPINNINGS OF TRADE UNION POLICIES

Besides questions related to social security, there are several other important issues on which trade unions feel strongly and upon which they have been exerting pressure on the Central Government. Some of these, such as opening of fair price shops, workers' education, workers' cooperatives, etc., are, no doubt, important to trade unions no less than to the government. On most of these the interests of trade unions coincide with those of the government even though the former may criticise the latter for acts of omission and commission. It is not possible to discuss all of these in a book of this kind without at the same time making for unmanageable size and distracting from the central theme. Instead of going into details we will concentrate on the central theoretical propositions which appear to underlie the positions taken up by the trade union centres on issues pertaining to national economic policies. The purpose is to state the important concepts, the logic that links them into a well rounded theory, and the policy precepts that flow from it.

Some of the economic doctrines of the trade unions are commonly shared throughout the movement. Others are specific to the political centres that advocate them. In respect of the latter the differentiae lie in their ideological

33. Despite the mutuality of interest, the housing programme continues to suffer from lack of support. In 1965, the INTUC publicly charged the State governments with diverting funds allotted to housing to unintended purposes. Many employers still do not feel that workers' housing is their responsibility. See *INTUC 16th Report*, December 24, 1965, p. 110.

moorings and the parties with which these are closely associated. For contrast it will be sufficient to consider the
INTUC and the AITUC only. The HMS is too split ideologically to develop a system of doctrines from which attitudes
or policies on issues of national importance can be derived.
The UTUC is ideologically so close to the AITUC that there
is hardly any difference between the two. Moreover, its
relative smallness has hampered the process of thinking
and articulation of policies that impart to an organised trade
union body its distinctive character.

The Theories of the INTUC

The distinctive characteristics of the INTUC doctrines
are brought out by five principal propositions that are stated
below:

(i) The development of the human factor is both the
objective and the principal means of economic growth.
Therefore, in a country committed to democratic
values, five year plans should lay greater stress not
only on avoiding the needless human suffering that has
been known to occur in the totalitarian countries,
but should also create and strengthen democratic
institutions and participation of working masses in
building their society. These democratic institutions
are cooperative societies, state-sponsored schemes for
workers' education, healthy industrial relations based
on mutuality between "strong, healthy and patriotic"
trade unions on the one hand and "humanised" and
socially responsible managements on the other.
The INTUC has also held that the industrial relations
machinery and other government departments dealing
with the public should be de-bureaucratised and
humanised. These strains of thought in the speeches
and writings of the INTUC leaders can be traced to
the Gandhian traditions to which it is historically
linked.[34]

4. See in this connection G. Ramanujam, *Industrial Relations, A Point of
View*, New Delhi, Indian National Trade Union Congress. Van Dusen
Kennedy associates this line of thinking with a peculiar brand of Hindu

(*ii*) The size of five year plans should be "realistic". The term "realistic" implies that a plan should not be bigger than the resources in sight, and furthermore, that it should be financed with minimum recourse to foreign aid and deficit financing. Accordingly, the INTUC has maintained that the development of agriculture, village and small-scale industries, and quick yielding projects should receive higher priority in the formulation of five year plans.

(*iii*) Workers, managements, and the government have a common interest in maximising production. Workers and their unions ought to contribute their utmost towards this end. But in return for this service their legitimate rights should be safeguarded. These include job security, including avoidance of retrenchment wherever possible, rising wages, and social security benefits. The INTUC holds that if workers are not properly protected and compensated for their efforts to expand output it will be difficult to ensure their continued cooperation in nation-building plans.

(*iv*) The government should steadfastly keep in view the goal of the socialist pattern of society. In order to reach this goal the government has the responsibility to show that (*a*) public sector undertakings will act as model employers, (*b*) monopoly power in the private sector is systematically curbed, (*c*) inequality in income distribution is reduced and, (*d*) the gains of economic development are widely shared geographically throughout the country. Furthermore, it also appears that the goal of a living wage is considered to be concomitant with socialism.

(*v*) As far as possible the settlement of bilateral disputes should be through constitutional and peaceful

---

tender-mindedness that is common among Indian leaders. See hi*
Unions, Employees and Government, (op. cit.), Chapter 1. It may b*
said, however, that what may appear to be tender-mindedness to a foreig*
visitor may in fact be a deliberate policy designed to meet the strains o*
development. From the point of view of the INTUC the concern fo*
human beings has probably a strong association with the values of demo*
cratic society.

methods. The strike weapon should be used only as a last resort. In all matters affecting labour relations the interests of the nation are supreme. The INTUC, while struggling for the rights and betterment of workers, cannot at any time ignore the national interests.

The AITUC Doctrines

By comparison with the Gandhian-cum-socialist orientation of the INTUC doctrines, the AITUC approach is explicitly Marxist. There is not even a remote reference to mutuality of interests between workers and employers. On the contrary, the emphasis is on class conflict between the two interests which are fundamentally irreconcilable. The government belongs to the bourgeoisie and the landed interests and must therefore side with the class enemy of workers. Nevertheless, due to historical forces, the national bourgeoisie is capable of playing a progressive role in the development of the economy. In this task it deserves the selective support of the working class. The latter must, however, always keep in view the ever-present danger of the government capitulating before the combined pressure of Anglo-American imperialism. The public sector and other progressive policies of the government should be safeguarded against the encroachment of vested interests. Accordingly, the AITUC declared:

We support the Plan in relation to the *country* and not in relation to the *class*, who owns the factories or forms the government. We oppose the power of the class but support the Plan, because the Plan builds an economy, an industrialisation which strengthens our economic base, a base of independence as against imperialism.[35]

The AITUC favours high priority for heavy industries in the plan and improvement of agriculture through radical land reforms. On foreign aid the position of the AITUC

35. S. A. Dange, *Report at Coimbatore*, (op. cit.), p. 25.

leadership is unequivocally in support of receiving it from the Soviet Union and her allies and in opposition to the Western countries. The plans should be big, bold, and ambitious although the burden of financing them should not fall upon the common man. They can be financed by taxing the rich and expropriating the capitalists, if necessary. The government should nationalise banks and insurance companies for the same purpose.

The AITUC does not appeal to the government to safeguard the interests of workers. It would rely on the organised strength and struggles of the working class to secure itself against the onslaughts of employers rather than be "merely conditioned by the profits of the bourgeoisie or the 'impartiality' of the arbitration tribunals".[36]

Unionism—A Common Factor

This theme runs through all the publications of the AITUC. The contrast between the INTUC and the AITUC approaches is seen throughout their respective philosophies, strategies, and tactics. Yet there are common factors which make for unity in action on many important issues affecting workers' interests and, if exploited skilfully, the respective leaders can together mount formidable pressure upon the government and the employers. On practical problems affecting workers, such as bonus, linking of dearness allowance with a revised index of consumers' prices, prompt implementation of awards made by national and industrial tribunals and of recommendations of wage boards, improved and expanded social security legislation, enlarged and better administered housing programmes, etc., the trade union leaders, their political affiliations notwithstanding, speak with one voice. However, they do not always act alike. Historically the AITUC unions are more conflict-prone than those affiliated to the INTUC, although, in this regard too, the difference is getting blurred. Where the two part company—and in this respect the gap is unbridgeable—is in their respective

36. S. A. Dange, "Trends in the Nainital Labour Conference", *Trade Union Record*, Vol. X, No. 7, November 1952, p. 5.

approaches to the socio-economic development of India from which flow their political attitudes and mutual hostility. These show up not so much in day-to-day working as in times of crisis or national emergency. The AITUC may be ahead of the INTUC in supporting the broad features of the Second and the Third Plans, but it has as yet given no commitment that the sectional interests of workers will be subordinated to the needs of the nation.

This may be the reason why important cabinet ministers attend the INTUC annual sessions and even encourage it to form unions in strategic industries.[37]   Since the relative growth of political centres has been held in high importance not only by the unions themselves but also by the government, it is necessary to devote more space to this problem. It is evident that from the latter's point of view it is not just the activities of union centres that matter, favourable or otherwise as these may be from time to time, but also their ultimate political goals.   Because of this vital concern with the security and the destiny of the country, the government cannot afford to remain neutral on matters affecting the strength and solidarity of trade unions, whether as a whole or in parts.

37. It is reported that the former Home Minister, G. L. Nanda, speaking at the 15th Session of the INTUC, "called upon the INTUC to expand its activities with a view to bringing in its orbit masses of workers employed in a large number of industries who were still not organised into trade unions. INTUC should pay special attention to organize the workers in a forceful and strategic manner in all those undertakings where still its message had not reached.   The fact that INTUC has about two million members could not be a matter of satisfaction as still there were undertakings of strategic importance without any attention. INTUC will have to give serious thought to this aspect among others, more particularly from the security point of view of the country." *INTUC, Fifteenth Session, A Brief Review*, p. 13.

CHAPTER 7

ORGANISATIONAL INTERESTS OF UNIONS

ORGANISATIONAL OBJECTIVES

Factors Conditioning the Formation of Objectives

THE ORGANISATIONAL OBJECTIVES OF TRADE UNIONS, LIKE those of any other organisation, are, in the order of importance, survival, growth, and maximisation of some utility function which in itself is composed of numerous sub-objectives. This can be illustrated by the example of a business corporation in a free society. The business corporation has to survive the rigours of market competition and, in a growing economy, must expand to retain its relative position, and, if possible, to improve it. At the same time it must make adequate profits, if not seeking literally to maximise them, watch the liquidity of its assets, maintain satisfactory dividends, promote a favourable public image of itself and do a variety of other things. These sub-goals may be deemed to comprise a set of utility functions which a representative corporation seeks to maximise. How are these goals set? They are set and re-set in response to a large number of influences that continually operate from the board of directors, from share and bond-holders, customers, unions, managers, and government, to list only the most important.

In the case of a union, its organisational objectives are crucially dependent upon the stage of its development. The objectives relate, besides survival and growth, to the maximising of workers' interests in terms of wages, job security, fringe benefits, promotion by seniority, the right to natural justice, and so on. In the wider sense they may relate to changing the government, the setting up of a dictatorship of proletariat, or the creation of a socialist democracy, international brotherhood, etc. How are these goals set? As in the case of the corporation, they are set by the interaction of varied influences emanating from leaders, political parties, government, and workers. At any point of time we find in the behaviour of unions a seeking towards goals as they have been set by these forces, and also a tendency towards their modification or a reordering of priorities. Trade unions, being dynamic organisations, are perpetually in the process of transition. In this chapter a partial analysis of this process is attempted.

What are the factors that generally govern or condition the formation of trade unions' objectives? The most important among these are: (i) the legal character of trade unions as voluntary associations of workmen; (ii) the state of potential conflict in which most unions generally find themselves, pitted mostly against employers, but sometimes also against the government and rival unions; (iii) the knowledge that the effectiveness of unions depends to a large extent upon their representative character, the authority of leaders over the rank and file, and public sympathy, if not active support to their demands; and (iv) the political (or socio-economic) goals to which the leadership is committed.

The first factor is a source of strength as well as of weakness. As democratic organisations, unions naturally enjoy the allegiance of their members. However, it is possible, as happens in India, that workers' allegiance to unions is weakened by union rivalry and discouragement by employers. In countries, such as the United States, where this problem is no longer serious, there is the opposite problem of workers' apathy leading to erosion of their moral authority. In order partially to offset these dangers, union leaders have traditionally fought for the right to union security (as provided by union shop contracts, if legal), or for the sole bargaining rights to the recognised unions, etc. Union leaders may also feel that a better way of ensuring organisational security is to organise employers.[1]

---

1. In the United States, as Ross says, organising the employer "was the more customary method prior to the National Labor Relations Act,

The latter may help the union for several reasons. The leaders of a "sweetheart" union may appear to be more reasonable than its rival with a more aggressive and militant leadership. Possibly, the managements have been directed by higher authorities, either in the same group of organisations or in the government, to deal with only one kind of unions and not others. On the other hand, some employers may feel that by helping the union organise workers they are buying trouble-free industrial relations, at any rate, for some time to come. There may be other reasons, too.

It is probably typical of unions in India that, though they have scored numerous victories, their primary struggle for survival is not yet over. The most important reason for the prevailing insecurity among unions is that, by and large, they are forced to organise workers rather than employers, in order to exist and function. Indeed the ever-present threat of rival unions cannot be eliminated even with the aid of obliging employers. Moreover, most unions are of the industrial rather than the craft type and as such cannot adopt the restrictive policies that their counterparts in the Western countries have traditionally followed for retaining membership support. The insecurity born of the purely voluntary character of trade unions in India has produced an extraordinary tendency among them to lean upon outside help and seek affiliations with stronger and more viable organisations.

The second factor is the very *raison d'etre* of trade unionism. Unions must struggle against employers for (*i*) securing the acceptance of workers' demand for better terms and conditions of work and employment, (*ii*) obtaining claims awarded to them by judicial and quasi-judicial bodies and the enforcement of laws favourable to labour, and

---

and is still widely practised. It is no longer legal for an employer to grant a closed shop or a union shop without consulting his workers, but he still has the right to recognise the union without proof of majority representation. Even without a 'sweetheart contract', the employer is in a position to give the union a great deal of assistance in the task of enrolling his workers if he himself has already been organised." A. M. Ross, *Trade Union Wage Policy*, (op. cit.), p. 101.

(*iii*) renewing the loyalty of members and the support of workers.[2] These struggles have to be carried on in India within the framework of laws that permit redressal of grievances and even settlement of disputes through the industrial relations machinery. Therefore, one of the basic organisational objectives is likely to be to secure sufficient support among workers to make the presence of the union felt both at the management and the government levels. Once this position has been attained, sights can be suitably raised whenever opportunities occur.

The third factor is crucially tied up with the first and the second. The level of effectiveness of unions varies with time and circumstances mainly because the variables upon which it is dependent do not remain constant. A union that is duly recognised by the company and the government as the sole bargaining agent of workers can set its organisational objectives at a wholly different level from another that is still struggling for these rights. The former can plan a whole range of welfare and community activities that will firmly establish it not just as a fighting organ of workers but as their service institution as well. In order to do these, a union needs not merely the support of workers but also of the employers and the government. The status of a recognised union with special rights and privileges has been, and probably will remain in the near future, the most important goal of most unions in India. Maybe the lack of assurance in this regard explains to some extent why some of the important goals of the five year plans, such as subsidised workers' housing, have not made satisfactory progress. Probably this also accounts for the non-fulfilment of plan expectations, in many industries, concerning union partici-

---

2. The third reason does not necessarily imply that unions deliberately engineer conflict situations to secure loyalty of workers. However, it has been observed that unions tend to be more militant when their security is threatened. Conversely, one of the reasons for the decline in strikes in Western countries is the disappearance of threat to union existence. See Richard A. Laster, *As Unions Mature, An Analysis of the Evolution of American Unionism*, Princeton, Princeton University Press, 1958, Chapters II and III, pp. 12-34; and A. M. Ross and P. T. Hartman, *Changing Patterns of Industrial Conflict*, (op. cit.), Chapter 5.

pation in programmes relating to the raising of productivity, reducing absenteeism, and the imparting among workers of a sense of discipline and commitment to the national purpose.

The fourth factor has been of great importance in determining the unions' organisational objectives in all democratic countries that have sizeable trade union movements. One reason cited by Ross and Hartman for the decline in the popularity of the strike in the United States and the Scandinavian countries is the increasing role of political activity in settling disputes of national importance.[3] In India, the conflicting ideologies of leaders have been largely responsible for the divided trade union movement. The government, too, has sought a favourable treatment of public sector enterprises by trade unions on ideological grounds. The government has also sought to establish new organisational goals for trade unions in India so that they may participate in the effective functioning of enterprises and thereby acquire a sense of partnership in the management of industry. The Joint Management Council Scheme was designed with this end in view. Other programmes, such as workers' education, slum clearance, the national productivity movement, etc., can also be viewed in this light. Accordingly, trade unions in India have been subjected to a sustained educational and propaganda barrage, at all levels, to move them nearer to the plan goals.

At this stage it cannot be clearly ascertained whether the government has succeeded, if at all, in these efforts. However, judged by the professions of leaders and the tenor of resolutions adopted at conventions, it would seem that the INTUC leadership has moved closer to the government in theory, if not in practice, than any other political centre. This may be attributed to the fact that the political goals of the INTUC leaders are similar to those of the party in power. In times of emergency, as prevailed in India immediately after the Chinese attack in October 1962, and the Indo-Pak armed conflict in September 1965, other trade union centres, too, temporarily abandoned some of their goals and moved

3. A. M. Ross and P. T. Hartman, (op. cit.), pp. 50-54.

closer to the government. However, in normal times the trade union centres that are nearer to the opposition parties have at best given qualified support, often interspersed with trenchant criticisms of government policies. Despite this mixed response, all trade union centres have participated in the formulation of policies affecting workers to a greater or lesser extent, and some have even collaborated in the execution of nationally approved programmes. To this extent it can be said that the government and trade unions have discovered common areas of national purpose and mutual cooperation at the highest level. It is not known, however, whether, and to what extent, these sentiments have percolated into the lower layers of organisations and have found their way into common beliefs and actions.

It is evident that none of the parties concerned, *viz.*, workers, employers, government, and political parties, can remain neutral on the question of organisational objectives of trade unions. Workers would like their unions to grow in strength, possibly more than one at a time, and to serve them in adversity as well as in fair weather. They may be more loyal to one than to another, or to none at all. On the other hand there are industries where workers, through long experience, have learnt the importance of having just one good union to which they give unflinching loyalty. In India, where "the law of uneven development" is the characteristic of the land, it is probably natural for workers to display varying degrees of commitment to the union as an institution. With the continuous influx of population from rural areas, the polyglot character of most of India's industrial cities, and the cultural distance that often separates the educated union leaders from the industrial workers, it cannot be expected that the unevenness among unions will either automatically or smoothly wither away. While it lasts, the other interested parties may not be able to resist the temptation to intervene in the process of union development with a view to moulding it in accordance with their own desires.

Next to workers, the employers as a group can play the most prominent role in building unions as organisations. In their regard a proposition can be safely stated, namely that the more resistant an employer is the more militant (and maybe irresponsible) a union he will get. In India many employers are still hostile to the idea of a union and even more to the concept that a workers' organisation should bargain with them on an equal basis. Cases are not unknown when employers have floated company unions either to forestall the formation of genuine unions or to wreck the ones that have already come into existence. It is possible that in several instances the phenomenon of inter-union rivalry is not a spontaneous reflection of political divergencies among leaders, but is sponsored and nurtured by other interests. On the other hand, in many industries employers have become more perceptive and mature and have helped in the development of stable unions. Indeed, the maturing process for the generality of unions and employers is concomitant and can be greatly speeded up when the initiative is with the latter. Alternatively, the government can play a decisive role in setting the direction for union-management relations and consequently the moulding of union objectives. In the United States, the controlling factor, since its enforcement, has been the Wagner Act. In India, the government has shown continuing interest in the problem, but the measures taken have either remained unenforced or have not been very effective. This aspect is taken up in the next section. The interest of political parties will be discussed thereafter.

GOVERNMENT INTEREST IN THE ORGANISATIONAL PROBLEMS OF TRADE UNIONS

Unions and the National Purpose

It has already been stated that the government has expressed its desire that trade unions should participate in the development of the economy, in implementing programmes of mutual interest and, above all, in maintaining industrial peace. The government has also realised that a weak and ineffective trade union movement cannot be expected to carry out these tasks effectively, and that it would require governmental assistance. In offering to extend the needed assistance, the government naturally expects the trade unions to use their power for the good of the country and in accordance with the priorities in the five year plans. This would not require the unions to abdicate their "social protest" function—a contrary policy could not possibly be carried out in a constitutional democracy—but to canalise workers' discontent along constructive lines and seek constitutional remedies for it. Since assurances along such lines could not be expected from trade union centres that are openly linked with opposition political parties, the government has felt unable to remain neutral in the matter of relative growth of union centres. The leaders of the government have, therefore, been openly partisan in supporting the INTUC against its rivals. To them this has no doubt appeared as the only way of reconciling the larger interests of the country with the necessity of strengthening the trade union movement for the purpose of securing the active support of the working class in building the economy.

But how can the government, and more particularly the governments in the States, support a part of the trade union movement without alienating others and without at the same time opening themselves to charges of partisan political interference? It appears that one way of doing it has been found. This has been for the government to use its discretionary authority to give recognition to unions in ambiguous situations as a means of political and administrative support but, at the same time, to recognise all the four trade union centres at the top for purposes such as nominating workers' representatives to the ILO, for political consultations, and for mutual give-and-take. Thus, in appearance, or so it is assumed, the government is free from any charge of partiality, at any rate at the Centre, and acquires moral authority by seeking the cooperation of all the union centres in well-structured forums of mutual consultations and by giving them opportunities to influence its policies. At the same time, through the elaborate machinery of membership verification and dispute settlement by conciliation and adjudication, often involving considerable exercise of administrative and political discretion, the governments of several States have tried to strengthen the INTUC unions at the grass roots level. This has been done despite much protest by other centres. To the authorities, therefore, it appears that the question of union recognition cannot be settled by the principle of equity alone since too much is at stake.

On the broader question of organising workers, government policy has been unequivocally favourable. In the First Five Year Plan, where labour policy was laid down in the greatest detail, it is said,

> The workers' right of association and collective bargaining is to be accepted without reservation as the fundamental basis of the mutual relationship. The attitude to trade unions should not be just a matter of toleration. They should be welcomed and helped to function as part and parcel of the industrial system. (p. 573)

The Plan also advocated the principle of determining a single bargaining agent in accordance with a prescribed legal framework and the fixing of responsibility for enforcing collective agreements. Even in respect of public sector enterprises the First Plan affirmed the need for forming unions. But these principles were never put into practice. In the Second Plan, this subject was given only passing attention. The Second Plan noted that "a strong trade union movement is necessary both for safeguarding the interests of labour and for realising the targets of production. Multiplicity of trade unions, political rivalries, lack of resources, and disunity in the ranks of workers are some of the major weaknesses in a number of existing unions." (p. 572) But the operational part emphasised the necessity of reducing the dependence of trade unions on outside leadership and the responsibility of the government for taking the requisite steps for training of workers in trade union philosophy and methods.

On the key question of trade union recognition, the Second Plan devolved the responsibility for making statutory provisions on the States. At the same time it was laid down that the criteria for recognition could not be merely the membership strength but something more. "In doing so the importance of one union for an industry in a local area requires to be kept in view. It is equally important that while mere members would secure recognition to a union, it should, for functioning effectively, exhaust the accepted procedure and the machinery for the settlement of disputes before it has recourse to direct action."[4]

The Codes in Relation to the Problem of Union Recognition

In retrospect, there is no doubt that the principal reason underlying the non-implementation of the policy on union recognition as stated in the First Plan was essentially the same that resulted in the non-enforcement of the Indian Trade Unions (Amendment) Act, 1947. The government has been simply unable to take the risk of recognising unions which, though representative in character, may not be committed to the national goals and to constitutional means. With the expansion in the public sector the risk has grown that militant unions in strategic industries may win workers' support by doing exactly the opposite of what the government may want them to do. Moreover, once a union got recognition it would be extremely difficult to have it dislodged. Government thinking has therefore probably developed on the following lines. Would it not then be better to leave the situation undefined where (i) inter-union rivalry is acute and the outcome of the verification of representative status is rather uncertain, and (ii) the union that is committed to the industrial relations policy of the government is relatively weak? Would it not also be better to let the managements negotiate with each union as circumstances determine, or perhaps just bypass all of them and deal directly with the workers and pray, strive, and hope that in the meanwhile the most reasonable union will continue to gather strength so as eventually to attain an unquestioned majority status? In any case if these questions had been asked the answer would probably have been in the affirmative. If so, it was desirable to give up all pretence of making statutory provision for nominating the most representative union as the sole bargaining agent of workers

4. *Second Five Year Plan*, p. 573.

for the purpose of engaging in collective bargaining and implementing agreements. A new method was needed that would involve trade union centres making a firm commitment to the industrial relations policy of the government and would maintain coexistence in the realm of inter-union relations. In return the government would in fairness give each recognised union centre an equal opportunity to avail itself of the industrial relations machinery for redressing workers' grievances. This method was developed to perfection by the then labour minister, Gulzari Lal Nanda, and was carried over into the Third Plan as the official policy of the government.[5]

As has already been described in Chapter 4, the new method lay in the adoption by the unions and the employers of the Code of Discipline and by the unions only of the Inter-Union Code of Conduct. The operative clauses of the Code of Discipline on the subject of union recognition provided, *inter alia*, that there should be voluntary recognition by employers of a union which had been functioning for at least one year and had no rival, and had (*i*) membership of at least 15 per cent of workers in the establishment, or (*ii*) 25 per cent of an industry in the local area where it claimed to be an industrial union, or (*iii*) whichever was the largest union by membership, and (*iv*) the maintenance of the *status quo* for at least two years after a union had been given recognition.

There are several qualifying clauses among which the most important is that "only unions which observed the Code of Discipline would be entitled to recognition".[6] Evidently, if a union fully subscribed to the Code of Discipline, including the no-strike clause in practice as well as in theory, the purpose of the industrial relations policy of the government would be served. Therefore, it would not matter if a trade union was affiliated with one political

---

5. *Third Five Year Plan*, Chapter XV entitled "Labour Policy", see in particular pp. 250-255.

6. Government of India, Ministry of Labour and Employment, Implementation and Evaluation Division, *Implementation and Evaluation Machinery, Its Functions and Procedures*, second edition, October 1953, p. 18.

centre or the other because the binding effect of the Code of Discipline would render them equally reasonable and co-operative in practice. This was no doubt expecting too much from the trade union centres that were committed to radical philosophies; but the government, nevertheless, thought that it might succeed.

The purpose of the Inter-Union Code of Conduct was to reinforce the Code of Discipline.[7] It barred unions from coercing workers to join them, abolished dual membership, required "unreserved acceptance of, and respect for, democratic functioning of trade unions", prohibited exploitation of the ignorance and "backwardness" of workers, and enjoined on the signatories to eschew casteism, communalism, and provincialism, and other evils. The moral tone of this Code is exceptionally high, and its remoteness from reality is also equally apparent. The wonder is not so much that the Inter-Union Code of Conduct was ever conceived and adopted, (who could refrain from affixing his signature to a document with such a high moral tone?), but that it was ever expected to work. And yet, this Code was put into practice, apparently in a sufficiently large number of cases, to justify the pronouncement in the Third Five Year Plan : "The deplorable consequences of inter-union rivalry both for industry and for the workers are well known. They have been mitigated to some extent by the Code of Conduct which was drawn up and accepted by the representatives of workers' organisations three years ago."[8] (p. 251)

The Code of Discipline has been instrumental in sorting out the problem of recognition in several instances. Some of its provisions have been codified by certain States and have acquired legal sanction. The Madhya Pradesh

7. *Ibid.*, p. 44.
8. The factual basis for this statement is furnished by the declining number of complaints on the violation of this Code by the labour ministry. The Central Implementation and Evaluation Division received 59 complaints in 1959, 35 in 1960, 30 in 1961, 27 in 1962, 30 in 1963, but only 8 in 1964. It may be noted that the declining trend in complaints under the Code of Conduct is in marked contrast to that under the Code of Discipline. See Ministry of Labour and Employment, *Report* for the respective years cited.

Industrial Relations Act, 1960, requires detailed steps to be taken by unions and the government in giving recognition to representative unions and associations of employers. One of the conditions laid down is that "the Registrar shall not recognise any union if at any time within six months immediately preceding the date of the application for recognition or thereafter the union has instigated, acted or assisted the continuation of a strike or stoppage which has been held or declared to be illegal." Similar conditions are attached to recognition in the Industrial Disputes (Rajasthan Amendment) Act, 1958.[9] In most States and at the Centre, where statutory provisions on this matter have not been made, the Implementation and Evaluation Machinery in the period 1960-1964 had secured the recognition of 23 unions in the Central sphere and 98 in the State sphere. Among these 51 were affiliated to the INTUC, 20 to the AITUC, and 8 each to the HMS and the UTUC, and the remaining were independent unions.[10]

It is, however, apparent that the battle of recognition is not over until the employers not only give this status to a union in formal terms but deal with it accordingly in practice. Progress has been much less satisfactory on the latter point. The trade unions have been critical of the Code of Discipline in this regard. In 1960, the HMS President S.C.C. Anthony Pillay complained: "Many representative unions have not been recognised, let alone employers negotiating with them in good faith, and lastly, the public sector has refused to accept and be bound by the Code."[11] The AITUC and the HMS leaders have said on numerous occasions since the adoption of the Code, that the government was "trying to favour its own trade union centre by boosting organisations that belong to INTUC even at the cost of industrial peace", or was "recognising

9. Government of India, Ministry of Labour and Employment, *Recognition of Unions under the Code of Discipline*, New Delhi, October 1963, pp. 31-39. Also see pp. 23-30.
10. Memorandum circulated by the Ministry of Labour and Employment to members of the Standing Labour Committee (24th Session), Annexure I, p. 7 (mimeographed).
11. Hind Mazdoor Sabha, *Report of the Eighth Annual Convention*, p. 18.

more than one union in an establishment" in order to rehabi-
litate the INTUC. It has been alleged that in certain
public sector undertakings "the INTUC union has been
recognised without bothering to see whether it fulfils the
criterion of minimum membership laid down in the Code of
Discipline".[12]

It is clear that the assessment of the working of the Code
of Discipline on the vital question of union recognition varies
widely from the government at one end, generally expressing
satisfaction with the INTUC standing close by and supporting the theory that "recognition to be really useful must be
voluntary and must reflect a change of heart and attitude
of both the parties,"[13] to the AITUC, the HMS, and the
UTUC, at the other end demanding in deep discontent
that statutory provision for the compulsory recognition of
representative trade unions through a secret ballot should be
introduced without delay. On the basis of this dichotomy
in appraisals, while it would be unfair to conclude that
valiant efforts have not been made through the implementation machinery set up under the Code of Discipline to render
the problem less intractable, yet the government officials
are just one among several parties concerned with the problem and can function well only under favourable circumstances.

The voluntary system of union recognition can work
only if the other parties are equally keen on it. This, moreover, implies that the competing unions are reconciled to
living with the outcome, no matter who wins or loses. However, under the prevailing political conditions it seems rather
improbable that any political centre will accept the prospect
of losing support, certainly not the INTUC. Had the contrary been the case, the problem of determining the most
representative character of competing unions in different
industries could have been settled for good by the enforcement of Chapters III-A and III-B of the Indian Trade
Unions (Amendment) Act, 1947. Alternatively, the volun-

12. Hind Mazdoor Sabha, *Report of the Tenth Annual Convention*, (op. cit.),
    p. 73, and *Report of the Eleventh Annual Convention*, (op. cit.), pp. 37-38.
13. *Labour Policy in the Third Five Year Plan*, (op. cit.), p. 29.

tary method, with which all parties are, in principle, in agreement, could also function satisfactorily. But the hard political realities of India, coupled with the breakdown of the rather facile assumptions underlying the Code of Discipline and the deepening of the economic crisis, have together combined gravely to weaken the effectiveness of policy that has been in operation since 1958. Since 1962, the INTUC and the AITUC have been at loggerheads, with each calling the other names in a manner that does scant justice to the moral precepts subscribed to in the Code of Conduct by both of them. Currently, the government has to deal with the problem of union recognition in an atmosphere that has been fouled with hostility and mutual hatred.

POLITICAL PARTIES AND TRADE UNION PROBLEMS

INTUC and the Communist Influence

On the question of union recognition, the INTUC has taken the position that only patriotic and responsible unions should be given this status even though these may at times fail to meet the criteria laid down by the Code of Discipline. In a memorandum to the government in 1965, the INTUC stated:

One union for one industry is an incomplete slogan. What is wanted is one *good* union for each industry. In trade unions "quality-first" must be the consideration.

The Code of Discipline treats the "anti-national" and nationalist unions on the same footing. It puts the truly democratic unions and those which utilise democracy to sabotage democracy also on the same footing. The recognition under the Code of Discipline should therefore be on "quality-based numbers" and not mere numbers. This will in the long run help unification of labour.

Recognition must be limited to the most representative organisation consistent with quality. Recognising all and sundry leads to perpetuation of disunity among labour. There should be a planned effort to create "impulses" for unity.[14]

According to the INTUC criteria of nationalism and "quality-first", a large number of trade unions, whether or not representative, have no right to exist. It has called the AITUC "an extension of the CPI to work out its policies among the working class....AITUC's role, therefore, in spite of its protestations to the contrary, is bound to be anti-national." Accordingly, the INTUC has demanded that the Communist Party of India, along with its various fronts, should be outlawed.[15] There is no doubt that if this demand was to be conceded, much of the problem of disunity in the trade union movement would also disappear and the INTUC would stand out sufficiently powerful to knock out or absorb the remaining rival centres. What other troubles would arise as a result is, however, a matter for grave speculation.

However, so far the government has not yielded to this demand. The AITUC itself has taken away much of the force of the INTUC criticism by rallying behind the government on the issue of "defence of motherland".[16] It has also demonstrated considerable diminution in conflict-proneness as the data themselves reveal. Moreover, while the AITUC criticises the government on certain issues, it also supports it on several others. Politically, the government might find it useful to have the backing of the Communist party and its various fronts, including the AITUC, in warding off potential threats from the right wing and communal parties. Thus, quite apart from the fact that in a democracy no party can be outlawed for its professions alone,

4. *Labour Policies and Programmes in the Fourth Five Year Plan*, p. 60.

5. *INTUC* 14th *Session, Report*, May 1963, Appendices, p. x.

6. In a resolution adopted by the AITUC General Council on November 16-18, 1962, the organisation called upon "all sections of the Indian working class to stand unitedly for the supreme task of defending the country's territorial integrity and defeating aggression." *Tasks of Trade Unions in National Emergency*, p. 1. Also see speech by S. A. Dange, *Our Statement on Imperialism and Indo-Pak War*, delivered before the Sixth World Congress of World Federation of Trade Unions in October 1965 in Warsaw.

the government has probably found it useful and expedient to let the left wing parties and unions function in their own right and neutralise the threat from the other extreme. In the trade union movement, in particular, the government probably realises that, in the very nature of things, conflict situations are not wholly unavoidable. Maybe it is better to let the discontent in workers find opportunities of self-expression through strongly worded resolutions, protests, and even strikes than to suppress such manifestations and face more deleterious consequences later on. Because of these and other related reasons, the INTUC strategy of achieving trade union unity through the abolition of undesirables has no chance of being considered, far less accepted and implemented, by the government.

The real significance of the INTUC stand on this point is not in its failure to secure its acceptance, but that it was at all seriously put forward. It has revealed the wide cleavage that has separated the two strongest trade union centres in India, since Independence, and the utter improbability of reconciliation. Ever since the trade union movement was split into four camps, there have been many unity talks but never between the INTUC and the AITUC. The reasons for a complete lack of *rapprochement* between the two are ideological,[17] and therefore virtually impossible of resolution.

The leaders of the INTUC have considered it as one of their primary missions to wean workers away from the communist influence. G. Ramanujam in his presidential address at the 11th Annual Session of the INTUC had this to say:

How could there be even one man or woman who could subscribe to any union controlled by the AITUC and the CPI, knowing that they are anti-national and that they do not really believe in democracy. I believe the so-called membership of the CPI unions at best represents only the number of discontented people the communists had succeeded in misleading. They are no there as a result of their understanding the communist

17. See Harold Crouch, (op. cit.), Chapter X entitled "Unity, Cooperatio and Rivalry", pp. 239-278.

and their designs. It is, therefore, our duty to carry on the light to them, disillusion them and bring them gently to our fold and let them forsake for ever the anti-national leadership. (p. 9)

This has been a running theme in the pronouncements of the INTUC leaders. For them the AITUC unions are not genuine ones. As can be expected, the AITUC leaders have returned the compliment. As viewed by them the INTUC unions have been set up with the slogan "Join Congress union and win your demands through the Tribunal which the Congress Government has set up for you," and with the purpose of diverting workers from the path of mass action to that of adjudication. The INTUC leaders have been publicly denounced as brokers of employers and strike-breakers.[18]

Since in most industries the INTUC and the AITUC unions have been challenging each other, it has become extremely difficult to settle purely "bread and butter" issues either through a tribunal or a process of collective bargaining. In the replies to the questionnaire of the Central Wage Board for the Iron and Steel Industry the AITUC disowned the agreements reached between the recognised INTUC unions and the managements on the ground that "the managements, both in private and public sectors, deliberately boost the INTUC unions with the purpose of signing agreements convenient to the managements". Indeed, the position was such that "non-recognised unions cannot even do elementary trade union work. We should like to lay a special emphasis on this aspect since it seriously affects the bargaining strength of the workers on the question of wages, etc." The AITUC further declared that "the question of determining the representative character of a union cannot be separated from the wage question. The present verification procedure is not adequate enough to determine the true representative character as the employers are in a position to use their influence in this regard and create

8. Indrajit Gupta, *Capital and Labour in the Jute Industry*, Bombay, AITUC, 1953, pp. 45-47.

obstruction in the way of expression of the real will of the people." (p. 23)

Effect on Unionism

The political conflict between the rival camps has imparted permanent instability to industrial relations in India. Behind this contest of wills are the organised political parties with their resources in men, money, and ideas. The real issue is not as to which trade union will represent the workers, but rather which ideology will do it. In a democracy, with all kinds of stresses and strains affecting political and economic stability, neither the government nor the ruling party can remain neutral on this question. In this struggle no one whose interests are involved can remain truly detached. Its nature is such that the outcome is closely bound up with the destiny of constitutional democracy itself.

If the inter-organisational combat is carried on at the present level, *i.e.*, without decisive intervention by the government on behalf of any interest, there cannot be a sole victor in the foreseeable future. This is unlikely for three important reasons. First, vast masses of workers are yet unorganised. Moreover, the total workforce is growing with the expansion in the economy. These will provide room for expansion to trade union centres of as many ideologies as may wish to contend. Second, trade unions do not just carry on ideological warfare but also function as service institutions. The constructive, or the social service, role of unions will enable union leadership in all the centres to retain organic ties with workers. This factor may actually grow in strength as workers gain in literacy or education organisational experience, and confidence so as to keep a proper balance between ideological and "bread and butter" unionism. Third, it is conceivable that managements, in the public as well as the private sector, will gradually recognise the merit of dealing only with those unions that enjoy majority support. As they gain in experience they may also learn to deal with more than one union, fairly and satisfactorily, in the interest of orderly industrial relations. It is quite probable that managements in their own interests would wish to stabilise not only labour-management relations but inter-union relations as well. Indeed, in course of time this factor may emerge as the most powerful one in working towards the goal of stability in inter-union relations.

What are the chances of political parties leaving trade unions to themselves? They are probably as bright as of the politicians renouncing their beliefs, goals, and methods! Moreover, in a democracy there is just no way of doing this. Left to themselves, why should politicians and their parties give up bases of power? Indeed, with spreading political consciousness and awareness of the nature of problems requiring political action of all types for safeguarding and enhancing their interests one expects an increase in the influence of political parties over workers. The two are likely to come closer rather than to drift apart. In this connection it may also be noted that communication with and consultation of the unions by the government are essentially political processes. Whether it is a question of setting up a wage board, or implementing an award, or mitigating the problem of technological unemployment, trade unions have to work on the government and *vice versa*. From the point of view of unions this requires organisational resources, representation in Parliament and State Legislatures, leaders who have access to the highest echelons of power, national media of publicity and organs that can seek public support or, if necessary, coalesce with other interest groups. Under Indian conditions, the trade unions by themselves are unlikely to be able to possess all of these and in sufficient measure. The experience hitherto has demonstrated the utility of wider affiliations. It has enabled trade union leaders to be elected to Parliament and Assemblies. The voice of the organised trade union movement can now reach all levels of the government, and even outside India. Trade unions, like other interest groups, would like to have friends in positions of power and influence. Through affiliation or close association with political parties, this goal is likely to be achieved with a maximum economy of effort.

The implications of close connections between political parties and trade unions should also be viewed in a larger context. The trade union movement in India, despite intramural fights, has been remarkably free from narrow communal, sectarian, and obscurantist tendencies. When the country was passing through the tragedy of communal carnage the trade union movement, by and large, maintained its balance and was a factor for peace and harmony. Similarly, in the linguistic agitations the trade union movement, wherever it was involved, stood for working class solidarity, protection of minorities, and peaceful methods. There is no doubt that in the post-Independence India the trade union movement has been a centripetal force. It is afferent, cuts across traditional loyalties and barriers, and is a force for modernity and democracy. It has accepted these goals and functions largely through close association with modern political movements and the ideologies they represent. On balance, this has been a benign influence which has moderated the anguish of transition through which India has been passing. In the democratic India these trends merit further strengthening.

On the other hand, it has also been observed that in some parts of India the trade union centres have been deeply infected by factionalism with whatever party they are closely associated. This is most evident in the INTUC in West Bengal and Bihar and to some extent in Madhya Pradesh. Alongside the party groupings parallel factions have appeared in the INTUC unions.[19] It is probable that factionalism has tended to reduce the effectiveness of unions. At the same time it may also have loosened their links with the political party whose organisational energies are being consumed in internal fights. The problem was considered serious enough by the INTUC leaders to warn their colleagues in the trade union movement to stay away from group rivalries in the Congress party.[20] It is well known that factionalism has deeply corroded the organisational solidarity

19. Van Dusen Kennedy, *Unions, Employers and Government*, (op. cit.), Chapter 6 entitled "Trade Union Politics", especially pp. 203-206.
20. *INTUC 15th Session, Brief Report*, Khandubhai Desai's speech, p. 7. The President of the INTUC, Kashi Nath Pandey, was even more explicit in recognising the evil that had already crept into the organisation: "Besides the political, economic and social difficulties, the wrangling inside was causing damage to the INTUC organisation. If the organisa-

of the AITUC.[21] The HMS has three distinct groups representing the Praja Socialist Party, the Samyukta Socialist Party, and the Congress. The UTUC, too, has its political factions. The general effect of these groupings on unions at the plant level will be determined by whether they are confined mainly to the top or cut vertically across the organisational structure. If it is limited to the former, it may show up in the weakening of ties between the central headquarters and the locals. But it has been observed that once factions have been formed they inevitably tend to grow and gradually envelop all layers of the organisation. This has probably happened in the AITUC. The organisation may still survive provided the factions can develop and operate rules for maintaining a state of permanent truce. Otherwise it will remain united in form but not in substance.

The above analysis shows that the benign effect of association with political movements is reduced to some extent by the diminution in the organisational effectiveness of trade unions that is caused by factionalism. There are other evil effects, too. These may, in broad terms, be said to be the misguiding of workers by politicians for their own ends, the growth of outside vested interests in trade unions, the possible misuse of funds, and the habit of dependence upon outside leaders. The government for its part appears to be convinced that, although outside leaders in the past have played a pioneering role in organising trade unions, this is no longer strictly necessary and that workers should be given opportunity as well as encouragement to develop

---

tion could not prevent division in their ranks, the future would be dark. He, therefore, appealed to the affiliated unions to recognise the truth that unity was strength and that organisations lived on the bonds of love and not when enmeshed with groups and factions." *Ibid.*, p. 24. Also see *INTUC 16th Report*, (op. cit.), pp. 28-29 and pp. 44-46.

21. This has reached a point where the AITUC workers have been involved in forming rival unions in the same industry. Recently the General Council of the AITUC has passed a resolution calling for the dissolution of rival unions. It has directed the State bodies to supervise elections and ensure the representation of different political trends in the unions' executives. See *Trade Union Record*, December 5, 1966, p. 5.

internal leadership. It has been the government's hope that the workers' education scheme will facilitate this process.

The Question of Developing Internal Leadership

Interestingly, the proposal for encouraging internal leadership has evoked only a lukewarm support from trade unions. The INTUC is favourably inclined towards workers' education provided the government will allow the unions themselves to manage the scheme with the aid of public money. Furthermore, the objective of the scheme should be to educate workers on their rights and responsibilities in relation to work, managements, and trade unions rather than to replace outside leaders. Only "bad outsiders" should be replaced and that task, too, must be left to the people themselves.[22]

The AITUC also favours reducing the dependence on outside elements provided "the union leadership is guaranteed protection from the victimisation in any form". Moreover, dismissed workers should not be considered as outsiders and those who retain jobs should be given one-fourth of their working time off for union work. Furthermore, the elimination of outsiders should be done on a selective basis in sectors where the internal cadre has developed suitably.[23]

It appears that, unwittingly, the trade unions, the government, and the employers are working towards the same goal. A responsible trade union leader, no less than a good manager, would, in the interest of organisation, develop a second line of leadership. If he is a political functionary, then, as a scarce resource, he can maximise returns to his party by developing internal leadership in unions that, if possible, will also develop ties with the party, and then move on to the next job. The more successfully he does this the more effective he is likely to be within his party by virtue of the large following that will have been acquired for himself and his organisation. There should, therefore, be no con-

---

22. G. Ramanujam, *Industrial Relations, A Point of View*, (op. cit.), pp. 41-45.
23. AITUC, *Seventeenth Tripartite*, 1959, p. 124.

flict between the union leadership and others on the goal of training of workers' cadres in unions. If so, the AITUC demands are eminently reasonable and could have been accepted. The fact that the argument persists indicates that the real reasons are different.

Probably neither the government nor the employers are so much desirous of developing internal working class leaders for professional trade unionism as of eliminating the influence of political parties on workers. In a democracy the second goal is clearly unattainable and probably not worth attempting. For one thing it is not clear beyond doubt whether the goal is to remove all political influence or only of the undesirable kind. If the latter, this goal practically synchronises with the policy of the INTUC to weed out "bad" leaders only and the political philosophy they propagate in the trade union movement. Uncertainty on the real goal has probably handicapped the functioning of government policy in this regard. However, there are long-run autonomous factors in operation which can be accelerated if the government aims at the professionalisation of trade unionism rather than the gradual elimination of outside political leadership. But this is crucially dependent upon the acceptance of a more basic assumption, *i.e.*, that the government considers a strong, self-reliant, and professional trade union movement as a desirable thing in itself.

Ambivalence in Government Policy
and the Dilemma of Unionism

As has been shown earlier, there is considerable uncertainty on the kind of trade unionism the government really desires. There is no doubt that, in the true spirit of the Constitution, the government unreservedly accepts trade unions as the vital part of a democratic society. But then it has also been repeatedly stated that the government would strive to secure the acceptance of certain essential goals by the entire trade union movement in order to facilitate rapid and orderly economic development. In our judgement the government has viewed the latter condition as absolutely vital and as an integral part of its long range plan for the country's development. On the other hand, it is equally evident that no trade union movement that accepts this condition can be genuinely independent. This is not to deny that trade unions that have grown independent by their own efforts may, in the larger interests of the country, accept certain restrictions on themselves for short periods. But, in India, the problem of development is not of short duration. It is, on the contrary, a long, indefinite spell of continuing emergency. Under these circumstances the success of government policy would involve a permanent restriction on the freedom and independence of trade unionism in India. This is the unresolved dilemma of trade unionism in a developing economy to which there is no unequivocal and lasting solution.

In India, as in most underdeveloped countries, the purpose of government policy is to develop, not strong and independent trade unionism, but generally autonomous and organisationally adequate labour organisations that can simultaneously represent the working class and live up to their responsibilities towards the planned economy. Most trade unions, at present, fall short of the criteria of autonomy and adequacy. The government would like to strengthen them in these respects. In so far as these short-term and limited goals are held in common by the government and the leaders of trade union movement, there is ample scope for united action.

CHAPTER 8

SUMMARY, CONCLUSIONS, AND POLICY PERSPECTIVES

IN THIS FINAL CHAPTER, FIRST THE SUMMARY AND CONCLUSIONS of the preceding discussions are given. Thereafter, some of the important gaps in our knowledge that require further research are listed. Finally, the necessity of reorienting government's policy on trade unions and industrial relations as also of reorganising the instruments of policy for serving the new goals is brought out.

SUMMARY AND CONCLUSIONS

As stated in Chapter 1, the principal purpose of this book is to analyse the interaction process between the trade union movement and the government's labour policy in the specific context of the stresses and strains of economic development caused by the successive five year plans. The period covered generally is 1950-1965, although for certain purposes the analysis goes back to 1946. The starting point of our thesis is that the progress of trade union movement and the peculiar characteristics of unionism in India are greatly conditioned by (*i*) the underdeveloped state of the economy, (*ii*) the leadership role assumed by the state for industrialising the country as rapidly as may be possible, (*iii*) the strong association of unions with political parties committed to different ideologies, and finally, (*iv*) the democratic, legal, and political system that gradually evolved under the British regime and formalised and reinforced by the Indian Constitution.

Factors (*i*) and (*ii*) together show the weak social base of the union movement, the inherent contradiction between the productionist goals of the government and the consumptionist (distribution-centred) outlook of trade unions, the immense possibilities of economic growth generating in turn equally powerful forces for the expansion of union membership and influence and the concomitant rise in industrial unrest, conflicts and social tension. The dominant factor is the government policy, which, through ever bolder development plans, has attempted to stretch the society's resources to the end of its tether, and in the process heightened social tensions far more than was probably necessary by sheer mismanagement of the economy. Inflation, acute shortages of essential commodities, growing unemployment, overcrowded urban centres blighted with slums, insanitation and inadequate supply of utility services, general decline in the standard of administration and rampant inefficiencies and corruption are the more notable symptoms of strains that the country has developed since the commencement of the planning era. These maladies have affected workers directly, as well as the internal structure of the trade union movement and its relationship with the state, and have contributed to general unrest, industrial disputes and conflicts.

The government, on its part, has tried to structure the relationship between itself and state organs on the one hand, and the unions on the other, on the basis of three principles. These principles are : (i) mitigating causes of conflicts between workers and employers on the basis of statute and voluntarily accepted codes of behaviour, (ii) widening the scope of cooperation between union leaders and the government, partly for the purpose of ensuring smooth running of the public sector undertakings, and (iii) controlling an important segment of the trade union movement politically with a view to facilitating (i) and (ii). These principles have been defined as well as sought to be implemented within the boundaries of the Constitution and the democratic polity it has created. Thus, the government has pursued the paradoxical policy of encouraging trade unions to grow and expand as the democratic institutions of the working masses and simultaneously controlling their behaviour to subserve the needs of a developing economy. Behind this paradox is the classic dilemma of a democratic government in an underdeveloped country. The dilemma is between the paramount necessity of economic development without which neither the security of the state nor the stability of the democratic polity is assured.

Indeed, the postulate of nationhood in a polyglot country, continually pulled apart by centrifugal tendencies, has no hope of realisation unless the economic wherewithal for the molification of contending demands also grows. On the other hand, the country has been committed to a democratic constitution. The future of democracy is secure only to the extent it is bolstered by democratic institutions and practices at the grassroot level. Independent trade unions functioning as representatives of workers and led by freely elected leaders are an organic part of the democratic society. The institutions of collective bargaining and voluntary arbitration have arisen in Western countries, to some extent in India as well, out of the free interaction of unions and employers. Nowhere has this process of development been free from conflict— in fact, a measure of tension sometimes resulting in work-stoppages of varying durations and intensities is inseparable from collective bargaining. Its development requires state support, considerable scope for the free interplay of unions and employers, and a corresponding assumption of risk of work-stoppages by the government. In Indian conditions, there has also been an attendant risk of letting the trade union movement pass under the control of communists and other radical elements whose avowed purpose is subverting democracy. So far the government has been unable to take these risks and, as such, has attenuated, dithered, and improvised in steering through conflicting goals. In practice the government has upheld the task of economic development as primal, and endeavoured to secure its acceptance by union leaders, but at the same time preserved their liberties and circumscribed their conduct.

In this paradoxical situation, the government has achieved a measure of success mainly because of three reasons. First, the government has on its own initiative taken the progressive line of legislating for workers' rights, or, at any rate, has appeared to go out of the way in meeting union demands. This has evoked from the employers' side the criticism of the government trying to appease labour, of passing a "plethora of legislation", and so on. Second, the growth of economy, such as it has been, has mitigated the problem of unemployment and greatly reduced the threat of retrenchment in traditional industries. This has also permitted the expansion of social security benefits to industrial workers. Third, the leftward ideological movement of the Indian National Congress and of the government, as a result thereof, has widened the scope of political cooperation between the latter and the trade union movement in its entirety. Lately this rapport seems to have weakened and its future is uncertain. The present state of affairs may be as much due to the prevalent economic stagnation as to the ideological confusion and the lack of sense of direction among the Congress leaders.

How has unionism responded to the opportunities of growth provided by the democratic constitution, the policy framework set up by the government, and the challenges posed by the developing economy? What are the factors that have conditioned the response of unionism and with what results? The latter question may be taken up first.

On the eve of Independence the trade union movement was already weak, internally split, highly politicised and articulate, and had won legal rights to organise and to secure the settlement of disputes through the industrial relations machinery as it existed, and the political right to influence government thinking through tripartite forums. Between 1946 and 1949, the trade union movement had further split into four centres. Recently, more centres have come up.

The policies of union leaders have been conditioned by the multiplicity of centres which are themselves the outcome of competition among political parties for workers' support. Our central proposition is that union rivalry is not rooted in conflict of interests among groups of workers but rather in the ideological distance among the leaders with differing goals and purposes. These have been accentuated by the desire of the government to secure political control over a sizable section of the union movement through the INTUC. Union rivalry has been stabilised by the government policy of recognising four centres, of registering and dealing with as many unions as may come into existence, of not giving the dominant unions legal protection and privileges including the right to bargain with employers, and, as has often been alleged, of discrimination in favour of the INTUC even though its unions may not represent the majority of workers.

Union rivalry has produced a dual effect upon the trade union movement. While pursuing quantitative expansion of membership, particularly in sectors that have not been unionised, it has also created permanent instability and flabbiness in the movement as a whole.

The disunity in the trade union movement can be analysed as a function of three variables : (i) the political distance among trade union leaders, (ii) the subordination of trade union interests to the ultimate goals of the movement as perceived by leaders,[1] and (iii) the probability that a sufficiently large number of employers have acquired vested interest in maintaining disunity.

The four prominent trade union centres, viz, the INTUC, the AITUC, the HMS, and the UTUC, represent conflicting ideologies, diverse political programmes, clashing party and personal interests, and even regional and caste loyalties. These form a shapeless quadrangle on the trade union "space" rather than a continuum. Although these together occupy only just over half of the aggregate union membership, their total weight in the trade union movement and on industrial relations is substantially greater. The "independent" unions, by their large numbers and considerable spread, have tended to maintain stability in the union movement.

The lack of viability of unions is testified by the decline in average membership, in the share of large unions with membership of 1,000 or above, and in the stagnation of income of the average union. In the context of rising prices, the latter denotes a fall in their economic strength. It is possible that

---

1. This is shown by strong ideological projections in their speeches and activities. A large number of union leaders are members of one party or another and carry the party line into union activities. The differences among them relate to the ultimate goal of the Indian society, i.e., whether it should be socialism, sarvodaya, communism or some variation of the traditional Hindu culture, the relative importance of constitutional and revolutionary forms of struggle, the strategy of forming united fronts, and so on. In fact, none of the splits in the trade union movement was due to differences among leaders on purely bread and butter issues.

the income figure is not wholly reliable, but it, nevertheless, points to the direction in which unions have been moving.

Now coming to the first question, it is clear that the spread of unionism has been aided by legal protection. The institutional machinery created by the government for consulting union leaders and employers has indirectly lent the former a status of equality with the latter as well as given them opportunities of influencing labour policies by arguing the case of their constituents on merits, citing not infrequently the conventions and resolutions of the ILO, past promises of leaders and often relevant data. Moreover, some give-and-take is inherent in the nature of the consultation machinery. Its continuation, therefore, rests on each party gaining positive returns from time to time. If the government is keen on securing unions' cooperation in the implementation of five year plans, it has to give something in return; and, furthermore, this should be sufficiently important for union leaders to make their support worthwhile. We have found that some *quid pro quo* has been established between the government and union leaders.

However, it is not clear whether, on balance, its net effect on unionism has been positive or negative. On the positive side, unions and their leaders have gained some accretion of social prestige and consequently may find it easier to negotiate with employers. This brings them workers' support. On the other hand, the advantages secured by the leaders have not involved popular action, or unions as organisations and, so, may have loosened the organic bonds between the latter and workers. On balance, it is probable that the consultation machinery has strengthened union leaders, benefited workers, but weakened the trade union movement.

The development of the economy, on the other hand, has directly contributed to the increase in union membership and influence. Rising employment and membership are highly correlated. But, why has the latter gone up faster than the former? We have hypothesised that the spread of unionism has been aided by erosion of real earnings on the one hand and threats to job security on the other. The gradual acceptance of unionism as a vocation and as a lever for social and political advancement has also strengthened it.

Trade union movement in India has grown in depth as well as in breadth. Between 1949-50 and 1963-64 the total number of registered unions has gone up by more than three times, those submitting returns by almost fourfold, and the membership of the latter by more than two times. The degree of unionisation has grown from 24.5 per cent in 1951-52 to 40.3 per cent in 1963-64. The union movement has spread to all States. Although geographical concentration of union membership has declined, its State-wise distribution correlates remarkably well with industrialisation. The States of Maharashtra and West Bengal accounted in 1963 for 40.1 per cent of the total average daily employment under the Factories Act and 40.9 per cent of the total membership of workers' unions.

Union membership is spread over practically every industry, but due to non-comparability of classifications for a large number of industries the sectoral data on the degree of unionisation can be compiled only for ten major sectors and thirty-one sub-sectors. Among these, textile industry is probably the most and gins and presses the least unionised. A crude measure of the relative position of an industry is its "rank variation" defined as the difference between the highest and the lowest ranks reached by an industry during 1951-1963. A general observation of the data indicates that rank variability is the least in highly unionisable industries identified by economic and historical characteristics and *vice versa*.

The logical connection of erosion of real earnings and threat of retrenchment with unionism can now be spelled out. The acceleration of investment in the aggregate has caused a less than proportionate increase in employment and a considerable rise in prices. In the manufacturing sector, employment has lagged behind output thereby raising worker productivity. On the other hand, while earnings have risen prices have moved up even faster causing real wages in most industries to either stagnate or fall. This trend has been most noticeable since 1956. These have affected unionism in three ways. First, the social base for union formation and membership recruitment has grown. Second, the rise in productivity has provided leaders with an economically feasible demand for higher wages. Third, rising prices and stagnating real incomes have provided leaders with a convenient battle-front to organise workers and to fight for their rights. The demand for protection of real income has been further reinforced by the fact that an increasing proportion of workers is getting less than the average earnings of all workers in the manufacturing sector implying that the standard of living of the majority of workers has been progressively falling. These trends have provided the material basis of discontent and consequently of union growth.

The correlation analysis shows that while simple correlation coefficients of the degree of unionisation and the consumer price index and earnings are significant, that of productivity and earnings are not. But the values of partial correlation coefficients of the first and the third sets with the CPI eliminated are not significantly different from zero The most important determinant of earnings is the CPI with which in most cases the dearness allowance is related in one way or the other. Since the dearness allowance acts as an escalator on earnings, the latter rise with the CPI. Formally, as well as statistically, the degree of unionisation and the CPI are independent variables. Nevertheless, unions can claim some credit for securing for workers the principle of dearness allowance. However, it is also evident that under conditions of subsistence living there could be no significant difference of opinions among the government, employers, and unions on the question of dearness allowance. Without it, the real wages of the large majority of workers would undoubtedly fall, with inflation, to intolerable levels. This would have adversely affected production and profits and consequently would have been against the best interests of employers themselves. Nevertheless, it is one thing to win a principle, and quite another to get it implemented. There is no doubt that behind the latter has been the active voice of unions.

The statistical analysis also shows that the degree of unionisation is highly correlated with the CPI. This is interpreted to mean that inflation promotes unionism through disillusionment among workers caused primarily by rising earnings being neutralised by higher prices and secondarily by the growing differential between wages and productivity.

The disillusionment leads to protests and agitations, some-times resulting in conflicts, and generally in the strengthening of unions. Thus, through the medium of leaders agitating for workers' rights, the unions gain in membership and in-fluence. It is curious that as compared to the Western indus-trialised countries where unionism has allegedly contributed to secular inflation by imparting to it a permanent, asymme-trical cost-push bias, the relationship discovered in India is exactly the opposite. We have termed it the "reverse effect". To the extent the relationship is of a general nature the line of causation flows from inflation to unionism, and not the opposite. This is evidently an asymmetrical relationship because in periods of declining prices the degree of unionisa-tion may not fall, at any rate significantly. Nor can it be expected that there is no limit to the postulated effect. Like most social phenomena the effect of inflation upon unionism, too, may be true under some boundary conditions. What the latter are, we do not know.

It is probable that the "reverse effect" operates only at a certain stage of union development. In the Indian context this may be identified as the one that falls between the stage when the union movement has just emerged and is still strug-gling for survival and the stage of maturity. If the Indian trade unionism may view its maturing stage in the image of its counterpart in the U.K. and the U.S.A. and its first stage in the period preceding Independence, the middle stage is the one through which it is currently passing. This has been a period of rapid proliferation of unions, wider social acceptance, greater effectiveness in terms of results achieved but yet characterised by grave organisational weaknesses, particularly the lack of independence and self-reliance among a large body of unions.

Inflation and the fearsome threat of unemployment have induced defensive postures among workers. The union leaders looking for membership and support have found workers ready for battles to safeguard their family bread and jobs. The economic circumstances have created a demand for unions which the relatively fixed stock of leaders have tried to supply to the best possible extent. Unions are forged on a set of demands, and they gain strength through conflicts and consolidate themselves by performing numerous services to members.

The above analysis is supported by the data on conflicts and membership. The data on "workers' participation in conflicts" and "membership involvement ratio" are revealing. The former shows a decline indicating that strike is spreading to firms of smaller size and generally correlates with the rapid growth of small unions. The latter has been falling, and it has been interpreted to mean that the proportion of union members in conflicts has been going up. This is suggestive of increasing union membership following strikes and corroborates the statistical finding that the degree of unionisation is positively related to the CPI. This line of reasoning is further reinforced by the data on causes of conflicts. These show that conflicts related to earnings are by far the most important and have been on the rise. By contrast the proportion of conflicts related to job security has been on the decline. The latter trend may be due to the legal protection afforded to workers against arbitrary retrenchment and the efficacy of the conciliation machinery in settling disputes. The decline in conflicts caused by personnel matters does not imply that these have become less important to either workers or unions. Moreover, personnel factors generate mostly disputes rather than conflicts.

The trend in conflicts is upward and is explained partly by the economic stress the country has been passing through, particularly since 1956, but is not wholly explained by it. The data by causes merely summarise numerous factors, not all of which are articulated, into convenient categories. These are generally recognised as factors in disputes that are, under ideal conditions, amenable to negotiations and eventual settlement. However, mandays are lost by quite another set of causes. Following the Labour Bureau, these are termed as "political and sympathetic strikes". These include the phenomenon of *Bundh*—a token general strike confined to a predefined locality and called mainly to protest against some government policies or actions that has given rise to general public discontent. The data on these are separately published by the Labour Bureau since 1962. To these have been added an altogether new feature called *Gherao*. It literally means "to surround". Lately, workers have downed tools, but rarely in the whole factory, to surround a prechosen senior management executive and deny him all facilities including water, food, and toilet. The seige is not lifted until the police or a high government official, often a minister, intervenes to save the executive. It may be repeated if workers' demands remain unconceded. The mandays lost in such protest activities should be included in the conflicts data. However, so far no detailed statistics on *Gherao* have been published. Since it is a post-1967 general election development, it is unlikely that the data on it will be published before two years.

The regular conflicts data taken together with political and sympathetic strikes show a disturbing trend. The variability of the latter factor is revealed by the fact that in 1963 when the official series shows a drop, and caused general satisfaction in the government, it staged a big climb. Taking the period 1962-1964, for which complete data are available, it is significant that the four union centres are responsible for leading a large majority of strikes. The average for the three years is 72 per cent.

Since Independence, the principal method of the government to prevent work-stoppages has been to refer disputes to the industrial relations machinery. A large majority of disputes, particularly those relating to employment and personnel matters, are settled at the conciliation stage. A few go for adjudication. But in many instances the industrial relations machinery has not been able to preserve peace. The breakdown rate, *viz.*, the ratio of conflicts to the total of disputes referred to the industrial relations machinery, has varied from approximately 4 per cent to 7 per cent. This may be symptomatic of organisational fatigue of the industrial relations machinery, or a diminishing inclination of the parties concerned to have disputes resolved through it. The former explanation is highly probable due to the growth of legislation on substantive matters which have tended to drive disputes from the bipartite arena to the industrial relations machinery. The failure of industrial relations machinery may also be due to unexplored social causes that lie hidden beneath the smouldering labour unrest.

The importance of the industrial relations machinery in providing indirect protection to unions is clearly evident in the process of conflict termination.   By intervening in conflicts, referring them to adjudication, through mediation and conciliation, and generally reducing their duration, the industrial relations machinery has saved numerous unions from collapsing from exhaustion.   Moreover, the quasi-judicial mode of its working enables unions to win some of their demands on merits.   The high success rate of unions in conflicts, despite their acknowledged weakness, is largely due to the functioning of the industrial relations machinery. Paradoxically, this policy has made the industrial relations machinery an important prop of unions, particularly the weak ones, and thereby may be providing tacit encouragement to strike-prone unions and stubborn employers.   On balance, in the long run, it may weaken the habit of self-reliance among unions in dealing with employers and, thereby, cause a slow-down of their maturing process.

In view of the high-proneness of unions to call strikes, can it be said that the government has not been successful in its industrial relations policy from which is derived its subsidiary policy on trade unions?   In order to answer this question, let us recapitulate the principal development in its thinking and the responses of unions.

The main concern of the government has been with maintaining industrial peace and securing the concurrence of union leaders on national objectives and instruments of planning, and, in a larger context, on the principle of reciprocity between rights and obligations.   As such, it could not permit free interaction of labour and employers.   It should be noted that on this stand it was supported by many trade union leaders.   In fact, the official policy of the INTUC coincided remarkably well with that of the government. Only during the Giri period an attempt was made to reverse the priorities in respect of maintaining industrial peace and promoting a self-reliant unionism, but it failed and was acknowledged as such by Giri even before he resigned from the cabinet.

With the onset of the Second Five Year Plan, the old

policy was presented in new idioms. The legal framework, with traditional priorities, was retained, but through the instruments of voluntary codes it was sought to be both supplemented and reinforced. Through the devices of the Code of Discipline, Workers' Participation in Management, and Workers' Education, the government tried to increase unions' commitment to national objectives, as expressed in the Plan, and widen the area of agreement between labour and management. In this attempt the government initially received some encouragement from union leaders, particularly of the INTUC, but gradually the facade of consensus has worn thin and even the tentative gains of this approach have tended to wither away.

Viewed from the side of unionism, the voluntary approach, both in its early success and later failure, has exposed the precarious existence of union leaders who are caught between the conflicting loyalties to the high principles, to which they cannot possibly object, and to the commitment to workers which in practice militates against them. The one material gain has been the assumption of moral responsibility by the labour ministry to process labour grievances and reduce dilatoriness in the implementation of labour laws in public sector enterprises. Unions have also won new legal and political rights, particularly in relation to job security and equal participation in the process of wage determination through the tripartite wage boards, etc.

The government considers the trade union as the principal intermediary which because of its popular character can enable the government to reach workers, attend to their needs, retain support, and maintain discipline. But, by and large, union leaders do not view themselves or their organisations in this light. As representatives of workers they make demands on the employers and the government, launch struggles, and exert political pressure to back these demands, but are generally ready to settle honourable compromises. The dichotomy in expectations and the conflict in roles as viewed by the government and union leaders have been responsible for several paradoxes in the Indian situation. This is best brought out by the working of the Code of Discipline. What appeared to the government as a solemn pledge was considered by a large section of union leadership as a package deal that was either mutually binding or not binding at all. Even the INTUC has started showing an increasing strike-proneness. It only shows the general incompatibility of dual loyalties. No union that is truly representative in character can abandon the strike weapon in the face of growing militancy of workers and continued insecurity on retaining the recognised status. There is, therefore, an air of unreality about the government postures in regard to its policy on voluntary codes and conference resolutions.

This is not to deny that there has been cooperation between unions and the government. In a way both have sought to enlarge the scope of cooperation, but on their own terms. The government has somehow believed that agreement on a larger purpose will gradually filter down to the ranks of unions and condition their behaviour. This is a naive assumption. It is possible that the union leaders themselves have wished the government well, but the compulsions of economic stress and the necessity to retain workers' support in a highly competitive situation have proved more powerful.

The relationship between the government and unions is an odd mixture of cooperation and clashes of interests. The goal of socialism with the underlying emphasis on public sector has brought many union leaders closer to the government. But, sharing of common objectives does not necessarily lead to common action. Even the INTUC leadership is disillusioned with planning in India. By contrast, the AITUC leaders have moved nearer to the government without abandoning their opposition platform, and have tried to make maximum capital through the two-pillar policy of supporting some aspects of the plan on the one hand and criticising on the other those features with which their views are ideologically at variance.

The conflicts of interests between union leaders and the government on the difficult subject of wages and employment have generally impaired cooperation between the two. The former have persisted in the untenable demand for raising real wages alongside employment. The government has naturally asked unions not to press for the former while employment is going up and the threat to job security is being reduced.   On the wage question, the concern of the government has been mainly with the rationalisation of wage structure and introducing "payment by results".   The unions are not satisfied with just this much and would like the wage level to rise with the national income; or, at any rate, want that there should be no fall in real wages.

The tasks of trade union leaders in India are exceptionally hard.   Their personal interests probably lie in retaining the allegiance of workers and the support of the government with a view to protecting themselves from the hostility of employers and the encroachment of rival unions.   The total leadership resources are very scarce.   This gives them a position of importance in respect of the government as well as union members.   They must somehow maintain balance between the two and serve both.   But the necessity of serving two masters with clashing interests has produced the classic dilemma of Indian unionism : Whether or not to seek independence?   There is really no clear escape from it in the short run and the result is a paradox.   In theory the union leaders profess deep faith in self-reliant unionism, in negotiating with employers on their own strength and disciplining workers in the interest of higher production, but in practice they work through the government and its machinery in a manner that cannot but postpone the realisation of the basic goal.   Since it is not an immediate goal anyway, and the day-to-day work must somehow go on, there is no need for haste.   This has produced an extraordinary situation in which schemes proposed by the government, such as, joint management councils, which may clash with the organisational interests of unions, are, nevertheless, accepted by union leaders with outward acclaim.   In practice, many such schemes are reckoned to have failed due to the inexplicable apathy of the concerned parties.

For the future of unionism it is important that the paradoxes in which it is caught are resolved with the help of the government.   Moreover, it must augment its key resources in leadership, stable membership, and total organisational energy which in most cases is extremely scarce.   At present much of the time and energy of unions are wasted on the existential struggles against employers and rival unions. This is bound to obstruct the formation of second and third lines of leaders, growth of service functions and, maybe, even the sense of social responsibility that everyone desires. It is generally recognised that union security is the foundation on which the edifice of a strong, constructive, and healthy unionism can grow. But, for many unions in India this is still a distant goal and will probably remain so for many years to come unless, in the meantime, significant changes occur in government policy, management outlook, and union practices. It should be the concern of all parties to industrial relations that while unions' resources are augmented some of the fronts on which they are currently engaged in futile battles are permanently closed. In other words, unions should be enabled to concentrate on more vital tasks by abandoning some which merely fritter away their energies.

Despite numerous weaknesses, the trade union movement as a whole has sources of vitality. These deserve to be identified and strengthened. Some of them have been commonly observed. Due to the operation of autonomous factors, such as, growth in employment, increasing stability in the industrial labour force, spread of education and modern ideas, rise in the consciousness of workers' rights in the industry as well as in the community, and experience with the functioning of trade unions there has come into existence a professional cadre of trade unionists in the country. These are whole-time functionaries who are completely devoted to their work in trade unions and have learnt the job of organising a union as well as keeping themselves in power. Many of them are politicians in addition to being trade unionists. But their strength lies in trade unions. In their dual capacity, some of them may be playing an important role in keeping the party and unions together and it is necessary to realise that for most of them political life is inseparable from union activities. However, the former derives its significance from the latter. Probably few of them would leave union work for the sake of party; but fewer still would like to give up political life altogether were it to clash seriously with their union interest. Some of them are known to have changed their political affiliations; sometimes the switch is from an extreme left wing party to one in the centre. In the HMS there are leaders who have in the past changed party affiliations but have stuck to their unions and also to the political centre. Besides them, there are also trade union functionaries who do not have any formal party affiliations, All these leaders, and the unions led by them comprise the core of professional unionism in the country. These are relatively more stable, probably less insecure, and derive their principal strength from workers who by experience have realised the worth of a strong union. It is this core that needs to be strengthened. Gradually as this segment grows in size the entire union movement will become stronger.

THE NEED FOR FURTHER RESEARCH

The analysis of the interaction of trade unionism with the government policy leads to several questions on which the existing data can throw, at best, insufficient light. These relate to the characteristics of unionism, the possible measures of union strength, the process of decision-making in unions, the relationship between the centres and the locals and the two-way flow of influence, and other related matters. Indeed, the stock of knowledge on this vital subject is too small compared to the area of darkness. Research in unionism is needed not merely to satisfy scholarly curiosity but, for the more important purpose of influencing attitudes and shaping policy based on informed judgement. In India, trade unions and their activities are still surrounded by controversy, and rational thinking in respect of them is unduly hampered by prejudices and archaic beliefs. There is no other way of countering these except by accumulating and disseminating more knowledge. In this perspective, we now list some of the more important questions that merit priority in research.

1.   An important gap in the existing literature relates to knowledge about the evolution of particular unions, the role of leaders in the organising strategy of unions, the two-way

influence process between the union and the political party and inter-union relations in overlapping jurisdictions. Investigations of these questions will throw light on the boundary conditions of union growth as well as on the probable effectiveness of agitational methods in enrolling new members and retaining their loyalties in situations characterised by inter-union rivalry.

2.   A related question with which we have grappled in the course of the present work is to determine with approximate accuracy a measure of union strength. This problem is particularly serious in India due to the varying interpretations of the purpose of unions in a developing economy advanced by union leaders themselves as well as the government. The INTUC leaders insist on some quality criteria, such as, allegiance to constitutional methods, cooperative relationship with employers, and loyalty to the country. On the other hand, for the AITUC leaders none of these criteria is at all relevant. It is struggle all the way until the communist ideology triumphs. In the thinking of the government an effective union is one that represents the majority of workers, disciplines and educates them and cooperates with management for raising output, productivity, and endeavours to maintain industrial harmony at all times. Now, it is obvious that none of these approaches is satisfactory. Instead of judging the effectiveness of a union on the normative criteria of behaviour laid down by outsiders, it is much better to find out positivist indicators of union strength. It has to be related to immediate or short-term goals which the union attempted to realise rather than to some ultimate purpose.

3.   A related question is : What are the characteristics of employers and unions in industries where unions have matured to the point of developing and maintaining service functions for members? These may take the form of union-sponsored cooperative societies of various kinds, active collaboration with management in building houses for workers, and expanding educational and training facilities for workers, etc. Is it possible that the growth of a union and its stability are highly correlated with the size and profitability of a firm? In the American context, Harold M. Levinson has advanced a proposition that has relevance to

India. He says that, "the greater the degree of concentration in an industry, the greater will be the union's ability to maintain a high degree of organisational strength and consequently the greater will be its rate of increase in wages".[2] This merits testing.

4.   It is common practice in India for the government to convene tripartite conferences at the apex level and secure consensus on important policy matters. We have adduced reasons for the union leaders lending their support to such decisions. For the government this procedure is of sufficient importance to consider measures that will strengthen the all-India organisations of employers and workers. Evidently, it hopes that somehow the participating organisations will acquire sufficient power over their constituents to be able to apply sanctions against the ones that have wilfully violated decisions to which these have been parties. In the case of unions this expectation raises two questions: (i) Can an apex organisation, such as the INTUC, the AITUC, the HMS, and the UTUC, that relies on the financial support from the constituent unions for its continued existence at all take disciplinary action and enforce it? Moreover, even if it has the ability, will it do so particularly if the recalcitrant member is a powerful one? If answers to these questions are in the negative, then the question arises: (ii) What should the government do to involve unions in the essential nation-building activities where the outcome is significantly dependent upon their cooperation? Quite obviously the stakes are too high for the government trying to either ignore or suppress unions, and as such a suitable method must be found. It may be hoped that researches will disclose that unions that can effectively cooperate with the government are the ones that enjoy the majority support, negotiate with managements, and generally rely on their own strength rather than the adjudication machinery for settling industrial disputes. On the other hand, unions that offer the highest cooperation but can deliver the least results

2. Harold M. Levinson, "Unionism, Concentration, and Wage Changes: Toward a Unified Theory", *Industrial and Labor Relations Review*, Vol. 20, No. 2, January 1967, pp. 204-205.

are the ones that are weak, insecure, lean on others and are not in a position to discipline workers. It may also be found that the former kind of unions exist mainly in industries that are managed by farsighted and responsible business leaders. This will no doubt put the issue of tripartite cooperation in relation to planning for development in a better perspective and suitable policies and methods can accordingly be structured to subserve the basic purpose.

5.   One of the important functions of unions in India has been to demand legislation in the interest of workers. It is, however, possible to argue that with growth in legislation the role of unions is bound to decline to mere law-enforcing agencies. For instance, on a substantive matter, such as, annual bonus, a company may conform to the letter of the law and yet may leave workers terribly dissatisfied. What does a union do then? It may call a strike and force the referral of dispute to adjudication. In such cases, the law, unions, conflicts, and adjudication become inextricably enmeshed with no hope of retrieve. The answer may be found either in going on with still more legislation and extended litigation that may result in the enunciation of judicial principles on the basis of which industrial tribunals may give awards, or in freezing the legislation at the current level and let collective bargaining do the rest.

A decision on this matter would be required since it is linked with another question : Against whom do the workers organise: is it the employers or the government or both? Who threatens the unions' solidarity most? Selected case studies may throw light on the process through which claims made against employers are gradually transformed into political demands on the government. What is, therefore, needed is a structure of protests mapped for magnitude, impact and revolutionary potential.[3] Workers' protests are acquiring new forms. Is there any relationship of the forms of protest with the state of union development on the one hard, and the nature of industrial relations in diffe-

---

3. See in this connection, Abraham J. Siegel, "Method and Substance in Theorizing about Workers' Protests" in National Bureau of Economic Research, *Aspects of Labour Economics*, Princeton, Princeton University Press, 1962.

rent regions and industries on the other?   Moreover, what happens to each of these categories when the government's conduct of the law and order function is deliberately modified in favour of workers?

SETTING A NEW GOAL

In view of the state of trade unionism in India as summed up above, what should be the goal of government policy. The principal reasons for asking this question in respect of the government rather than the managements and the unions are two : (i) In India there has been a government policy that has played an important role in shaping the course of trade union development. Moreover, if the government can lay down a new goal for trade unions, formulate suitable policies that find general acceptance at the Centre as well as in the States, in the employing ministries no less than in the labour ministry, it can also influence the working of trade unions and the attitudes of managements. Once the much needed reorientation in government thinking has occurred, and gets widely known, the other parties will gradually adjust themselves to the new milieu. (ii) For managements and trade union leaders the problem of setting new goals and structuring methods of working that are rationally derived from them is somewhat more complicated and involves a different approach. Not only the numbers involved are very large but the outlooks of managements and unions are greatly determined by their respective experiences, industrial conditions, and philosophies. In this context, the problem of goal-setting is essentially an educational one. It is a laborious and time-consuming process which is, nonetheless, as desirable as it is effective. However, the success of such efforts as may be required to serve this purpose is crucially dependent upon the change in the *milieu* that the revised thinking in the government will bring about. The latter will validate the former, so to say, in a manner that a large number of courses and seminars cannot.

The new goals of policy must meet two important criteria. First, these should be fully consistent with the spirit of the Constitution. It probably needs no emphasising that the trade union policy should be in harmony with the democratic system of government and the widely upheld purpose of extending it to the functioning of society. Second, as far as possible these should be reconciled with the developmental objectives of the government. Ideally one goal should not be at cross-purposes with the other.

The basic goal towards which we would like the government policy to be reoriented is the development of professionalism within the existing framework of trade union movement which at present comprises political centres, coalition unions, and truly independent unions. In addition to these, there may also be company unions which are formally constituted of worker-members but in effect are no more than appendages of management structures. The goal is not to work against political influence, whether or not desirable, favour one kind of philosophy as against others, seek to abolish outside leadership gradually or otherwise and to give protection to weak and strong unions alike. These are essentially negative purposes. Instead, the government should affirm a positive purpose and devote its energies to achieving it.

The experience in this country so far has demonstrated that it is possible neither to eliminate the political factor in the trade union movement nor to maintain agreeable peace among the contending centres. The first cannot be achieved within the framework of the Constitution. The second is predicated on the first, and so, depending upon the policies of the centres, may or may not be attained even for temporary periods. It is, therefore, necessary to strive towards the goal of professional trade unionism within as well as outside political centres and through the existing leadership. While much has been said against them, it can be definitely said in their favour that they have served the cause of trade unionism with dedication and zeal and have come to possess sophistication, expertise and experience that should count as assets of great value. It is in the interest of the country in general, and of the trade union movement in particular, that the positive aspects of the present leadership should be utilised in full.

The goal of professional trade unionism will not be found

inimical by the present leadership because this does not threaten them directly nor the political philosophies in which they may believe. In fact, it coincides remarkably well with their organisational goals, *viz.*, to train up second and third line leaders in the unions they lead. However, it is possible that there may be suspicion and distrust in some quarters which with perseverance can be allayed and overcome.

Professional trade unionism is consistent with democracy not only in respect of the functioning of the political superstructure but also in the deeper sense of building a network of people's institutions that comprise its real bastion. It has three essential features. First, these are democratic organs of workers whose primary function is to regulate employers. Second, unions to be effective must eliminate, as far as possible, the bargaining power of individual workers and indiscipline in their ranks. To this extent these also operate as worker-regulating devices. Third, for the sake of workers' solidarity and the efficacy of union organisation these instinctively side with forces working for natural and social justice and other progressive ideals. Because of these characteristics trade unions led by professionals are a positive factor in a democratic society. This is also because trade unionism is egalitarian and forward looking on the one hand and disciplinarian and law-enforcer on the other.[4]

Professional trade unions are also likely to better appreciate the problems of industry and the economy. Rational leaders set achievable goals and they can be expected to be pragmatic on the use of tactics. There are union goals that can be conceded without involving the managements concerned, or the country as a whole, to any economic cost whatsoever; and there are economic policies that will not probably invoke negative union responses. Among the former are demands related to union security and the individual worker's right to natural justice. Among the latter are fiscal and monetary policies that are designed to develop the economy without unleashing unbearable inflation. Unwise economic policies have a far greater potential of upsetting industrial relations

4. E. Wight Bakke, *Mutual Survival, The Goal of Unions and Management*, New York, Harper & Brothers, 1946, pp. 1-18 and pp. 79-82.

than all the irresponsible trade union leaders put together.

The assumptions upon which the policy of developing professional trade unionism rests are basically three. These are :

1.   The socio-economic system remains stable and viable. It is clear that if the economy does not grow at a satisfactory rate or the political system develops fissures or internal instability, this policy is unlikely to be put into practice. Professional trade unionism can grow in India provided the environment is favourable and the government can take practical steps on the basis of stable expectations.

2.   This goal finds wide support in the party in power, in the opposition parties, and within the government. In order that this goal is genuinely accepted and not merely formally endorsed, it should be routed through the democratic process of free discussion.

3.   The goal of professional trade unionism should be accepted, again, through the democratic process by large segments of trade union leadership and managements. These are the principal parties to industrial relations and should be able to develop positive attitudes towards it. The change in attitudes is in itself a democratising process and can be accelerated by active participation of interested outsiders, *viz.*, educators, researchers, journalists, lawyers, etc.

INSTRUMENTS OF POLICY

The goal of promoting professionalism among trade unions can be achieved by effective coordination of four policy instruments. These are : (*i*) legislation, (*ii*) administration, (*iii*) political persuasion, and (*iv*) workers' education. The functions of each of these instruments may be briefly discussed.

The function of legislation is to establish create rights and obligations for managements, workers, and trade unions and it is the responsibility of the government to enforce them. The trend of legislation, so far, has been to impose liabilities upon employers, restrict their powers and prerogatives, and provide for adjudication of mutual rights and obligations. The government has constituted a National Commission on

Labour with wide terms of reference.[5] We suggest that the Commission should also concern itself with those aspects of labour statute which can be suitably amended with the purpose of strengthening trade unions and promoting bipartite industrial relations without either impairing or restricting the existing rights and benefits that have been statutorily made available to workers or increasing the obligations of employers.

In our view the law would need to be amended in significant respects. These may relate to issues as wide as the definition of "industrial dispute", the procedure for the formation of works committees, and as narrow as the provision that a public utility will be notified only on due inquiry and will include reasons that should be justiciable. The Commission may also examine the feasibility of implementing, though belatedly, the Indian Trade Unions (Amendment) Act, 1947. Indeed, the Act may require further amendment to provide for contingencies where more than one union may be recognised for bargaining purposes and the rights of unrecognised unions. Similarly, the possibility of making a statutory provision for voluntary check-off may also be explored. Furthermore, the Commission may consider the desirability of amending the Industrial Employment (Standing Orders) Act, 1946, to incorporate the principle that in undertakings where a recognised union with bargaining power exists the framing of standing orders and their revision are subject to bipartite settlement which, once mutually agreed upon, may be registered with the labour commissioner's office without the necessity of formal certification. In this context the Commission might consider suggesting amendments to the Industrial Disputes Act that will provide for a procedure for the opening of bipartite negotiations, notice periods for the revocation and renewal of collective agreements, the legal sanction behind them, their jurisdiction and the settlement of jurisdictional disputes and related matters. An enabling provision for arbitration with binding awards may also be considered to cover disputes on the interpretation

. See the Resolution of the Government of India as reproduced in *Indian Journal of Industrial Relations*, Vol. 2, No. 3, January 1967, pp. 408-409.

of agreements.

It is evident that the purpose of promoting professional trade unionism cannot be adequately served by legislation alone. However, the government can implement its policy better if it forms part of the statute. In any event, legislation merely declares an intent; it is for the administration to carry it out. Labour administration in India is generally well-staffed and has acquired considerable experience in handling industrial disputes. It has not been above reproach, and in several States the charge of favouritism has been openly levelled against it. It is important that personnel charged with the responsibility of implementing the labour policy should endeavour to rise above partisanship and carry out their tasks fairly and efficiently. There is no reason to believe that once the political arm of the government is keen on carrying out the new policy, and the environment in the country is favourable towards it, the administration will not rise to the occasion.

The role of the government in persuading employers and union leaders is the key to the success of this policy. Indeed, this task commences even before the laws have been amended and continues until the underlying philosophy has found wide acceptance. The government has been performing this function for nearly two and a half decades in the tripartite conferences and committees. This process may not be merely continued but be carried in depth to factories and unions at the grassroots. This task is not as easy as it may sound. The experience hitherto, particularly since 1957, amply demonstrates that the persuasion function has to be carried at four levels, *viz.*, (*i*) employing ministries in the government, (*ii*) State governments, (*iii*) employers, and (*iv*) union leaders. It may be expected that the policy will face resistance at each level. It is also clear that until the policy has been effectively sold at all the four levels, the results will fall short of expectations. To this, unfortunately, there are no short-cuts. It is, thus, possible that several years will elapse in the development of the principal building blocks on which the policy is structured, in securing wide acceptance of the goal as well as the means and its general implementation.

The fourth function, *i.e.*, workers' education, is probably only next in importance to legislation for the success of the policy. In this context the government should consider practical steps for reorienting the present workers' education programme and the feasibility of letting trade unions do a part of the job. The latter aspect is tied up with the principle of accountability for public funds and the responsibility of the government to ensure that the funds will be funnelled into trade unions for *bona fide* reasons and will be spent for the intended purpose only. This aspect is rather important because lapses in this regard will engender grave risks to the future development of trade union movement. First, the risk of political abuse of public monies in the form of personal patronage and partisan support to the favoured unions will increase manifold. Second, if it is possible to safeguard against the first risk by elaborate rules and procedures, there is the danger of unions getting irretrievably enmeshed in the bureaucratic swamp. Instead of promoting professionalism such a development would actually tend to defeat it. It, therefore, appears that on balance the risks are too great and consequently not worth taking. The demand of the INTUC leaders to conduct the workers' education programme with the aid of government money should be viewed in this context. The government should not accede to this demand.

The purport of the above passage is not to deny that in ideal circumstances trade unions would be most suited to plan and implement the scheme of workers' education but rather to argue against their use of public funds for this purpose. The fact remains, however, that the present circumstances are far from ideal and, furthermore, that, if left to unions themselves, the scheme is unlikely to go very far. The government might, therefore, consider the feasibility of persuading the universities, some post-graduate colleges, and the leading educational and research institutions in the country to participate in this venture and seek grants-in-aid for the purpose. For coordinating their work, maintaining standards, integrity and fairness in selection, teaching and evaluation of worker-students, an all-India committee of experts may be constituted. This may consist of all the interest groups that are deeply involved in the success of the programme. These groups are: (*i*) unions of all shades of political opinion, (ii) employers in the public and private sectors, (iii) Central and State governments, and (iv) educationists. The principal advantage of letting the universities implement this programme is that they are likely to be more free from political pressures emanating from any interest group than any other party. The participation of unions and employers at the policy level will be the best guarantee that the programme will not be divorced from reality and that its purpose will be kept constantly in view. There will also be a side advantage in taking the workers' education scheme to the universities and colleges. So far these have taken little interest in this idea. Nevertheless, in the interest of the country, men of learning should be given an opportunity of purposive involvement in an important nation-building activity. It will enable them to shed their isolation and apply their concepts and tools to a real life problem. In the long run the results may be expected to be mutually beneficial.

APPENDIX

TABLE

Union Membership, Average Daily Employment and Degree

Industry Code No.	Industry	1951		
		A	B	C
0.1	Plantations	113	1236	9.1
0.2	Gins & Presses	1	131	0.8
1.	Mining and Quarrying	133	549	24.2
2.0-2.2	Food, Beverages and Tabacco	123	588	20.9
2.3	Textiles	349	1119	31.2
2.5-2.6	Wood, Cork & Furniture & Fixtures ..	3	37	8.1
2.7	Paper and Paper Products	7	27	25.9
2.8	Printing, Publishing & Allied Industries	30	79	38.0
2.9	Leather & Leather Products except Footwear	4	18	22.2
3.0	Rubber & Rubber Products	5	24	20.8
3.1	Chemicals & Chemical Products ..	31	90	34.4
3.2-3.3	Non-metallic Mineral Products including Products of Petroleum and Coal ..	23	162	14.2
3.4	Basic Metal Industries	76	102	74.5
3.5	Manufacture of Metal Products ..	10	62	16.1
3.6	Manufacture of Machinery	11	107	10.3
3.7	Manufacture of Electrical Machinery, Apparatus, Appliances and Supplies ..	3	32	9.4
3.8	Transport Equipment	1	207	0.5
7.2	Railways	407	923	44.1
7.6	Posts & Telegraphs	64	193	33.2

Notes: A=Workers' Union Membership ('000)
        B=Average Daily Employment ('000)
        C=Degree of Unionisation (%)

of Unionisation in Selected Industries (1951-52—1963-64)

1952			1953			1954		
A	B	C	A	B	C	A	B	C
165	1245	13.3	194	1175	16.5	237	1215	19.5
1	127	0.8	..	132	..	1	142	0.7
147	559	26.3	188	594	31.6	205	568	36.1
150	541	27.7	163	536	30.4	200	574	34.8
470	1182	39.8	442	1166	37.9	455	1172	38.8
4	41	9.8	5	37	13.5	5	39	12.8
8	28	28.6	11	26	42.3	8	29	27.6
27	79	34.2	27	74	36.5	26	80	32.5
8	18	44.4	9	21	42.9	9	20	45.0
6	24	25.0	7	24	29.2	9	26	34.6
38	89	42.7	44	90	48.9	37	94	39.4
37	158	23.4	38	153	24.8	49	132	37.1
55	101	54.5	50	92	54.3	58	94	61.7
11	66	16.6	17	58	29.3	17	59	28.8
14	96	14.6	16	92	17.4	20	95	21.1
4	31	12.9	6	29	20.7	5	31	16.1
7	228	3.1	2	231	0.9	4	242	1.7
366	932	39.3	159	931	17.1	190	965	19.7
64	212	30.2	64	236	27.1	3	242	1.2

(Continued)

TABLE

Industry Code No.	Industry	1955		
		A	B	C
0.1	Plantations	311	1250	24.9
0.2	Gins & Presses	1	149	0.7
1.	Mining and Quarrying	198	591	33.5
2.0-2.2	Food, Beverages & Tobacco	211	590	35.8
2.3	Textiles	418	1177	35.5
2.5-2.6	Wood, Cork & Furniture & Fixtures ..	7	42	16.7
2.7	Paper & Paper Products	8	30	26.7
2.8	Printing, Publishing & Allied Industries	34	82	41.5
2.9	Leather & Leather Products except Footwear	12	20	60.0
3.0	Rubber & Rubber Products	4	27	14.8
3.1	Chemicals & Chemical Products ..	35	102	34.3
3.2-3.3	Non-metallic Mineral Products including Products of Petroleum and Coal ..	53	139	38.1
3.4	Basic Metal Industries	67	103	65.0
3.5	Manufacture of Metal Products ..	20	66	30.3
3.6	Manufacture of Machinery	23	107	21.5
3.7	Manufacture of Electrical Machinery, Apparatus, Appliances & Supplies ..	7	34	20.6
3.8	Transport Equipment	8	245	3.3
7.2	Railways	205	990	20.7
7.6	Posts & Telegraphs	35	262	13.4

Notes: A=Workers' Union Membership ('000)
B=Average Daily Employment ('000)
C=Degree of Unionisation (%)

1 (Contd.)

1956			1957			1958		
A	B	C	A	B	C	A	B	C
266	1294	20.6	279	1274	21.9	497	1260	39.4
1	110	0.9	1	164	0.6	1	125	0.8
257	629	40.9	242	655	36.9	308	649	47.5
248	504	49.2	292	560	52.1	325	567	57.3
441	1134	38.9	538	1153	46.7	643	1098	58.6
7	30	23.3	12	40	30.0	16	45	35.6
9	28	32.1	16	29	55.2	19	35	54.3
44	77	57.1	44	81	54.3	47	87	54.0
10	20	50.0	8	19	42.1	15	18	83.3
3	26	11.5	12	29	41.4	7	30	23.3
40	87	46.0	53	94	56.4	46	109	42.2
53	121	43.8	68	145	46.9	64	157	40.7
61	103	59.2	92	110	83.6	111	130	85.4
21	70	30.0	39	78	50.0	25	95	26.3
27	114	23.7	29	128	22.7	63	133	47.4
18	34	52.9	11	40	27.5	6	43	14.0
9	228	3.9	10	251	4.0	16	275	5.8
123	1031	11.9	264	1063	24.8	333	1119	29.8
50	282	17.7	40	287	13.9	34	309	11.0

(Continued)

Industry Code No.	Industry	1959			1960		
		A	B	C	A	B	C
0.1	Plantations	490	1269	38.6	486	1223	39.7
0.2	Gins & Presses	1	162	0.6	1	157	0.6
1.	Mining & Quarrying ..	312	618	50.5	313	652	48.0
2.0- 2.2	Food, Beverages & Tobacco	299	575	52.0	343	610	56.2
2.3	Textiles	756	1101	68.7	655	1128	58.1
2.5- 2.6	Wood, Cork & Furniture & Fixtures	14	50	28.0	14	52	26.9
2.7	Paper & Paper Products ..	19	35	54.3	20	39	51.3
2.8	Printing, Publishing & Allied Industries	50	87	57.5	49	92	53.3
2.9	Leather & Leather Products except Footwear	20	20	100.0	16	19	84.2
3.0	Rubber & Rubber Products	12	31	38.7	12	35	34.3
3.1	Chemicals & Chemical Products	57	118	48.3	66	125	52.8
3.2- 3.3	Non-metallic Mineral Products including Products of Petroleum and Coal ..	78	169	46.2	92	182	50.5
3.4	Basic Metal Industries ..	171	135	126.7	147	148	99.3
3.5	Manufacture of Metal Products	39	98	39.8	50	111	45.0
3.6	Manufacture of Machinery	64	141	45.4	61	169	36.1
3.7	Manufacture of Electrical Machinery, Apparatus, Appliances & Supplies ..	17	55	30.9	24	67	35.8
3.8	Transport Equipment ..	19	299	6.4	32	292	11.0
7.2	Railways	328	1155	28.4	527	1160	45.4
7.6	Posts & Telegraphs ..	54	328	16.5	42	354	11.9

Notes: A=Workers' Union Membership ('000)
B=Average Daily Employment ('000)
C=Degree of Unionisation (%)

Sources: (i) Indian Labour Gazette, Vol. XV, July-June 1958, pp. 906-941.
(ii) Indian Labour Year Book, 1951-52, p. 154 and 1952-53, pp. 153-154.

1 (*Contd.*)

	1961			1962			1963	
A	B	C	A	B	C	A	B	C
348	1210	28.8	159	1183	13.4	181	1132	15.9
- 1	150	0.6	..	150	..	2	155	1.9
308	671	45.9	355	684	51.9	360	698	51.6
278	739	37.6	316	754	42.0	328	765	43.1
597	1206	49.5	586	1236	47.6	627	1272	49.4
15	40	21.7	14	75	18.7	10	87	11.5
22	42	52.4	22	47	46.8	21	49	42.9
47	95	43.1	51	111	45.9	45	115	39.1
17	20	85.0	15	22	68.2	25	26	96.1
12	39	30.8	20	44	45.5	24	49	43.2
74	146	50.7	68	157	43.3	76	176	43.9
103	186	48.8	105	222	47.3	104	237	49.5
152	178	85.4	123	194	63.4	133	230	57.8
67	135	49.6	63	151	41.7	68	176	38.6
70	215	32.6	80	235	34.0	70	258	27.1
26	87	29.9	35	107	30.6	37	122	30.3
58	358	16.2	90	377	23.9	52	404	12.9
561	1163	48.2	281	1180	23.8	424	1216	34.9
37	373	9.9	46	387	11.9	52	427	12.2

(*iii*) *Indian Labour Statistics*: (*a*) 1959, pp. 14-20; 28; 86-91, (*b*) 1963, pp. 24-25 & 99, (*c*) 1964, pp. 28-29; 30; 32-33 & 95-100, (*d*) 1965, pp. 32-33, (*e*) 1966, pp. 32-33; 36; 38-39 & 105-116.

Average Annual Money Earnings of Factory Workers earning

Industry Code No.	Industry	All India Average Annual	
		1951 Rs. 1036.0	1952 Rs. 1112.0
0.2	Gins & Presses		185
2.0-2.2	Food, Beverages & Tobacco ..	..	598
2.3	Textiles	1044	1122
2.5-2.6	Wood, Cork & Furniture & Fixtures	797	751
2.7	Paper & Paper Products	958	1019
2.8	Printing, Publishing & Allied Industries	1053	1156
2.9	Leather & Leather Products.. ..	752	719
3.0	Rubber & Rubber Products ..	1525	1340
3.1	Chemicals & Chemical Products ..	868	974
3.2	Products of Petroleum & Coal ..	1132	1157
3.3	Non-metallic Mineral Products (Excluding Products of Petroleum & Coal)	699	696
3.4	Basic Metal Industries	1366	1533
3.5	Metal Products (Excluding Machinery & Transport Equipment)	917	991
3.6	Machinery (Excluding Electrical)	998	1030
3.7	Electrical Machinery, Appliances & Apparatus	1238	1296
3.8	Transport Equipment	1171	1671

2

less than Rs. 200 per month by Selected Industries (1951-1964)

		Earnings for all Industries		
1953 Rs. 1111.0	1954 Rs. 1111.0	1955 Rs. 1174.0	1956 Rs. 1187.0	1957 Rs. 1234.0
170	189	157	211	195
623	624	620	652	692
1116	1090	1191	1306	1243
800	858	676	739	843
998	948	1063	1036	1158
1123	1214	1152	1189	1218
879	815	837	757	890
1432	1336	1368	1502	1497
1036	1021	957	981	1147
1408	1340	1493	1686	1990
824	740	782	833	835
1711	1613	1673	1483	1463
942	1025	1048	1120	1145
1032	1118	1100	1136	1189
1309	1275	1340	1314	1438
1164	1392	1430	1473	1482

(*Continued*)

TABLE

Industry Code No.	Industry	All India Average Annual	
		1958 Rs. 1285.0	1959 Rs. 1310.0
0.2	Gins & Presses	197	203
2.0-2.2	Food, Beverages & Tobacco ..	686	767
2.3	Textiles	1306	1405
2.5-2.6	Wood, Cork & Furniture & Fixtures	814	837
2.7	Paper & Paper Products	1226	1276
2.8	Printing, Publishing & Allied Industries	1210	1316
2.9	Leather & Leather Products.. ..	1118	1045
3.0	Rubber & Rubber Products ..	1326	1274
3.1	Chemicals & Chemical Products ..	1308	1367
3.2	Products of Petroleum & Coal ..	1850	2195
3.3	Non-metallic Mineral Products (Excluding Products of Petroleum & Coal)	885	920
3.4	Basic Metal Industries	1557	1529
3.5	Metal Products (Excluding Machinery & Transport Equipment)	1186	1253
3.6	Machinery (Excluding Electrical) ..	1322	1216
3.7	Electrical Machinery, Appliances & Apparatus	1470	1490
3.8	Transport Equipment	1458	1473

Sources: (i) *Statistical Abstract of India*, 1952-53.
 (ii) *Indian Labour Statistics*, 1961, p. 50.
 (iii) *Indian Labour Statistics*, 1964, p. 44.
 (iv) *Indian Labour Statistics*, 1966, p. 59.
 (v) *Indian Labour Statistics*, 1965, 1966, pp. 50 & 50 respectively.

2 *(Contd.)*

	Earnings for all Industries			
1960 Rs. 1385.0	1961 Rs. 1417.0	1962 Rs. 1459.0	1963 Rs. 1433.0	1964 Rs. 1528.0
207	227	245	260	278
776	876	750	755	808
1405	1491	1574	1572	1669
945	996	1007	1115	1157
1294	1254	1209	1598	1620
1226	1326	1365	1342	1347
944	1180	1140	1289	1470
1414	1542	1403	1488	1517
1334	1449	1452	1579	1590
2042	1855	1876	1969	1767
1008	1020	994	1022	1077
1499	1814	1566	1522	1445
1304	1323	1360	1324	1335
1228	1330	1418	1382	1401
1435	1496	1467	1483	1452
1422	1547	1552	1621	1874

For All India Average Annual Earnings of all industries

(*i*) *Indian Labour Statistics*, 1961 and 1964, pp. 51-52 and 38-39 respectively.

(*ii*) *Indian Labour Statistics*, 1966, p. 47 (computed).

TABLE

Trends in Industries (earning less than Rs. 200 per month) whose Average for All Industries (1951-1964)

Industry Code No.	Industry	Average Annual Money			
		1951		1952	
		1036	A	1111	A
0.2	Gins & Presses	155	—	185	—
2.0-2.2	Food, Beverages & Tobacco ..	614	—	598	—
2.3	Textiles	1044	+	1122	+
2.5-2.6	Wood, Cork & Furniture & Fixtures	797	—	751	—
2.7	Paper & Paper Products	958	—	1019	—
2.8	Printing, Publishing & Allied Industries	1053	+	1156	+
2.9	Leather & Leather Products.. ..	752	—	719	—
3.0	Rubber & Rubber Products ..	1525	+	1340	+
3.1	Chemicals & Chemical Products ..	868	—	974	—
3.2	Products of Petroleum & Coal ..	1132	+	1157	+
3.3	Non-metallic Mineral Products (Excluding Products of Petroleum & Coal)	699	—	696	—
3.4	Basic Metal Industries	1366	+	1533	+
3.5	Metal Products (Excluding Machinery & Transport Equipment) ..	917	—	991	—
3.6	Machinery (Excluding Electrical) ..	998	—	1030	—
3.7	Electrical Machinery, Appliances, Apparatus, etc.	1238	+	1296	+
3.8	Transport Equipment	1171	+	1671	+

Notes: $A = \begin{cases} \text{Higher } (+) \\ \text{or} \\ \text{Lower } (-) \end{cases}$

3

Annual Money Earnings are Higher or Lower than the Average Annual Income

(in rupees)

Earnings for all Industries							
1953		1954		1955		1956	
1111	A	1111	A	1174	A	1187	A
170	—	189	—	157	—	211	—
623	—	624	—	620	—	652	—
1116	+	1090	—	1191	+	1306	+
800	—	858	—	676	—	739	—
998	—	948	—	1063	—	1036	—
1123	+	1214	+	1152	—	1189	+
879	—	815	—	837	—	757	—
1432	+	1336	+	1368	+	1502	+
1036	—	1021	—	957	—	981	—
1408	+	1340	+	1493	+	1686	+
824	—	740	—	782	—	833	—
1711	+	1613	+	1673	+	1483	+
942	—	1025	—	1048	—	1120	—
1032	—	1118	+	1100	—	1136	—
1309	+	1275	+	1340	+	1314	+
1164	+	1392	+	1430	+	1473	+

(Continued)

Industry Code No.	Industry	Average Annual Money			
		1957		1958	
		1234	A	1285	A
0.2	Gins & Presses	195	—	197	—
2.0-2.2	Food, Beverages & Tobacco	692	—	686	—
2.3	Textiles	1243	+	1306	+
2.5-2.6	Wood, Cork & Furniture & Fixtures	843	—	814	—
2.7	Paper and Paper Products	1158	—	1226	—
2.8	Printing, Publishing & Allied Industries	1218	—	1210	—
2.9	Leather & Leather Products	890	—	1118	—
3.0	Rubber & Rubber Products	1497	+	1326	+
3.1	Chemicals & Chemical Products	1147	—	1308	+
3.2	Products of Petroleum & Coal	1990	+	1850	+
3.3	Non-metallic Mineral Products (Excluding Products of Petroleum & Coal)	835	—	885	—
3.4	Basic Metal Industries	1463	+	1557	+
3.5	Metal Products (Excluding Machinery & Transport Equipment)	1145	—	1186	—
3.6	Machinery (Excluding Electrical)	1189	—	1322	+
3.7	Electrical Machinery, Appliances, Apparatus, etc.	1438	+	1470	+
3.8	Transport Equipment	1482	+	1458	+

Notes : $A = \begin{cases} \text{Higher } (+) \\ \text{or} \\ \text{Lower } (-) \end{cases}$

3 (Contd.)

Earnings for all Industries											
1959		1960		1961		1962		1963		1964	
1310	A	1385	A	1417	A	1459	A	1433	A	1528	A
203	—	207	—	227	—	245	—	260	—	278	—
767	—	776	—	876	—	750	—	755	—	808	—
1405	+	1405	+	1491	+	1574	+	1572	+	1669	+
837	—	945	—	996	—	1007	—	1115	—	1157	—
1276	—	1294	+	1254	—	1209	—	1598	+	1620	+
1316	+	1226	+	1326	—	1365	—	1342	—	1347	—
1045	—	944	—	1180	—	1140	—	1289	—	1470	—
1274	—	1414	+	1542	+	1403	—	1488	+	1517	—
1367	+	1334	—	1449	+	1452	+	1579	+	1590	+
2195	+	2042	+	1855	+	1876	+	1969	+	1767	+
920	—	1008	—	1020	—	994	—	1022	—	1077	—
1529	+	1499	+	1814	+	1566	+	1552	+	1445	—
1253	—	1304	—	1323	—	1360	—	1324	—	1335	—
1216	—	1228	—	1330	—	1418	—	1382	—	1401	—
1490	+	1435	+	1496	+	1467	+	1483	+	1452	—
1473	+	1422	+	1547	+	1552	+	1621	+	1674	+

Sources:

(i) *Indian Labour Statistics*, 1961, p. 50.

(ii) *Indian Labour Statistics*, 1964, p. 44.

(iii) *Indian Labour Statistics*, 1966, p. 59.

For All-India Average Annual Earnings of all Industries

(i) *Indian Labour Statistics*, 1961 and 1964, pp. 51-52 and 38-39 respectively.

(ii) *Indian Labour Statistics*, 1966, pp. 50-51 (computed for 1963).

TABLE

Trends in Average Annual Money Earnings of Factory Workers

Industry Code No.	Industry	Average	Annual	Money
		1959 Rs. 1186	1960 Rs. 1226	
0.2	Gins & Presses	370	368	
2.0-2.2	Food, Beverages & Tobacco	769	849	
2.3	Textiles	1218	1266	
2.5-2.6	Wood, Cork & Furniture & Fixtures ..	915	934	
2.7	Paper & Paper Products	1192	1172	
2.8	Printing, Publishing & Allied Industries	1282	1320	
2.9	Leather & Leather Products	991	1134	
3.0	Rubber & Rubber Products	1172	1219	
3.1	Chemicals & Chemical Products ..	1360	1360	
3.2	Products of Petroleum & Coal ..	2320	2208	
3.3	Non-metallic Mineral Products (Excluding Products of Petroleum & Coal) ..	960	1061	
3.4	Basic Metal Industries	1268	1376	
3.5	Metal Products (Excluding Machinery & Transport Equipment)	1354	1352	
3.6	Machinery (Excluding Electrical) ..	1263	1321	
3.7	Electrical Machinery, Apparatus & Appliances	1280	1275	
3.8	Transport Equipment	1269	1398	

Sources:

    (a) *Indian Labour Statistics*
        (i) 1961, see pp. 68-73.
       (ii) 1962, see pp. 46-49.
     (iii) 1963, see p. 46.
     (iv) 1964, p. 49.
      (v) 1965, p. 56.
     (vi) 1966, pp. 56-69.
    (b) *Indian Labour Year Book*
        (i) 1962, see p. 45.
      (ii) 1963, see p. 44.
     (iii) 1964, see p. 44.

4

earning less than Rs. 400 per month by Selected Industries (1959-1964)

Earnings for all Industries			
1961 Rs. 1426	1962 Rs. 1491	1963 Rs. 1587	1964 Rs. 1449
502	431	490	454
869	1001	903	897
1547	1648	1658	1429
1045	1061	1186	1148
1337	1331	1739	1492
1445	1473	1474	1544
1216	1461	1763	1518
1827	1729	1870	1387
1646	1676	1808	1676
2423	2481	2536	2349
1071	1032	1082	1236
1869	1585	2107	1583
1449	1937	1666	1452
1210	1582	1546	1554
1640	1679	1716	1862
1719	1741	1850	1607

Notes:

Annual Average Money Earnings for (*a*) Industries during 1959, 1960 and 1964; (*b*) Industry Group No. 0.2 and 2.0 to 2.2 and, (*c*) All Industries computed on the basis of the data available.

Index Numbers of (a) Employment, (b) Productivity,

(Base Year:

Indus-try Code No.	Industry	1952			
		A	B	C	D
2.0-2.2	Food, Beverages & Tobacco ..	92.0	108.7	..	132.5
2.3	Textiles	105.6	98.3	109.2	127.6
2.5-2.6	Wood, Cork & Furniture & Fixtures	110.8	114.9	146.8	121.0
2.7	Paper & Paper Products ..	103.7	100.4	108.1	110.4
2.9	Leather & Leather Products ...	100.0	80.1	92.7	200.0
3.0	Rubber & Rubber Products ...	100.0	90.3	103.8	120.2
3.1	Chemicals & Chemical Products	98.9	108.7	114.5	124.1
3.2	Products of Petroleum & Coal ...	93.1	100.7	104.3	...
3.3	Non-metallic Mineral Products (other than Products of Petroleum & Coal)	97.8	109.7	101.0	..
3.4	Basic Metal Industries	99.0	103.6	115.8	73.2
3.5	Metal Products (Excluding Machinery & Transport Equipment)	106.5	93.7	108.6	103.1
3.6	Machinery (Excluding Electrical)	89.7	88.1	100.8	141.7
3.7	Electrical Machinery, Apparatus & Appliances	96.9	116.9	106.9	137.2
3.8	Transport Equipment	110.1	78.2	144.3	620.0

Notes: A=Employment
B=Productivity
C=Real Wages
D=Degree of Unionisation

5

(c) *Real Wages, and* (d) *Degree of Unionisation* (1952-1964)

1951 = 100)

1953				1954			
A	B	C	D	A	B	C	D
91.2	103.6	..	145.5	97.7	99.9	..	166.5
104.2	106.6	105.5	121.5	104.7	109.8	108.0	124.4
100.0	88.3	98.9	166.7	105.4	105.3	113.1	158.0
96.3	111.6	102.6	163.3	107.4	114.0	105.1	106.6
116.7	68.1	118.2	193.2	111.1	73.2	97·3	202.7
100.0	94.6	108.2	140.4	108.3	102.8	106.9	166.3
100.0	114.8	117.6	142.2	104.4	111.0	125.2	114.5
87.9	111.9	121.6	..	99.6	258.8	123.6	..
94.9	115.0	117.4	..	79.8	155.6	111.1	..
90.2	107.4	113.9	72.9	92.2	123.4	122.3	82.8
93.5	114.4	101.7	182.0	95.2	167.2	115.3	178.9
86.0	97.0	98.2	168.9	88.8	143.2	111.7	204.9
90.6	132.1	103.9	220.2	96.9	138.2	110.6	171.3
111.6	80.8	100.3	180.0	116.9	91.9	123.7	340.0

(Continued)

Indus-try Code No.	Industry	1955			
		A	B	C	D
2.0-2.2	Food, Beverages & Tobacco ..	100.3	111.4	..	171.3
2.3	Textiles	105.2	113.0	123.4	113.8
2.5-2.6	Wood, Cork & Furniture & Fixtures	113.5	139.7	101.2	206.2
2.7	Paper & Paper Products ..	111.1	129.8	120.5	103.1
2.9	Leather & Leather Products ..	111.1	76.5	113.1	270.3
3.0	Rubber & Rubber Products ..	112.5	108.4	113.7	71.2
3.1	Chemicals & Chemical Products	113.3	116.6	125.9	99.7
3.2	Products of Petroleum & Coal ..	110.3	1100.7	145.7	..
3.3	Non-metallic Mineral Products (other than Products of Petroleum & Coal)	83.7	162.4	122.3	..
3.4	Basic Metal Industries	101.0	114.6	133.6	87.2
3.5	Metal Products (Excluding Machinery & Transport Equipment)	106.5	166.6	124.5	188.2
3.6	Machinery (Excluding Electrical)	100.0	184.3	113.8	208.7
3.7	Electrical Machinery, Apparatus & Appliances	106.3	155.1	118.7	219.1
3.8	Transport Equipment	118.4	132.3	131.8	660.0

Notes : A=Employment
B=Productivity
C=Real Wages
D=Degree of Unionisation

5 (*Contd.*)

1956				1957			
A	B	C	D	A	B	C	D
85.5	145.0	..	235.4	95.2	137.6	..	249.3
101.3	126.0	116.2	124.7	103.0	123.6	112.4	149.7
81.1	223.0	97.2	287.6	108.1	174.1	107.9	370.4
103.7	145.0	110.5	123.9	107.4	153.4	117.2	213.1
110.0	82.0	90.9	225.2	105.6	80.6	104.3	189.6
108.0	123.0	114.4	55.3	120.8	114.3	114.1	199.0
103.4	133.0	118.1	133.7	104.4	132.1	124.1	164.0
136.3	114.6	146.9	..	139.1	1283.9	166.0	..
90.1	172.0	117.8	..	101.4	175.5	119.3	..
100.9	116.0	113.2	79.5	107.8	110.6	107.4	112.2
112.9	163.0	117.4	186.3	125.8	142.9	114.4	310.6
106.5	208.0	113.8	230.1	119.6	239.5	108.5	220.4
106.0	216.0	107.7	562.8	125.0	217.6	159.8	292.6
110.1	197.0	124.6	780.0	121.3	188.5	121.6	800.0

(*Continued*)

Industry Code No.	Industry	1958			
		A	B	C	D
2.0-2.2	Food, Beverages & Tobacco ..	96.4	142.2	..	274.2
2.3	Textiles	98.1	127.9	106.8	187.8
2.5-2.6	Wood, Cork & Furniture & Fixtures	121.6	156.7	106.3	439.5
2.7	Paper & Paper Products ..	129.6	147.6	121.7	209.7
2.9	Leather & Leather Products ..	100.0	186.5	116.1	375.2
3.0	Rubber & Rubber Products ...	125.0	114.7	95.9	112.0
3.1	Chemicals & Chemical Products	121.1	131.9	123.3	122.7
3.2	Products of Petroleum & Coal	140.7	1362.6	155.6	..
3.3	Non-metallic Mineral Products (other than Products of Petroleum & Coal)	105.4	189.6	114.1	...
3.4	Basic Metal Industries ..	127.5	100.2	103.4	114.6
3.5	Metal Products (Excluding Machinery & Transport Equipment)	153.2	123.0	111.4	163.4
3.6	Machinery (Excluding Electrical)	124.3	264.0	108.7	460.2
3.7	Electrical Machinery, Apparatus & Appliances	134.4	212.6	109.4	148.9
3.8	Transport Equipment	132.9	155.9	104.1	1160.0

Notes : A=Employment
B=Productivity
C=Real Wages
D=Degree of Unionisation

5 (*Contd.*)

	1959				1960		
A	B	C	D	A	B	C	D
97.8	147.4	..	248.8	103.7	154.3	..	268.9
98.4	132.2	104.9	220.2	101.7	131.3	113.1	186.2
135.1	183.6	107.0	345.7	140.5	190.2	110.2	332.1
129.6	168.7	118.9	209.7	144.4	180.6	97.1	198.1
111.1	83.5	117.8	450.5	105.6	99.7	120.5	379.3
129.2	121.2	87.0	186.1	145.8	128.5	96.6	164.9
131.1	137.1	120.1	140.4	138.9	145.9	124.4	153.5
140.4	1473.5	170.8	..	143.3	1610.5	151.5	..
118.6	191.1	114.0	..	125.2	208.5	110.1	..
132.3	125.4	105.4	170.1	144.1	152.6	105.1	133.3
158.1	114.3	113.8	247.2	179.0	108.8	118.8	279.5
131.8	311.9	99.9	440.8	157.9	331.7	101.8	350.5
131.8	232.2	106.6	328.7	209.4	192.6	98.1	380.9
144.4	147.6	100.3	1280.0	141.1	183.6	98.8	2200.0

(*Continued*)

Indus-try Code No.	Industry	1961			
		A	B	C	D
2.0-2.2	Food, Beverages & Tobacco ..	125.7	138.0	..	179.9
2.3	Textiles	107.8	128.0	116.8	158.6
2.5-2.6	Wood, Cork & Furniture & Fixtures	108.1	251.0	69.0	267.9
2.7	Paper & Paper Products ..	155.6	176.0	112.7	202.3
2.9	Leather & Leather Products ..	111.0	95.0	121.9	386.4
3.0	Rubber & Rubber Products ..	162.5	128.0	104.4	148.1
3.1	Chemicals & Chemical Products	162.2	144.0	131.1	147.4
3.2	Products of Petroleum & Coal	163.6	149.5	126.6	..
3.3	Non-metallic Mineral Products (other than Products of Petroleum & Coal)	173.9	161.0	130.7	..
3.4	Basic Metal Industries ..	174.5	125.0	105.2	114.6
3.5	Metal Products (Excluding Machinery & Transport Equipment)	217.7	129.0	122.9	308.1
3.6	Machinery (Excluding Electrical)	200.9	296.0	107.8	316.5
3.7	Electrical Machinery, Apparatus & Appliances	271.9	154.0	106.8	318.1
3.8	Transport Equipment	172.9	164.0	128.3	3240.0

Notes : A = Employment
B = Productivity
C = Real Wages
D = Degree of Unionisation

5 (Contd.)

1962				1963			
A	B	C	D	A	B	C	D
128.2	88.6	..	201.1	130.1	65.6	..	206.2
110.5	130.9	121.2	152.6	113.7	135.4	117.9	158.3
202.7	150.8	104.4	230.9	235.1	154.0	105.5	142.0
174.1	164.9	107.1	180.7	181.5	187.9	99.5	165.6
122.2	93.5	103.9	307.2	144.4	94.3	126.5	432.9
183.3	122.6	116.4	218.8	204.1	121.5	101.9	240.4
174.4	144.9	125.6	125.9	195.6	143.1	134.7	125.6
143.3	1844.9	139.0	..	143.3	2143.7	136.4	..
136.6	250.3	116.5	..	146.6	216.8	114.7	..
190.2	141.7	105.0	85.1	225.5	137.9	101.1	77.6
243.5	155.7	123.7	259.0	283.9	130.2	115.4	239.6
219.6	295.4	112.0	330.1	241.1	337.0	107.7	263.1
334.4	144.8	101.9	347.9	381.2	143.9	93.7	322.3
182.1	180.3	109.9	4780.0	195.2	168.0	107.2	2580.0

(Continued)

TABLE

Industry Code No.	Industry
2.0-2.2	Food, Beverages & Tobacco .. ..
2.3	Textiles .. ..
2.5-2.6	Wood, Cork & Furniture & Fixtures .. ..
2.7	Paper & Paper Products .. ..
2.9	Leather & Leather Products .. ..
3.0	Rubber & Rubber Products .. ..
3.1	Chemicals & Chemical Products .. ..
3.2	Products of Petroleum & Coal .. ..
3.3	Non-metallic Mineral Products (other than Products of Petroleum & Coal) .. ..
3.4	Basic Metal Industries ... ...
3.5	Metal Products (Excluding Machinery & Transport Equipment)
3.6	Machinery (Excluding Electrical) .. ..
3.7	Electrical Machinery, Apparatus & Appliances .. ..
3.8	Transport Equipment .. ..

Notes : A=Employment
B=Productivity
C=Real Wages
D=Degree of Unionisation

Sources :

(a) *Index of Employment*
Based on Average Daily Employment data collected under the Factories Act. See
(i) *Indian Labour Gazette*, March 1958, pp. 906-941.
(ii) *Indian Labour Statistics*, 1959, 1963, 1964, 1965, and 1966, pp. 14-20, 14-19, 14-23, 20-29, 20-29.

(b) *Index of Productivity*
Based on Index of Industrial Production (base shifted to 1951). See (i) *Monthly Statistics of the Production of Selected Industries in India* (for January & February, 1966), C.S.O., pp. 235-245.

(c) *Index of Real Wages*
Based on Index of Money Earnings and All-India Consumer Price Index. See
Indian Labour Statistics, 1966, pp. 60 and 198.

(d) *Index of Degree of Unionisation*
Based on (1) Average Daily Employment and (2) Membership of Workers' Unions. For (2) See

5 (*Contd.*)

| | 1964 | | |
A	B	C	D
133.8	144.0	..	206.2
118.6	139.0	116.2	158.3
245.9	149.0	121.3	142.0
200.0	179.0	103.2	165.6
144.4	88.0	137.2	432.9
204.2	129.0	90.0	240.4
195.6	157.0	115.1	125.6
154.5	213.2	103.2	..
198.2	169.0	103.7	..
241.2	129.0	75.6	77.6
304.8	136.0	102.2	239.8
260.7	349.0	93.3	263.1
412.5	157.0	87.1	322.3
201.9	207.0	94.2	2580.0

(*i*) *Indian Labour Year Book*, 1952-53, pp. 153-154.
(*ii*) *Indian Labour Statistics*, 1959, 1963, 1964 and 1966, pp. 86-91, 99, 99-100, 105-116.

Notes:

(*a*) *Index of Productivity* is derived by dividing the Index of Production by the Index of Employment.

(*b*) *Index of Real Wages* is derived by deflating the Index of Money Earnings by the All-India Consumer Price Index. The formula is $\dfrac{\text{Money Wages}}{\text{Consumer Price}} \times 100$

(*c*) *Index of Degree of Unionisation* is constructed on the basis of workers' union membership divided by Average Daily Employment. The formula is

$$\frac{\text{Workers' Union Membership}}{\text{Average Daily Employment}} \times 100$$

Trends in Average Size of Employment per Factory, Average Size of Union

Industry Code No.	Industry	1951			1952		
		A	B	C	A	B	C
2 & 3	Manufacturing	87	26	731	85	32	966
2.0-2.2	Food, Beverages & Tobacco	39	10	344	41	14	251
2.3	Textiles	294	99	1213	303	137	1518
	(a) Cotton	380	152	1468	445	221	1931
	(b) Others, (Jute, Silk & Woollen) ..	556	134	508	478	202	532
2.4	Clothing, Footwear and Made-up Textile Goods ..	51	78	N.A.	46	79	N.A.
2.5-2.6	Wood, Cork & Furniture & Fixtures	32	3	N.A.	31	4	N.A.
2.7 2.8	Paper & Paper Products .. Printing, Publishing & Allied Industries	230 39	71 17	} 222	207 38	70 14	} 305
2.9	Leather & Leather Products (Except Footwear) ..	32	8	140	28	17	169
3.0	Rubber & Rubber Products	201	45	N.A.	170	48	N.A.
3.1	Chemicals & Chemical Products	81	32	249	71	37	340
3.2-3.3	Non-metallic Mineral Products (Including Products of Petroleum and Coal) ..	90	17	169	89	30	250
3.4	Basic Metal Industries ..	138	110	740	144	87	868
3.5	Manufacture of Metal Products	36	6	N.A.	35	7	N.A.
3.6	Manufacture of Machinery (Excluding Electrical) ..	60	7	N.A.	48	8	N.A.
3.7	Manufacture of Electrical Machinery, Apparatus & Appliances	136	14	415	129	17	408
3.8	Transport Equipment ..	203	1	N.A.	186	7	N.A.
3.9	Miscellaneous Industries ..	57	26	N.A.	33	15	N.A.
5.0	Electricity, Gas, Water and Sanitary Services ..	65	77	276	58	108	144

Notes: A=Average Daily Employment per Factory
  B=Average Union Membership per Factory
  C=No. of Workers Involved per Dispute

6

Membership per Factory and No. of Workers Involved per Dispute (1951-1963)

1953			1954			1955		
A	B	C	A	B	C	A	B	C
112	41	646	106	33	612	117	44	501
50	19	364	47	21	278	48	21	222
422	182	838	383	170	883	369	148	784
756	403	883	707	306	1124	717	236	735
489	140	776	426	223	646	372	231	852
101	133	N.A.	84	94	N.A.	83	60	N.A.
39	6	N.A.	37	6	N.A.	37	7	N.A.
213	101 ⎫		309	70 ⎫		198	62	N.A.
41	17 ⎬ 375		42	51 ⎬ 1608		42	19	N.A.
48	21	67	46	22	164	48	30	68
191	60	N.A.	189	73	N.A.	184	30	N.A.
97	56	253	93	44	670	94	38	10
107	38	183	105	49	269	107	51	308
158	95	224	166	111	185	168	118	371
41	13	N.A.	43	13	N.A.	46	15	N.A.
58	12	N.A.	58	14	N.A.	62	15	N.A.
134	33	935	128	24	362	129	29	459
227	2	N.A.	224	4	N.A.	213	8	N.A.
126	36	N.A.	120	45	N.A.	119	43	239
60	121	145	58	130	206	58	108	75

(Continued)

Industry Code No.	Industry	1956			1957		
		A	B	C	A	B	C
2 & 3	Manufacturing	86	31	638	93	40	569
2.0-2.2	Food, Beverages & Tobacco	50	19	545	48	21	342
2.3	Textiles	332	129	1108	279	122	864
	(a) Cotton	566	156	1213	520	161	892
	(b) Others (Jute, Silk & Woollen) ..	272	187	744	227	189	707
2.4	Clothing, Footwear and Made-up Textile Goods ..	62	38	N.A.	69	50	N.A.
2.5-2.6	Wood, Cork & Furniture & Fixtures	25	5	N.A.	32	7	N.A.
2.7	Paper & Paper Products ..	174	58 ⎤	⎰ 104	185	87	672
2.8	Printing, Publishing & Allied Industries	35	20 ⎦		36	18	N.A.
2.9	Leather & Leather Products (Except Footwear) ..	42	22	54	42	16	50
3.0	Rubber & Rubber Products	166	21	N.A.	135	52	N.A.
3.1	Chemicals & Chemical Products	82	38	191	89	44	267
3.2-3.3	Non-metallic Mineral Products (Including Products of Petroleum & Coal) ..	90	39	236	100	40	392
3.4	Basic Metal Industries ..	140	84	259	143	110	648
3.5	Manufacture of Metal Products	41	12	N.A.	46	21	N.A.
3.6	Manufacture of Machinery (Except Electrical)	56	13	N.A.	60	12	N.A.
3.7	Manufacture of Electrical Machinery, Apparatus & Appliances	111	26	677	127	30	383
3.8	Transport Equipment ..	177	7	N.A.	198	7	N.A.
3.9	Miscellaneous Industries ..	98	36	N.A.	99	54	403
5.0	Electricity, Gas, Water & Sanitary Services	48	117	150	56	158	477

Notes: A=Average Daily Employment per Factory
B=Average Union Membership per Factory
C=No. of Workers Involved per Dispute

6 (*Contd.*)

1958			1959			1960		
A	B	C	A	B	C	A	B	C
84	39	536	80	40	468	80	37	70
44	21	522	41	18	420	42	20	70
250	141	1059	222	141	833	219	122	1394
448	172	1133	428	236	1016	418	213	1624
207	228	950	163	161	142	156	120	1167
69	58	N.A.	64	51	113	68	31	116
30	8	N.A.	30	6	202	28	6	144
174	95	423	181	88	400	169	84	328
36	18	N.A.	34	17	59	34	16	37
42	31	276	42	42	556	42	34	69
119	27	N.A.	110	39	832	106	33	230
98	38	125	94	41	193	97	46	136
100	37	136	100	41	257	97	43	218
146	122	1168	147	164	528	136	127	563
50	12	N.A.	49	17	201	49	20	179
54	23	N.A.	52	21	284	57	18	111
104	13	329	111	31	364	118	37	318
186	10	N.A.	173	10	629	173	16	992
69	51	166	70	44	190	69	17	89
57	171	473	58	169	215	58	143	250

(*Continued*)

TABLE

Industry Code No.	Industry	1961		
		A	B	C
2 & 3	Manufacturing	84	32	393
2.0-2.2	Food, Beverages & Tobacco	39	17	592
2.3	Textiles	221	105	687
	(a) Cotton	406	283	775
	(b) Others (Jute, Silk & Woollen) ..	150	212	823
2.4	Clothing, Footwear & Made-up Textile Goods	86	29	87
2.5-2.6	Wood, Cork & Furniture & Fixtures ..	21	4	147
2.7	Paper & Paper Products	158	74	418
2.8	Printing, Publishing & Allied Industries	36	16	242
2.9	Leather & Leather Products (Except Footwear)	50	34	63
3.0	Rubber & Rubber Products	104	47	52
3.1	Chemicals & Chemical Products ..	98	43	159
3.2-3.3	Non-metallic Mineral Products including Products of Petroleum and Coal	85	42	299
3.4	Basic Metal Industries	137	87	124
3.5	Manufacture of Metal Products	51	21	126
3.6	Manufacture of Machinery (Except Electrical)	57	19	160
3.7	Manufacture of Electrical Machinery, Apparatus & Appliances	129	42	316
3.8	Transport Equipment	162	39	293
3.9	Miscellaneous Industries	68	17	442
5.0	Electricity, Gas, Water & Sanitary Services	62	124	588

Notes: A=Average Daily Employment per Factory
B=Average Union Membership per Factory
C=No. of Workers Involved per Dispute

Sources : (i) *Indian Labour Gazette* :
    (a) Vol. XI, July-June 1953-54, pp. 248-271.
    (b) Vol. XV, July-June, 1958 pp. 906-941.
   (ii) *Indian Labour Statistics*:
    (a) 1959, pp. 86-91.
    (b) 1963, pp. 22-23, 99, 150-153.
    (c) 1964, pp. 26-27, 95-100, 156-163.

6 (*Contd.*)

1962			1963		
A	B	C	A	B	C
80	34	373	77	31	389
42	16	311	38	16	307
217	107	630	224	108	684
427	185	565	388	110	731
144	42	1068	161	41	909
79	30	40	105	39	73
27	6	98	23	3	50
164	86	258	153	65	188
35	15	36	36	78	73
44	37	220	57	52	42
101	31	238	104	51	330
97	49	182	102	44	148
92	45	226	91	40	388
138	118	227	145	83	153
50	25	365	15	20	251
57	18	382	59	16	149
120	36	945	129	39	209
168	27	655	163	21	714
71	12	665	68	19	264
61	140	224	69	165	825

(d) 1965, pp. 32-33, 171-184.
(e) 1966, pp. 32-33, 105-116, 171-184.

(iii) *Indian Labour Year Book*:
 (a) 1951-52, p. 154.
 (b) 1952-53, pp. 153-154, 451-470.
 (c) 1953-54, pp. 433-449.
 (d) 1954-55, pp. 354-380.
 (e) 1955-56, pp. 414-430.

TABLE 7

Trends in (a) Workers Involved per Dispute, (b) Frequency Rate, (c) Severity Rate, (d) Membership Involvement Ratio, and (e) Index of Industrial Unrest

Year	All Industries		Manufacturing Sector only				
	Workers Involved per Dispute	Membership Involvement Ratio	Workers Involved per Dispute	Membership Involvement Ratio	Frequency Rate	Severity Rate	Index of Industrial Unrest (Base Year= 1951= 100)
1951 ..	645	53.9	731	68.7	0.105	424	100
1952 ..	840	38.6	996	66.5	0.192	310	73
1953 ..	605	22.2	646	37.1	0.071	383	90
1954 ..	568	22.0	612	45.8	0.084	400	94
1955 ..	453	23.3	501	36.3	0.094	563	133
1956 ..	594	30.1	638	49.0	0.097	597	141
1957 ..	545	29.6	569	41.0	0.097	400	94
1958 ..	610	25.6	536	30.9	0.088	414	97
1959 ..	453	17.7	468	24.2	0.086	421	99
1960 ..	623	24.7	702	41.4	0.093	533	126
1961 ..	377	12.9	389	20.0	0.094	421	99
1962 ..	473	19.2	373	23.1	0.087(E)	432(E)	102(E)

Source:

    Indian Labour Year Book 1962, p. 93.

Notes:

    (*i*) *Membership Involvement Ratio* $= \dfrac{\text{Workers involved in Disputes}}{\text{Union Membership}} \times 100$

    (*ii*) *Frequency Rate* is the number of industrial disputes to one lakh of mandays scheduled to work.

    (*iii*) *Severity Rate* is the ratio of total mandays lost due to industrial disputes to one lakh of mandays scheduled to work.

    (*iv*) *Index Numbers of Industrial Unrest* are the percentages of ratio of mandays lost to mandays scheduled to work for the given year as compared to the similar ratio for the base year, *i.e.* 1951.

    (*v*) E=Estimated.

TABLE 8

*Total Wages and Value Added by Manufacture for All Industries
According to C.I.M. & A.S.I. (1950-1962)*

Year			Total Wages (in Million Rs.)	Value Added (in Million Rs.)	Ratio of Total Wages to Value Added by Manufacture
1950	..	..	1365	2839	0.480
1951	..	..	1535	3472	0.442
1952	..	..	1627	3150	0.516
1953	..	..	1647	3343	0.493
1954	..	..	1712	3729	0.459
1955	...	...	1752	4195	0.418
1956	..	..	1925	4687	0.411
1957	..	..	1993	4679	0.426
1958	..	..	1950	4899	0.398
1959	..	..	3004	7590	0.396
1960	..	..	3424	8644	0.396
1961	..	..	3868	9776	0.396
1962	..	..	4423	11156	0.396

Sources: (a) 1950 to 1958 except for 1957, *Census of Indian Manufactures,* 1954, 1955, 1956 & 1958.

(b) 1957 & 1959-61, *Statistical Abstract of India*, 1962, 1963 & 1964.

(c) 1962, *Annual Survey of Industries*, 1962, Vol. I, p. 48.

TABLE 9

Trends in Index Numbers of Average Annual Money Earnings of Factory Workers According to (a) Census of Indian Manufactures & Annual Survey of Industries and (b) Payment of Wages Act

(Base Year=1951=100)

Year				Index Numbers of Average Annual Money Earnings	
				C.I.M. & A.S.I.	Payment of Wages Act
1952 ..	..	..	..	104.7	107.1
1953 ..	..	..	..	107.8	107.7
1954 ..	..	..	..	107.4	107.7
1955 ..	..	..	..	106.1	113.1
1956 ..	..	..	..	110.4	115.4
1957 ..	..	..	..	114.4	120.8
1958 ..	..	..	..	117.3	118.8
1959 ..	..	..	..	115.2	121.7
1960 ..	..	..	..	127.7	130.1
1961 ..	..	..	..	136.0	138.6
1962 ..	..	..	..	147.4	144.0
1963 ..	..	..	..	154.9	145.2
1964 ..	..	..	..	N.A.	147.7

Sources: (i) *Indian Labour Statistics* 1966, p. 198.
　　　　　 (ii) *Census of Indian Manufactures* 1951 to 1958.
　　　　　 (iii) *Annual Survey of Industries* 1959 to 1963.

Notes: Index Nos. of *Money Earnings* based on C.I.M. & A.S.I. (computed on the basis of available data).

TABLE 10

List of Industries for which Wage Boards have been set up

(Up to May, 1967)

Name of the Industry/ Employment	Date on which the Board was constituted	Date on which report was submitted
1. Cotton Textile	30th March, 1957 (Second Wage Board constituted on 12-8-1964)	1st December, 1959
2. Sugar	26th December, 1957 (Second Wage Board constituted on 16-11-1965)	28th November, 1960
3. Cement	2nd April, 1958 (Second Wage Board constituted on 2-9-1964)	7th October, 1959 (1965-1966 Interim Relief)
4. Jute	25th August, 1960	4th September, 1963
5. Tea Plantations	5th December, 1960	June, 1966
6. Rubber Plantations	7th July, 1961	June, 1966
7. Coffee Plantations	7th July, 1961	1966
8. Iron & Steel	5th January, 1962	1966
9. Coal Mining Industry	10th August, 1962	*Interim Recommendations* 1965-1966 (2nd Interim Relief)
10. Iron Ore Mining	3rd May, 1963	
11. Limestone & Dolomite Mining Industries	3rd May, 1963	
12. Non-journalist employees of Newspaper Establishments	25th February, 1964	
13. Port & Dock Workers	13th November, 1964	1965-66 (Interim Relief)
14. Engineering	12th December, 1964	1966 (Interim Relief)
15. Heavy Chemicals & Fertilizers	3rd April, 1965	May, 1967 (Interim Relief)
16. Leather & Leather Goods	21st March, 1966	November, 1966 (Interim Relief)
17. Road Transport	28th May, 1966	
18. Electricity Undertakings	28th May, 1966	

Implementation of recommendations

The recommendations of the Wage Boards are being implemented mainly through persuasion.

The implementation in the case of industries falling in the State sphere is secured through the concerned State government.

The organisation of the Chief Labour Commissioner has been entrusted with the work of securing implementation in the industries in the Central sphere, *viz.,* coal mines, iron ore, limestone & dolomite mines.

A rough appraisal puts the implementation ratio at about 50 per cent of the recommendations made (*Deccan Herald*, 30th April, 1967; *Times of India*, Bombay, 1st May, 1967).

SELECT BIBLIOGRAPHY

PUBLIC DOCUMENTS

INDIA. CABINET SECRETARIAT. STATISTICS (Department of—). CENTRAL STATISTICAL ORGANISATION. *Estimates of national income*, 1948-49 to 1962-63. Delhi, Manager of Publications, 1964. iii, 23 p.

———. *Estimates of national income*, 1963-64 (provisional). Delhi, Manager of Publications, 1966. 6 p.

———. *Statistical abstract of the Indian Union.* Delhi, Manager of Publications. 1949—. New series 1—.

INDIA. EMPLOYEES' PROVIDENT FUND ORGANISATION. CENTRAL PROVIDENT FUND COMMISSIONER. *Statistical abstract.* Delhi, Manager of Publications, 1965. 32 p.

INDIA. INDIAN LABOUR CONFERENCE. *Summary of the proceedings of the conference.* Delhi, Manager of Publications.

Sixth session held at New Delhi on 27th and 28th October 1944. 71 p.

Eighth conference held at New Delhi on 21st and 22nd April 1947. 178 p.

Twelfth session held at New Delhi on 13th July 1963. 113 p.

Thirteenth session held at Mysore in January 1954. 161 p.

Fifteenth session held at New Delhi on 11th and 12th July 1957. 97 p.

Sixteenth session held at Nainital on 19th and 20th May 1958. 168 p.

Nineteenth session held at Bangalore on 9th and 10th October 1961. 26 p.

INDIA. LABOUR (Ministry of—). *Summary of proceedings of the Standing Labour Committee (Tenth session) held in New Delhi on the 15th, 16th and 17th April 1948.* Delhi, Manager of Publications, 1948. 139 p.

INDIA. LABOUR AND EMPLOYMENT (Ministry of—). *Annual reports*, 1959-60 to 1965-66. New Delhi, Manager of Publications.

INDIA. LABOUR AND EMPLOYMENT (Ministry of—). *Implementation and evaluation machinery—its functions and procedures.* 2nd ed. Delhi, Manager of Publications, 1963. 47 p.

———. *Recognition of unions under the code of discipline.* Delhi, Manager of Publications, 1963. 41 p.

———. *Reports on the working of joint management councils.* New Delhi, Manager of Publications, 1965. 179 p.

INDIA. LABOUR AND EMPLOYMENT (Ministry of—). LABOUR BUREAU. *Indian labour statistics,* 1959 to 1966. Delhi, Manager of Publications. (Annual publication)

———. *Indian labour year book.* Delhi, Manager of Publications. 1946—. (Annual publication)

———. *Trade unions in India,* 1953-54 to 1960-61. Delhi, Manager of Publications. (Annual publication)

INDIA. LABOUR AND EMPLOYMENT (Ministry of—). STUDY GROUP ON SOCIAL SECURITY. *Report.* Delhi, Manager of Publications, 1958. 98 p.

INDIA. PLANNING COMMISSION. *First five year plan.* Delhi, Manager of Publications, 1952. xvi, 670 p.

———. *Second five year plan.* Delhi, Manager of Publications, 1956. xiv, 653 p.

———. *Third five year plan.* Delhi, Manager of Publications, 1961. xiv, 774 p.

———. *Third plan mid-term appraisal.* Delhi, Manager of Publications, 1963. ii, 179 p.

———. *Fourth five year plan : a draft outline.* Delhi, Manager of Publications, 1966. xiii, 430 p.

INDIA. PLANNING COMMISSION. COMMITTEE ON PLAN PROJECTS. *Report on literacy among industrial workers.* Delhi, Manager of Publications, 1964. iii, 56 p.

INDIA. REGISTRAR GENERAL (Office of the—). *Census of India* 1961. V. 1, Pt. II-A(i) : General population tables. Delhi, Manager of Publications, 1964. vi, 691 p.

INTERNATIONAL LABOUR OFFICE. *Employment objectives in economic development : report of a meeting of experts.* Geneva, the Author, 1961. xi, 255 p. (*Its* studies and reports, new series, no. 62)

———. *Labour costs in European industry.* Geneva, the Author, 1959. viii, 170 p. (*Its* studies and reports, new series, no. 52)

RESERVE BANK OF INDIA, Bombay. *Reports on currency and finance*, 1951-52 to 1965-66. Bombay, the Author. (Annual publication)

UNITED NATIONS. *Economic survey of Asia and the Far East*, 1964. Bangkok, the Author, 1965. x, 281 p.

BOOKS

ALL INDIA TRADE UNION CONGRESS, New Delhi. *Report and resolutions* : *Twenty-fourth session, Calcutta, May* 27-29, 1954. New Delhi, the Author, 1954. 220 p.

————. *Crisis and workers* : *report to AITUC General Council, Bangalore session, January* 14-18, 1959. New Delhi, the Author, 1959. iv, 186 p.

————. *General report at Ernakulam* : *Silver jubilee session, December* 25-29, 1957. New Delhi, the Author, 1958. 104 p.

————. New Delhi. *Our statement on imperialism and Indo-Pak war* : *speech by S. A. Dange on behalf of Indian delegation at Sixth Congress of World Federation of Trade Unions, Warsaw, October* 19, 1965. New Delhi, the Author, 1965. 18 p.

————. *Report and resolutions* : *Twenty-fourth session, Calcutta, May* 27-29, 1954. New Delhi, the Author, 1954. 220 p.

————. *Report at Coimbatore* : *Twenty-sixth session, January* 6-12, 1961. New Delhi, the Author, 1961. 71 p.

————. *Sixteenth tripartite*. New Delhi, the Author, 1958. 86 p.

————. *Seventeenth tripartite*. New Delhi, the Author, 1959. v, 135 p.

————. *Twenty-first tripartite*. New Delhi, the Author, 1963. 140 p.

————. *Tasks of trade unions in a national emergency*. New Delhi, the Author, 1962. 16 p.

BAKKE, Wight K. *Mutual survival* : *the goal of unions and management*. New York, Harper, 1946. ix, 82 p.

BRADLEY, Philip D., *ed. Public stake in union power*. Charlotesville, University Press of Virginia, 1965. x, 382 p.

CHOUDHURI, Sunil Rai. *Sickness insurance in India and Britain*. Calcutta, World Press, 1966. xvi, 318 p.

————. *Social security in India and Britain*. Calcutta, World Press, 1962. xv, 328 p.

CROUCH, Harold. *Trade unions and politics in India*. Bombay, Manaktalas, 1966. x, 315 p.

DWARKADAS, Kanji. *Forty-five years with labour*. Bombay, Asia, 1962. 315 p.

FONSECA, A. J. *Wage determination and organized labour in India*. London, Oxford University Press, 1964. 241 p.

GALENSON, Walter, ed. *Labour in developing economies*. Berkeley, California, University of California Press, 1962. x, 299 p.

GHOSH, Subratesh. *Trade unionism in the underdeveloped countries*. Calcutta, Bookland, 1960. ii, 410 p.

GIRI, V. V. *Labour problems in Indian industry*. 2nd ed. Bombay, Asia, 1962. xviii, 520 p.

GUPTA, Indrajit. *Capital and labour in the jute industry*. Bombay, All India Trade Union Congress, 1953. 62 p.

HIND MAZDOOR SABHA, Bombay. *Report of the annual convention*. Bombay, the Author.

Seventh convention held at Nagpur on December 24-28, 1958. 115 p.

Eighth convention held at Delhi on February 19-24, 1960. 108 p.

Ninth convention held at Calcutta on December 24-28, 1960. 62 p.

Tenth convention held at Coimbatore on May 5-8, 1962. 172 p.

Eleventh convention held at Dalmianagar, April 11-15, 1962. 129 p.

INDIAN NATIONAL TRADE UNION CONGRESS, New Delhi. *Brief review of the seventh annual session, Nagpur, January* 1955. New Delhi, the Author, 1955. 55 p.

————. *Summary of proceedings : seventh session, Nagpur, January* 1955. New Delhi, the Author, 1957. 55 p.

————. *Report, May* 1956 *to November* 1957 : *Ninth annual session, Madurai, January* 1-2, 1958. New Delhi, the Author, 1958. 112 p.

————. *Report, May* 1962 *to April* 1963 : *Fourteenth annual session, Jaipur, May* 25-26, 1963. New Delhi, the Author, 1963. vii, 151, xxxiii p.

————. *Brief review of the fifteenth annual session, Hyderabad, December* 30-31, 1964. New Delhi, the Author, 1964. 112 p.

————. *Report, May* 1963 *to December* 1964 : *Fifteenth annual session, Hyderabad, December* 30-31, 1964. New Delhi, the Author, 1964. xiv, 165, xxxxi, 70, xviii p.

INDIAN NATIONAL TRADE UNION CONGRESS, New Delhi. *Report, December* 1964 *to December* 1965 : *Sixteenth annual session, Bhilai, December* 24, 1965. New Delhi, the Author, 1966. 104 p.

————. *Labour policy in third five year plan* : *memorandum by INTUC.* New Delhi, the Author, 1960. 56 p.

————. *Labour policies and programmes in the fourth five year plan* : *INTUC suggestions.* New Delhi, the Author, 1965. 66 p.

JOHRI, C. K. *Monetary policy in a developing economy.* Calcutta, World Press, 1965. xv, 283 p.

KARNIK, V. B. *Indian trade unions* : Bombay, Labour Education Service, 1960. 273 p.

KASSALOW, Everett M., *ed. National labour movements in the postwar world.* Illinois, Northwestern University Press, 1963. xv, 256 p.

KNOWLES, H. William. *Industrial conflict and unions.* Berkeley, California, University of California, Institute of Industrial Relations, 1961. (reprint no. 159)

KOTHARI, G. L. *Labour law and practice in India.* Bombay, Tripathi, 1964. xxi, 1106 p.

KUMAR, C. B. and ANSTEY, Vera. *Development of industrial relations in India.* Bombay, Orient Longmans, 1961. xv, 250 p.

LABOUR FORUM, New Delhi. *Planning for labour : a symposium.* New Delhi. Labour Publication Trust, 1947. xxii, 500p.

LESTER, Richard A. *As unions mature : an analysis of the evolution of American unionism.* Princeton, Princeton University Press, 1958. xi, 171 p.

LEWIS, H. G. *Unionism and relative wages in the United States* : *an empirical enquiry.* Chicago, University of Chicago Press, 1963. xvii, 308 p.

MATHUR, J. S. *Indian working-class movement.* Allahabad, the Author, 1964. xvi, 424 p.

MORRIS-JONES, W. H. *Government and politics of India.* London, Hutchinson University Library, 1964. 236 p.

MUKHTAR, Ahmad. *Factory labour in India.* Madras, Annamalai University, 1930. 828 p.

MYERS, Charles A. *Industrial relations in India.* Bombay, Asia, 1960. xx, 376 p.

NATIONAL COUNCIL OF APPLIED ECONOMIC RESEARCH, New Delhi. *Growth without inflation.* New Delhi, the Council, 1965. xi, 148 p.

NATIONAL COUNCIL OF APPLIED ECONOMIC RESEARCH, New Delhi. *Saving in India*, 1950-51 to 1961-62. New Delhi, the Council, 1965. vii, 185 p.

NEHRU, Jawaharlal. *Speeches*. New Delhi, Ministry of Information and Broadcasting, Publications Division. V. 1, 1946-49. 1949. xi, 388 p.

OLGA, L. Aikin. *Legal perspectives* (*In* Roberts, B. C., *ed. Industrial relations* : *contemporary problems and perspectives*). Bombay, Asia, 1962. pp. 195-226.

ORANTI, Oscar A. *Jobs and workers in India.* Ithaca, New York, Institute of International Industrial and Labor Relations, Cornell University, 1955. xiv, 215 p. (Cornell international industrial and labor relations reports, no. 3)

PALEKAR, Shreekant A. *Problems of wage policy for economic development with special reference to India*. Bombay, Asia, 1962. xviii, 343 p.

PUNEKAR, S. D. and MADHURI, S. *Trade union leadership in India*: *a survey*. Bombay, Tata Institute of Social Sciences, 1965. (mimeographed)

RAMANUJAM, G. *Industrial relations* : *a point of view*. New Delhi, Indian National Trade Union Congress, 1965. xi, 127 p.

RAO, A. V. Raman. *Mediation, conciliation and arbitration*: *U.S.A. and India—a comparative study*. Bombay, Popular, 1963. xvi, 232 p.

RAO, B. Shiva. *Industrial worker in India*. London, Allen and Unwin, 1939. 263 p.

RAO, V. K. R. V. and others, *eds. Papers on national income and allied topics*. Bombay, Asia, 3 v.
V. 1. 1960. xii, 298 p.
V. 2. 1962. xviii, 115 p.
V. 3. ed. by N. S. R. Sastry and others. 1965. xii, 264 p.

RASTOGI, J. L. *Industrial relations in Uttar Pradesh*. Lucknow, the Author, 1965. ii, 266 p.

REES, Albert. *Economics of trade unions*. Chicago, University of Chicago Press, 1965. xiv, 208 p.

ROSS, Arthur M. *Trade union wage policy*. Berkeley, California, University of California Press, 1956. viii, 133 p.

ROSS, Arthur M. and HARTMAN, Paul T. *Changing patterns of industrial conflict*. New York, Wiley, 1960. x, 220 p.

ROSS, Philip. *Government as a source of union power : the role of public policy in collective bargaining.* Providence, Rhode Island, Brown University Press, 1965. xiv, 320 p.

SHAH, K. T., *ed. Labour : Report of the Sub-Committee of the National Planning Committee.* Bombay, Vora, 1947. 195 p. (National Planning Committee series)

SHARMA, G. K. *Labour movement in India : its past and present.* Jullundur, University Publishers, 1963. iii, 250 p.

SINGH, Hari Kishore. *History of the Praja Socialist Party, 1934-59.* Lucknow, Narendra Prakashan, 1959. 239 p.

SINGH, V. B. and SARAN, A. K., *eds. Industrial labour in India.* 2nd ed. Bombay, Asia, 1963. xx, 664 p.

SRIVASTAVA, P. C. *Social security in India.* Allahabad, Lokbharti, 1964. 376, xxx p.

SUFRIN, Sidney C. *Unions in emerging societies: frustration and politics.* Syracuse, N.Y., Syracuse University Press, 1964. vii, 124 p.

THAKKAR, G. K. *Labour problems of textile industry : a study of labour problems of the cotton mill industry in Bombay.* Bombay, Vora, 1962. xiv, 175 p.

UNITED TRADE UNION CONGRESS, Calcutta. *Report at the 3rd All-India session, Quilon, April* 2-6, 1958. Calcutta, the Author, 1958. 51, 42 p.

———. *Report at the 5th All-India session, Bombay, August* 28-30, 1964. Calcutta, the Author, 1964. v, 42 p.

VAID, K. N. *Growth and practice of trade unionism—an area study.* Delhi, Delhi School of Social Work, University of Delhi, 1962. 200 p. (Studies in social work, publication no. 15)

———. *Industrial disputes in India.* New Delhi, Shri Ram Centre Press, 1965. vii, 36 p. (Industrial relations statistical series, no. 5).

———. *State and labour in India.* Bombay, Asia, 1965. xii, 279 p.

———. *Trade unions in India.* New Delhi, Shri Ram Centre Press, 1965. vii, 48 p. (Industrial relations statistical series, no. 4)

———, *ed. Labour management relations in India : a symposium.* Delhi, Delhi School of Social Work, University of Delhi, 1960. 118 p. (Studies in social work, publication no. 11)

VENKATASUBBIAH, H. *Indian economy since independence.* 2nd ed. rev. Bombay, Asia, 1961. xi, 359 p.

WEINER, Myron. *Politics of scarcity : public pressure and political response in India.* Bombay, Asia, 1962. xv, 271 p.

ZINKIN, Maurice. *Some aspects of change in Indian society,* 1938-60: *reminiscence.* (*In* Sovani, N. V. and Dandekar, V. M., *eds. Changing India.* Bombay, Asia, 1961. pp. 329-345.)

ARTICLES AND PERIODICALS

DANGE, S. A. "Trends in the national labour conference". *Trade Union Record,* V. 10(7), November 1952.

GADGIL, D. R. "On rephasing the second five year plan". *Indian Economic Journal,* V. 5(4), April 1958: 353-368.

Indian Labour Journal. Simla, Labour Bureau, Ministry of Labour and Employment. 1960—. V. I—(Formerly Indian Labour Gazette, 1943-1959)

JOHRI, C. K. and AGARWAL, N. C. "Inter-industry wage structure in India, 1950-1961: an analysis". *Indian Journal of Industrial Relations,* V. 1(4), April 1961: 377-414.

KENNEDY, Van Dusan. "Sources and evolution of Indian labour relations policy". *Indian Journal of Industrial Relations,* V. 1(1), July 1965: 15-40.

MATHUR, A. S. and RAMAN. "Trade union leadership in Agra". *Agra University Journal of Research* (Letters), V. 10(1), January 1962.

MATHUR, K. "Bonus legislation in India". *Indian Journal of Industrial Relations,* V. 1(4), April 1966: 457-475.

MEHTA, Asoka. "Dynamics of the labour movement". *Indian Journal of Economics,* V. 4(1), April 1966.

———. "Mediating role of the trade union in under-developed countries". *Economic Development and Cultural Change,* V. 7(1), October 1957.

Monthly Statistics of the Production of Selected Industries in India. Calcutta, Cabinet Secretariat, Department of Statistics, Central Statistical Organisation. 1949—. (Monthly)

MUNSON, F. C. and NANDA, A. C. "Influence of legal framework on labour leaders and their unions". *Indian Journal of Industrial Relations,* V. 2(1), July 1966: 3-33.

SHENOY, B. R.   "Indian economic scene—some aspects".   *Indian Economic Journal*, V. 5(4), April 1958: 327-352.

SHIVAMAGGI, H. B.   "Trends in money and real wages in India: 1951-61".   *Reserve Bank of India Bulletin*, V. 1 8(4), April 1964: 421-439.

SOVANI, N. V.   "Planning and planners in India."   *Indian Economic Journal*, V. 13(4), January-March 1966: 477-497.

YEGNARAMAN, Y. S.   "On the comparability of addition to working population during the first and second plans—1961 census and plan estimates".   *Asian Economic Review*, V. 5(3), May 1963.

INDEX

Adarkar, B. P. 183
Agarwal, N. C. 80*n*, 82*n*
Agra University Journal of Research (letters) 13*n*
Ahmedabad Textile Labour Association 14*n*
Aikin, Olga L. 131*n*
All India Trade Union Congress 14*n*, 15*n*, 27, 46, 47, 48, 49, 50*n*, 51, 119, 159, 161, 163, 165, 181, 189, 191, 192, 193, 206, 207, 208, 210, 211, 215, 216, 223, 232, 236, 237
  Silver Jubilee Session, 1957 174
  and Communists 10, 46, 159, 173, 209-10
  and social security 191-2
  and socialist pattern of society 173-5
Annual Survey of Industries 141
Arora, H. C. 3*n*
As Unions Mature 197*n*
The Asian Economic Review 32*n*
Asiatic Labour Conference, 1929 46
Aspects of Labour Economics 238*n*

Bakke, E. Wight 241*n*
Bank Credit 69, 70
Banks, Nationalisation of 175, 192

Bharatiya Mazdoor Sangh 28, 50
Bombay. Congress Ministry, 1938 107
Bombay Industrial Disputes Act, 1938 98
Bombay Industrial Relations Act, 1946 98
Bombay Plan 170
Bonus 20, 22, 83, 84, 93, 148, 149, 154, 164, 166, 167, 192
  Supreme Court decision 154
Bonus Act 154
Bonus Commission, 1961 154
Bradley, Philip D. 20*n*
Breakdown rate 134, 135, 136, 229
British Trade Disputes Act, 1906 131
Budget 67, 69, 70
Budgetary deficit 67, 69, 70
Bundh
  See Strikes, Political
Business corporation Organisation 194

Capital and Labour in the Jute Industry 211*n*
Census of India 1961 1*n*
Census of Manufacturing Industries 141
Central Industries Advisory Council 9